BODIES ON THE LINE

CONTEMPORARY NORTH AMERICAN POETRY SERIES

Series Editors Alan Golding, Lynn Keller, and Adalaide Morris

BODIES *on the* LINE

Performance and the Sixties Poetry Reading

by Raphael Allison

UNIVERSITY OF IOWA PRESS | IOWA CITY

University of Iowa Press, Iowa City 52242

www.uiowapress.org
Printed in the United States of America

Design by April Leidig

The University of Iowa Press is a member of Green Press Initiative and is committed to preserving natural resources.

Printed on acid-free paper

Library of Congress Cataloging-in-Publication Data
Allison, Raphael, 1970–
Bodies on the line : performance and the sixties poetry reading / by Raphael Allison.
p. cm. — (Contemporary North American poetry series)
Includes bibliographical references and index.
ISBN 978-1-60938-303-9 (pbk)
ISBN 978-1-60938-304-6 (ebk)
1. Oral interpretation of poetry—United States—History.
2. American poetry—20th century—History and criticism.
I. Title.
PN4151.A45 2014
808.5'45097309046—dc23 2014010228

Contents

Acknowledgments

This book began on a rainy November afternoon in 2003 in the Woodberry Poetry Room at Harvard University. New to the campus, I had recently discovered this magical place, full of warm light and blond wood paneling and, of course, endless shelves of poetry volumes. I would spend odd hours at the Woodberry reading, though one day—I can't quite remember how this happened—I came across a cardboard box full of cassettes, a dozen or so, labeled hastily in ballpoint pen with titles like "Robert Frost Reading His Poetry" and "Robert Frost Reads for NBC 3/28/54." I asked for a playback machine and settled into one of the Woodberry's oversized armchairs for a listen. It was a thrill. I had never heard Frost's voice before, and I was stunned. He was a great performer—old, yes (most of these recordings were made in the final decade of his life), and maybe a little hammy at the microphone, preening even, and yet a masterful and effective showman. After listening to a few of the Frost cassettes, I poked around and found that many of the poets I was scrutinizing so intensely in my scholarly life were there too, and each had an unusual vocal signature—Marianne Moore's flat American tongue, Wallace Stevens's Episcopal baritone, the surprising nasality of the mighty Charles Olson.

I say this book began by listening to these Woodberry tapes, though really it didn't. It wasn't until a year later, as I was driving down Route 9 near Bard College, heading to my office there, that I had what I've always doubted writers really have—an epiphany. Why not, said a voice from nowhere, write a *book* about *poetry recordings*? Had this ever been done before? My god, there are a dozen tapes of Robert Frost just sitting in a box in Cambridge, and no one seems to know they exist. Frost! The most picked-over American poet of the twentieth century, and all this fresh material moldering in a closet. Upon reaching my building, I marched into the office of my colleague Derek Furr and suggested we begin research, together, on poetry recordings. And so we began driving up to Cambridge for marathon listening sessions, sleeping in spare beds at my friend Lisa Szefel's apartment, hashing out the big themes we were discovering over coffee and Indian food in Harvard Square. It was fun and exciting, and it felt like we were on to something big and new—or at least, as big and new as things get in the placid estuaries of literary studies. In any case, to begin to acknowledge those who worked with or alongside me on this book, I must begin with Derek and Lisa. This whole investigation wouldn't have gotten off the ground without them.

As I moved forward with my research, others were so helpful in locating and helping me access resources, including Don Share from the Woodberry Room, as well as Michael Collier, who went so far as to dub and send along CDs of recordings he'd made himself of William Meredith reading at Bread Loaf. To the staff at the Bread Loaf library in Middlebury, Vermont, where I spent two summers researching and writing large portions of this book, thank you for your patient and cheerful assistance. Thanks to Melissa Watterworth Batt at the Thomas J. Dodd Research Center at the University of Connecticut, as well as the folks at the Sound Reference Center at the Library of Congress; the Bancroft Library at the University of California, Berkeley; and the Schomburg Center for Research in Black Culture and the Dorothy and Lewis B. Cullman Center, both of the New York Public Library. Big thanks also to Barbara and Norty Garber for setting me up in their Vermont cabin for a week of uninterrupted writing, and to Andrew Epstein for corresponding about the process of book publication.

Sometimes brief conversations were extremely useful, pointing me in new directions that turned out to be fruitful. Early discussions with Joan Retallack and Michael Ives at Bard College were formative. Jan Heller Levi talked with me about disability, Donna Masini helped me work through my developing thoughts on Gwendolyn Brooks, and Tom Sleigh's idea to listen to William Carlos Williams as I was researching my chapter on disability was a crucial and brilliant suggestion at a time when I needed crucial and brilliant suggestions.

I am always amazed at the willingness of friends and colleagues to read and comment upon long and sometimes muddled drafts. Enormous and heartfelt thanks to Derek Furr, Kristin Dombek, Andrew Mossin, and Jaime Alves for offering such extraordinary feedback on the book's major chapters. Thanks to Aaron Freundschuh, Andrea Scott, Keith Shaw, and all the other readers from the Work-in-Progress Colloquium at Princeton University, who not only provided smart commentary but kick-started my motivation to finish the manuscript. Thanks also to the two anonymous readers for the University of Iowa Press, whose thoughtful suggestions have made this book stronger. I also can't thank enough Dee Morris, Alan Golding, Lynn Keller, and Elisabeth Chretien at Iowa for making the process of getting this book into print a pleasure.

When I began to look into possible publishers I met my former dissertation adviser and now friend, Ross Posnock, for lunch. As usual, Ross gave me his smart advice and encouragement. Ross, thank you for all your help and support over the years in matters professional and personal. Your work sets the mold, in my opinion, for what good scholarship looks like.

For their consistent support, I'd like to thank my mother and father, Millicent and Joel Allison, and my brother, Ben Allison. My parents gave me the love of books and art, which has shaped me.

In the midst of writing this book, my wife at the time, Justine Salton, died suddenly. After this, I was lost and confused, and I abandoned this project for six years. Justine was the type of scientist—if there is such a type—who started her courses in evolutionary biology by having students read Walt Whitman's "When I Heard the Learn'd Astronomer." She provided astute commentary on my first crack at this project—advice that was wise and intolerant of artifice. Justine, you will always have a place in this world as long as I am in it.

I would like to thank my wife, Tracy K. Smith, who believes in everything worth believing in. I love you and thank you for your trust and belief in me. This book quite simply would not be here if not for you.

And finally, to my Atticus, Naomi, and Sterling—three tiny voices that make the world the bright place it is. This book is for you.

Preface | Tomás and Adam

Leaving the Atocha Station, a 2011 novel by the poet Ben Lerner, tells the story of Adam Gordon, a young American living on a fellowship in Madrid. Adam is a poet, though one entirely unsure of his commitments to art, spending his days reading Tolstoy, smoking spliffs, and writing pastiche poems by scrambling and revising fragments from Lorca. In an early scene, he is compelled to participate in a reading with an earnest poet named Tomás, who goes first: "Tomás looked less like he was going to read poetry and more like he was going to sing flamenco or weep; he did not say thank you or good evening or anything but instead paused dramatically as if to gather his strength for what would be by any measure a heroic undertaking. He had shoulder-length hair that kept falling in his eyes as he arranged his papers and he kept smoothing it back with a gesture I found studied; he struck me as a caricature of himself, a caricature of El Poeta" (Lerner 35).

This description captures a reading style that will likely be familiar to many. Its central conceit is that reading aloud reunites the poem with the emotion or creative energy that originally summoned it into being. This style demands access to whatever set the poem in motion and reanimates the poem's actual, physically expressed dramatic essence. Reading aloud, Tomás's style seems to announce, is a time machine: the speaking voice transports the reader back to a moment of pain or sorrow or joy or excitement, even boredom or alienation—whatever forged the poem—and reconstitutes it as a glowing aura or presence. Witness Tomás, "gripping the podium as though the waves of emotion breaking over him might wash him from his feet" (Lerner 37).

When Adam reads, things change. He doesn't make a dramatic entrance or fail to thank the audience like the fragile Tomás does. Nor is he self-assured; he stalls, in fact, by pouring himself a glass of water before nervously approaching the podium: "I said thank you into the microphone and began to read my poem, to read it in a deadpan and monotonic but surprisingly confident way, considering my knees were shaking and my hands were freezing, to read it as if either I was so convinced of the poem's power that it needed no assistance from dramatic vocalization, or, contrarily, like it wasn't poetry at all, just an announcement of some sort: this train is delayed due to trackwork ahead, etc." (Lerner 38).

Whereas Tomás delivers in heightened theatrics what Adam later calls "an Esperanto of clichés" (Lerner 39), Adam's reading wards off such pitfalls by consciously distancing the speaker from emotional dramatization. The use of "as if" and "like" suggests this reading is comparable to, but not actually, authentic speech; Adam considers, but is not committed to, the poem's essential force and understands the poem is built from the vocabulary of daily monotony, like announcements on commuter trains. If Tomás's reading requires its audience to believe, Adam wonders if such belief is possible. Adam is modern, Tomás premodern.

And yet, a little reflection upends this neat dualism. Though Tomás strives for an immediacy and presence, Lerner's description is a clear parody of a turgid, self-conscious reader, one whose every gesture is already coded in conventional terms. Tomás "paused dramatically," indulged in "studied" mannerisms. The description's comedy derives from its familiarity—we've all seen this joker before. So Tomás's style, which seems to radiate authentic presence, has been transformed into an anthology of predictable, gestural motifs. Conversely, Adam's performance turns against its own pretensions to disaffection. Though he studiously avoids suggesting his reading is self-revelation—he reads "deadpan and monotonic"—something slips from his grasp, and he discovers that meaning is produced almost without his consent. After Adam reads his poems in English, his friend Arturo repeats them in Spanish, something that Adam initially imagines will insure his poems' detachment: "Translation would further keep my poems in contact with the virtual" (Lerner 37). And yet as Arturo speaks "in what he must have thought was the midpoint between my style and Tomás's, gripping the podium like the latter, but modeling my detachment," something unexpected happens: "[A]s the poem went on I slowly began to recognize something like my voice, if that's the word, a recognition made all the more strange in that I'd never recognized my voice before" (39). As he puts it later, "[I]t was like seeing myself looking down at myself looking up" (39). Despite every effort at disengagement, Adam's spoken poem leads him directly back, with vertiginous refraction, to himself; and despite every effort at "being there," Tomás's poem fates him to a thousand prefabricated stylistic grooves.

THOUGH LERNER'S novel is firmly rooted in a present-day landscape of befuddled American culture kids like Adam, it takes its name from the title of a poem in John Ashbery's *The Tennis Court Oath,* published in 1962. The date is significant: it's the argument of this book that a showdown like the one between Tomás and Adam—a high noon face-off between real and phony, authenticity and performance, feeling and fakery, commitment and dissolution, body and spirit—describes a condition that suffused poetry readings beginning in the 1950s, had major expression in the 1960s, and is still with us today. Lerner's comic scene helps characterize two central strains of live poetry reading that I'll spend the rest of this book detangling. The first I'll call the *humanist* strain, the legacy of a style of 1960s poetry reading that became mainstreamed through the Beats and their imitators. It's characterized by what at first glance looks like faith in the power of "presence," its sources and dividends, its belief in the possibilities of aesthetic or personal coherence, and the power of poems to enact themselves and all their incongruous energies fully, faithfully, and at once. This term itself—"presence"—should be familiar to scholars of postwar poetry. It serves as a critical term of favor, a password of sorts for a range of writings on the 1960s in general. Making quoted reference in the pages of *Critical Inquiry* to the Language poet Charles Bernstein, Marjorie Perloff ticks off familiar keywords of 1960s poetics, what she calls an "Official Verse Culture, with its 'sanctification' of 'authenticity,' 'artlessness,' 'spontaneity,' and claims for self-presence, the notion, widely accepted in the poetry of the 1960s, that 'the experience is present to me'" ("Language" 405). Perloff is describing a set of terms that later avant-garde poets like Bernstein would find undertheorized, earnest, and naive. Still working under the sign of 1960s counterculture, Charles Altieri's *Enlarging the Temple* (1979) depicts what he calls the period's "poetics of presence," a rejection of high modern imperiousness:

> In 1962 it seemed tremendously important to rebel against an aesthetic of impersonality that required poets to use overtly mythical or meditative themes and subjects and to develop these themes in complex linguistic and formal patterns. Then it was revolutionary to present an intensely personal voice dealing with topical and topological materials in forms that approximated direct statement before exploding into moderately surreal images. Then originality consisted in refusing the demands for poems that had to be given elaborate interpretations, in fostering poems based on the direct voices of oral readings, and above all in denying the authority of tradition and the balancing meditative mind while exploring directly religious sacramental aspects of secular experience. (15)

While the real motive of Altieri's study is to deepen and develop this prevailing narrative with "philosophical depth and relevance" and to construct "a coherent philosophical poetics" (16), he leaves more or less intact the decade's master narrative of presence. More recently, Michael Davidson has made the crucial link between such a poetics of presence and the voice itself, one that Altieri only hints at, describing a period style that provides "unmediated access":

> For poets of the 1950s and 1960s, a new oral impulse served as a corrective to the rhetorically controlled, print-based poetry of high modernism. Whereas "voice" for T. S. Eliot and Ezra Pound is a rhetorical construct produced through personae and irony, for postwar poets it becomes an extension of the physiological organism. . . . Orality signifies unmediated access to passional states, giving testimony to that which only *this* poet could know. We can see this oral imperative in Olson's "Projective Verse" essay, Allen Ginsberg's theories of mantric breathing, Jack Kerouac's "spontaneous prose," Frank O'Hara's "personism," Michael McClure's "beast language," and Denise Levertov's theories of organic form. (*Ghostlier* 196–97)

Fused to images of 1960s art and culture and parodied by Lerner as the glib theatrics of Tomás, a poetics of presence is arguably what many mainstream poetry readings subsist on today—what crowds (or largish groups) come to witness, what performers typically proffer.

The second strain of live poetry reading, what I'll call the *skeptical* strain, is what this book is really about. If humanist reading has won out, it can't eclipse its counterforce, a kind of reading characterized by what at first glance looks like lively, ludic resistance to pieties of humanism—a sense of openness and possibility of meaning, lack of stability or consistency, and ironic detachment. I say "at first glance" because, as the dramatics of Tomás and Adam reveal, these strains—the word is etymologically linked to "thread"—easily braid, twist, and tie each other in knots of contradiction and interdependence. Doesn't the sincere Tomás turn out to be the consummate performer? And doesn't the flaccid postmodern gamesmanship of Adam lead toward something like self-discovery? Neither humanist nor skeptical styles of reading exist independently or with full coherence; rather, such terms are useful, though somewhat abstract, pegs for pinning to the wall tendencies, conditions of reading, emphases, and accents. This book argues that the dialectic between humanism and skepticism—skeptical humanism?—is audible in poetry reading from major figures from the postwar era in a variety of ways and that the iconographic image of the authentic humanist emoter demands considerable complication.

This book has a historical dimension as well, one that will be stitched throughout: skeptical humanism was born out of the crucible of 1960s culture, when presence meant literally "putting your body on the line," a defining personal and political gesture that resonated throughout American life. The importance of presence in poetry readings can be linked, for example, to the sit-in, a mode of nonviolent resistance to white power pioneered by southern blacks. As early as 1957, there had been sit-ins in sixteen American cities, and by 1960 that number had more than tripled (Gitlin 81–82); merely occupying public space with one's body could constitute an act of social awareness and political commitment. More generally, what the sociologist Todd Gitlin, in his historical memoir *The Sixties*, calls "direct action"—physical involvement demonstrating ideological convictions—defined the 1960s as a decade of being out there, in the world, and on view. Is it frivolous to wonder that Jacques Derrida's early, influential meditation on "the metaphysics of presence"—a critique of the Western hermeneutical tradition—was published in 1967? Perhaps, but as Gitlin points out, always in play was an abiding ambivalence about the new, participatory mode of democratic civility, one that echoes the kind of Tomás-and-Adam theatrics in its "decade-long dialectic between total immersion and skittish withdrawal" (108). If poets were reading alongside civil rights protesters and student demonstrators, if readings presented poets with platforms, literally, upon which to publicize their work and generate engagement, poets were simultaneously coming to realize the wages of such publicity. Resistance to exposure, ambivalence about speech, and a general puncturing of the aura of immediacy readings seemed to promise were all on consistent display in readings by the period's most notable figures.

As goes the nation, so goes the poetry reading. The postwar years saw a boom in most everything, as we all know, but especially babies and poetry readings. The small but growing number of critical works devoted to poetry in performance—books by Lesley Wheeler, Derek Furr, Daniel Kane, Susan Somers-Willett, and Tyler Hoffman—has already begun to establish this fact, if it wasn't clear enough from the historical record. Allen Ginsberg's 1955 reading of an early draft of *Howl* at San Francisco's Six Gallery is the most well-known event, though others discussed in this book are equally important to the development of a postwar culture of poetry reading: Robert Frost's saying from memory "The Gift Outright" at John F. Kennedy's inauguration in 1961 and his numerous appearances throughout the United States as a reader-performer; Charles Olson's maniac reading juggernaut at the Berkeley Poetry Conference in 1965; Gwendolyn Brooks's appearance at the Second Black Writers' Conference at Fisk University in 1967, an event that transformed her poetic and personal convictions; and performances and recordings by William Carlos Williams and Larry Eigner, both of whom struggled with fluid verbal articulation due to speaking disabilities. Suddenly, meteorically, a poet reading his or her work in front of an assembled group of listeners had become crucial not only to the poet's own career and creation of a poetic identity and legacy but also to poetry itself. Poetry may still have spoken to private matters, been composed in solitude, even read quietly in bedrooms and on campus quads, but increasingly the public reading had begun to take on definite cultural forms alongside other modes of public gathering—antiwar protests, civil rights marches, sit-ins and be-ins and teach-ins, music festivals, the "encounter movement," collective drug trips and therapies, revolutionary gangs, Yippie street theater, Digger theater and the Merry Pranksters, avant-garde "happenings," to name just some—to constitute the heart, rather than the periphery, of sixties poetry. A fact too little known is that this heart was split.

The following chapter describes how readings and sixties culture converged. First, I sketch with more depth the two major nodes of the reading dialectic described above by briefly examining performances by Allen Ginsberg and John Ashbery; then, I provide grounding in the 1960s culture of presence; finally, I offer a brief description of how theoretical conceptualizations of voice, performance, and orality help to orient our listening to the poets discussed in the book's subsequent chapters. Along the way and as a recurring example, I focus on Ginsberg, who, with Charles Olson (the subject of chapter 3), was the most visible and vocal poet making claims about voice during this period and one of the most frequent performers of poems in public.

BODIES ON THE LINE

1

The Antinomies of Sixties Reading

Allen and John

Of all sixties poets, perhaps Allen Ginsberg lays the greatest original claim to a poetics of presence, immediacy, and physical *thereness*—and that is how his legacy is still articulated. At the end of *Voicing American Poetry* (2008), Lesley Wheeler claims that Ginsberg's reading at London's Royal Albert Hall in 1965—an event that constituted "a warning about distancing technologies and a celebration of embodied voices"—indicates "what embodied voices have the potential to *do*: create community through ritual, inspire peace, call audiences to arms in a sensual rather than a military way" (166). Likewise, in his chapter on Beat performance in *American Poetry in Performance* (2011), Tyler Hoffman reads Ginsberg as a poet of physical immediacy, citing the "presence associated with [Ginsberg's] live performance" (139), and he writes of Ginsberg's famous Six Gallery reading on October 13, 1955: "What impressed many in the audience at the Six Gallery that October night was the 'insurgent' political power of the spoken word and the body behind it" (129). Ginsberg's most celebrated poem does indeed prefigure its relationship to live speech repeatedly, with his ecstatic "best minds" (*Collected* 126) who "talked continuously seventy hours from park to pad to bar to Bellevue," "yacketayakking screaming," who "wailed down Wall" (127) and, with more libidinal thrust, "howled on their knees" and "screamed with joy" (128). Conversely, silence is linked with humiliation: the "who" of part 1 stands at the end, "speechless and intelligent and shaking with shame" (130).

Ginsberg was convinced of the necessity of the live voice and breath for performance and composition. Voice often served as a poem's starting or was figured as the spark for formal structures. Ginsberg claimed in "Notes Written on Finally Recording *Howl*" that his great poem "developed out of an extreme rhapsodic wail I once heard in a madhouse" (*Deliberate* 231) and had lines structured around "a single breath unit" (230). In "Abstraction in Poetry," Ginsberg notes how Kerouac's prose in *Visions of Cody* sometimes found its start in "actual recorded tape conversations" that were later transcribed and revised (*Deliberate* 243). For Ginsberg, performance or articulation of the poem as actual speech was elemental and crucial. In a postscript penciled on a 1955 letter to William Carlos Williams, Ginsberg instructs even his mentor poet (who was ironically suffering from increasing expressive aphasia at the time) that his poems "are best & clearest read aloud" (*Howl Facsimile* 150). Live reading seemed to offer Ginsberg the chance to leap from print to create community through a ritual of "ecstatic" speech where performance was prior to written text. In a studio-made recording at the Poetry Center at San Francisco State University in 1956, Ginsberg cautioned future listeners that they were missing a crucial element of the poem—its "ecstatic" "transmission":

> The way it should be read is, um, with people or in front of people, the way I, I have been reading it recently, this way, except I've read it too much and so the heart has gone out of me for reading it. However, the way it should be read is, um, kind of ecstatically, if possible, but it would take ecstasy to read it. Uh, what I'm going to do is read it quietly and give it, uh, give it a, uh, silent chance, and then if I can work up into any kind of, of real rhythm I'll try to deliver that, which I would like to do, but it's very difficult to do because it requires a certain kind of openness on my part [pause] and a sense of openness on the audience part too, actually, for a transmission, really.

Ginsberg reads the version of *Howl* that follows this caveat well, and the second section builds into a stirring peroration, though some of Ginsberg's live performances are indeed suffused with much greater sense of rollicking, engulfing presence not captured in this canned recording.

Ironically, much of Ginsberg's fame and reputation as a live reader stem from an *unrecorded* performance, the Six Gallery reading of *Howl* in San Francisco, held on October 7, 1955, almost precisely a year before the Poetry Center recording. This means that *Howl*'s first and most indelible incarnation was also its most significant form of publication to date. The first draft was written in early August of that year and revised heavily up to the Six Gallery reading, and what Ginsberg brought to that event would undergo more revising before actually being published by Lawrence Ferlinghetti's City Lights press a year later. Despite or because of its status as a work in progress, accounts of this reading often emphasize the sense of momentous change it generated, often noting a "surprise" that indicates a new and unregulated force. Writing about the Six Gallery readers in the third person (and with characteristic immodesty) in an article coauthored with Gregory Corso, Ginsberg reported that the reading as a whole was "a violent and beautiful expression of their revolutionary individuality . . . conducted with such surprising abandon and delight by the poets themselves . . . that the audience . . . was left stunned" (*Deliberate* 240). "The reading was delivered by the poet," Ginsberg writes about his own performance of *Howl*, "rather surprised at his own power, drunk on the platform, becoming increasingly sober as he read, driving forward with a strange ecstatic intensity" (*Deliberate* 241). In his memoir *Scratching the Beat Surface* (1994), Michael McClure claims that the Six was a transformative event of "wonder" in which Ginsberg's physical voice and body sped forth a larger sense of social upheaval:

> Allen began in a small and intensely lucid voice. At some point Jack Kerouac began shouting "GO" in cadence as Allen read it. In all of our memories no one had been so outspoken in poetry before. . . . Ginsberg read on to the end of the poem, which left us standing in wonder, or cheering and wondering, but knowing at the deepest level that a barrier had been broken, that a human voice and body had been hurled against the harsh wall of America and its supporting armies and navies and academies and institutions and ownership systems and power-support bases. (168)

Wonderment, surprise, astonishment, transformation: for Ginsberg and his circle, reading equated to authenticity and the power of physical presence of body and voice.

Later recordings bear this out, and one in particular—the Big Table Reading in 1959 in Chicago—has Ginsberg declaiming *Howl* in a peremptory style that is truly affecting. His voice is pitched high and cleaves, during the entire reading, which lasts over twenty minutes, to this somber, measured, vatic tone. Yet he also modulates his voice carefully, taking measure of the poem's underlying movements of feeling, which build over the three parts in a slow crescendo. Sometimes, phrases are emphasized with staccato syllables, as when he spits out rapid-fire, "until the noise of wheels and children brought / them down shuddering mouth-wracked and battered bleak of brain / all drained of brilliance." Other passages are given wailing emphasis, as when he truly howls the final word in the phrase "shocks of hospitals and jails and wars," or in part 2, when he declaims his lines on Moloch with implosive force, almost crying the words in deliberative accusation. The exclamation "monstrous bombs!" is shouted. Part 3 is saturated with an accrued sense of emotional weight, especially in the line "O skinny legions run outside O starry / spangled shock of mercy the eternal war is / here." All of this emphatic, oracular power is underscored by tiny, but telling, edits: Ginsberg cuts the phrase "this actually happened" from an anecdote about someone who leapt from the Brooklyn Bridge ("who jumped off the Brooklyn Bridge this actually happened and walked / away unknown and forgotten" [*Complete* 129]), as if his presence alone is sufficient to verify the story's truth; and he elides the word "here" in one line from part 1 ("putting down here / what might be left to say in time come after death" [131]), again as if the deictic "here" of the page has been supplanted by the "here" of the room. Minus the audience's few careful coughs and complicit chucklings—at the lines about throwing potato salad at CCNY lecturers on Dadaism, for example, or at the comic list "occupational therapy pingpong & amnesia"—all of this resounds in a room that is silent, attentive, and wildly enthusiastic in its final applause.

And yet other recordings of *Howl* tell a different story. Perhaps most striking is an abbreviated performance of the poem from the Vancouver Poetry Conference recorded in the summer of 1963. Comparing the Big Table and Vancouver readings is shocking. Ginsberg's voice in Vancouver is deflated, flat, and almost querulous. He moves sequentially through his poems, reading in a bored, laconic mumble. He introduces *Howl* as a mere chronological inevitability: "The next on that, in that series is *Howl*. That's kind of long for me." There is laughter, then Ginsberg asks for the time and says, "I'll read it until I get bugged or bored." This version of *Howl* begins softly, as if punctured and lacking sufficient air. His voice is slow, enunciating, dry, and plodding, and when he gets to the end of line 5 ("tenement roofs illuminated") he simply cuts off and says, "Actually I don't want to read that, I don't see why I should. Fuck you. Yeah, hung up on that. I was just trying to be nice." The entire episode runs less than two minutes.

A later reading of *Howl* in San Francisco in 1971 at the Intersection for the Arts is neither oracular nor deflated. It's lively, comic, edited (possibly spontaneously), interspersed with comments from Ginsberg and laughter from the audience. Compared to the Big Table performance, it's also tonally polyvalent. His voice begins with energy and force, though soon, small substitutions for phrases can be heard, some of them seemingly references to location. The line "burning their money in / wastebaskets and listening to the Terror through the wall" (*Collected* 126) becomes "burning their money in wastebaskets amid the rubbish of memorable Berkeley manifestoes listening to the terror through the wall." An attentive listener soon notices that sizable chunks of the poem are simply excised, that some lines are read in jumbled order, that many small changes to the City Lights version are peppered throughout the reading. Sometimes, Ginsberg stops abruptly to proffer a comment, as when he says of one line ("who chained themselves to subways" [126]) that "the principle of a line like that is to go from A to Z in rhythm," or when he explains the line ending "seeking visionary indian angels who were visionary indian angels" (127) is really "the center perception of the whole poem." As the poem moves forward, the audience can be heard laughing more, as if authorized by the reader himself, who increasingly shifts into a clownish mode. The words "incomprehensible leaflets" (127), referring to counterculture literature being snooped by the FBI, is read hilariously, the fourth syllable of "incomprehensible" given a gouging emphasis, as if to embody for a moment a noninitiate's description of protest literature. Because of blue laws prohibiting vulgar public speech (Hoffman, *American* 133), the poem's many obscenities are redacted by the word "censored," which Ginsberg clearly uses for comic emphasis; thus "blew and were blown" becomes "censored and were censored." In the long passage beginning "who copulated ecstatic and insatiate," the many intrusions of the word "censored" are funny, and Ginsberg's loopy, reeling enunciation suggests how far from a Big Table–style, hieratic reading of the poem we are.

Tyler Hoffman, who has written the only full-scale interpretive analysis of

Ginsberg's live readings, argues repeatedly that Ginsberg's style of "Beat performance" was "freewheeling, improvisatory, and dialogic" and that his "humane vocal presence" was achieved in unregulated and ecstatic moments of live reading (*American* 127). This perspective is not unlike Ginsberg's self-descriptions or his traditional reception. Referring to the poet's self-interruptions and comic twists, Hoffman says Ginsberg was dialogic in Bakhtin's sense of the word, erupting in "mockery," acts of "discrowning," and "spectacles of inversion that expose the unstable and temporary nature of any hierarchy" (134). It's worth questioning this judgment with some care. First, is Ginsberg's performance polyvalent and heteroglossic, as Hoffman suggests, or does it in fact erode the authority of spoken poetry that he demonstrated elsewhere? Hoffman himself notes Paul Blackburn's article in *Big Table* (the magazine that sponsored Ginsberg's 1959 reading), in which Blackburn distinguishes between "drunken directness" and "drunken playing for cheap laughs" and says that in one recording, Ginsberg pandered to the crowd and debased his poem (133). And yet by listening across readings, can't we hear a little Adam in Ginsberg's Tomás? Inserting local place-names to titillate an audience is a tactic more typically associated with rock bands on tour in Cleveland; interrupting the flow of the poem with comments and jokes casts the high-flown, declamatory, prophetic voice into relief as a *performed* voice by contrast, robbing it of any claim to authentic presence.

I don't claim here that such deviations from a more singular "ecstatic" reading of the poem are more or less meaningful than others, but I do claim that they suggest—through serial listening—that the image of Ginsberg as a poet of endless, heroic public power is a limited framework of reception. Is it possible that Ginsberg's fluctuations as a reader have less to do with dialogism or bad humor and more to do with a subterranean resistance to live reading? "I have quit reading in front of live audiences for a while" (*Deliberate* 231), Ginsberg wrote in 1959, burned out before even the starter's pistol kicked off the sixties heyday. "[I]t's become more a trap and duty than the spontaneous ball it was first" (231). Yet if we imagine the poetry reading as a crucible of live "transmission," as Ginsberg so often urged us to, we miss a crucial point: that along with Ginsberg, preeminent poet of directness, immediacy, presence, authenticity, and embodied liveness, sixties poets actually resist such an ethos. As much as live reading was courted by poets of the sixties—even the most oracular among them—it was also forsworn. A skeptical counterforce to humanist sixties reading was audible in the Dharma Lion himself.

Yet if performer-readers like Ginsberg were touched by the antinomies of sixties reading, others were more fully committed to a style in which presence was not only out of fashion (or perhaps not yet in fashion) but studiously avoided. The New York School poet John Ashbery will serve as one example—appropriately so, if we key his style to Lerner's Adam Gordon. Ashbery engages in what might be termed "metareading," a style that, unlike the wailing reverberations of Ginsberg, puts distance between voice and poem and from the reader's or listener's own relationship to it. This is accomplished both through tone of voice and simple, directive comments. For example, Ashbery introduces his poem "To a Waterfowl" at a reading at the Living Theatre in New York on September 16, 1963, by foregrounding its genre, which is itself significant: the poem is a cento, an Italian found-poem form that collages lines from other poems into a cobbled new lyric (the title itself is taken from William Cullen Bryant's heavily anthologized lyric). Ashbery's note to the audience that "I hadn't known this when I wrote it," however, suggests his remoteness from what has come to be the poem's formal logic, which is itself an act of bricolage, of stripping the poem's genesis of its own originality; his words serve as a framing device that cools the poem down by suggesting the poet's own belatedness of enterprise. More significant is Ashbery's form of reading, which, unlike Ginsberg's, lacks inflection or dynamic vocal range. He says virtually nothing before or after poems (the previous comments are all the gloss we get in the Living Theatre reading, which lasts close to an hour), and his voice's flatness and freedom from affective pitch are remarkable—almost a performance of nonperformance. While it's hard not to hear Ashbery practically straining to steer clear of the semiotics of emotion, in a 1999 interview with Daniel Kane, Ashbery frames his experience as a reader after returning from Paris in the early 1960s as unpracticed amateurism. In fact, his reading at the Living Theatre marked Ashbery's American return, as Kenneth Koch makes clear at the outset of his introduction to Ashbery that evening. Ashbery tells Kane, "When I left [America for Paris], poetry readings were solemn and official events given by elder statespersons of poetry, like Auden or Eliot and Marianne Moore. Then the 'Beat revolution' happened to take place while I was away, and when I got back—although I wasn't aware of it—

everyone was giving poetry readings everywhere. I was astonished at being asked to give one, until I realized I was one of about a hundred poets one could have heard that night in New York" (xvii). Obviously not a part of Ginsberg's "revolution"—which Ashbery associates here most generally with performative reading—the poet's self-image is still, decades later, that of the wide-eyed outsider entirely unskilled at live reading. And it shows. His readings at the Washington Square Art Gallery on August 23, 1964, and his performance on March 27, 1967, at the YM-YWHA reveal a voice indistinguishable from the Living Theatre reading in almost every way. Their uniformity testifies to the lack of occasion readings seemed to offer Ashbery.

If we can hear a grinding resistance to liveness in Ginsberg, can we hear eruptions of presence in Ashbery? Even under the spell of Ashbery's affect-free monotone, the audience can be heard providing (and projecting) the kind of aura he negates. Audio recordings only reveal, of course, a limited dimension of actual live reading, and it's instructive to take into account the voices of others, as readings are communal events. Laughter, for example, vents occasionally and erratically into Ashbery's readings, sometimes at moments when it's difficult to discern why. In his introduction to Ashbery at the Living Theatre, Koch says, "My own opinion is that he's writing the best poetry that anyone is now writing in the English language. Um, I think as an influence—" but here he gets a huge laugh. "Why is that funny? I don't understand," he continues, sounding genuinely confused. Obviously, something has occurred within the room outside Koch's control, perhaps simply a surplus of excitement at the prospect of hearing this important voice. (The possibility that it's something more trivial is also apparent, as Koch can be heard to then say, "Clarice, you're very silly," before going on; this is most likely directed at Clarice Price, Larry Rivers's wife.) When the audience laughs during the reading itself, the effect can be equally disorienting. A lusty, collective guffaw follows some of the better-known lines from the cento—as when Ashbery reads Stevens's line "late coffee and oranges in a sunny chair"—suggesting that laughter may serve as a participatory gesture indicating knowledge of literary history. Other laughs are cloaked in total mystery. Ashbery reads the following lines describing rivers from "Into the Dusk-Charged Air"; they are free of any kind of editorializing perspective. Can you guess where the laughs fall?

The Ebro
Is blue, and slow. The Shannon flows
Swiftly between its banks. The Mississippi
Is one of the world's longest rivers, like the Amazon.
It has the Missouri for a tributary.
The Harlem flows amid factories
And buildings. The Nelson is in Canada,
Flowing. (*Rivers* 18)

I didn't think so. Answer? The audience titters after the line "like the Amazon" and sends up quite a big laugh after "The Nelson is in Canada, / Flowing," a line whose comic dimensions could be argued to emerge from the present participle "flowing," which might sound absurdly simple after the repetition of all the other "flows." Yet without question the audience is alert, attentive, and sensible of its own role in the reading. It fills in for the laconic reader a sense of presence and "being there" that his own performance won't avow.[1]

In a recording of Ashbery reading at the YM-YWHA in 1967, the poet Richard Howard introduces Ashbery by referring to this Living Theatre performance in legendary terms. According to Howard, Ashbery read with extreme dramatic flair that night, "striding up and down, smoking, wreathed in clouds of smoke," stunning his audience: "Some of you may have seen him on that occasion. He gave an extraordinary reading, uh, at the Living Theatre on the set for *The Brig* [a play about a soldier in the brig that went up in May of the same year] behind a lot of barbed wire. It wasn't certain on that occasion whether the wire was to keep him from us or us from him." None of this is remotely apparent from the recording of this event, nor is there any evidence for Howard's judgment that the reading was "a tremendous movement forward, into, and upon his audience" (except, of course, for the poems themselves, which may have created their own major effects). Howard also notes that "John Ashbery, I think, is the first poet in history in whose work anxiety, with all its shaping and climax-reaching concerns, has no place at all." Extraordinary, incursive, explosive, and unprecedented, but without the sense of anxious presence that marked so many other writers—all, in fact, "in history" so far. Yet we can hear it, and imagine it, from these traces left on tape (and, now, bumped to digital formats and available online): the eruptions of laughter in the descriptions of scenes we can't fully reconstruct attest to a struggle in live reading between the necessities and rewards of unmediated presence, as well as an opposite, atavistic return to the text itself. This return is what this book is about.

Authenticity, Orality, and Performance

Can readings really tell us anything important? The poet Ron Silliman argues that the speaking voice is a form of presence—the "power of presence," or "POP," as he calls it—that actually restricts meaning:

> No event invokes the power of presence like a reading. The performer literally POPs off the stage and *is* the page from which the words of the text emanate, if not actually from which the words themselves appear to have been inscribed. The reading, even the projectivist event at its most rigorous (Duncan whispering linebreak counts), seems particularly structured to invite this sort of ventriloquism, the narrowing of multiple possibilities down to a single, narrow "interpretation." By their very nature, readings problematize multiplicity and ambiguity, simply by virtue of this supplement, the body and physical voice of the reader. (373)

Silliman's idea of readings' winnowing loss is not without precedent. Charles Bernstein points out that trends in scholarship through the 1980s and 1990s often dismissed oral performance in literary studies due to "the prevalent notion that the sound structure of language is relatively arbitrary" (5). Acoustic effects are regularly regarded as inconsequential epiphenomena with no real value, mere accidents of throat, larynx, mucous membranes, regional upbringing, or lung capacity—all contingencies too arbitrary to serve as bases for interpretation—or they are events marginal to the authority of print's textuality and circulation. In his study of the spoken text, *Reading Voices* (1990), Garrett Stewart characterizes this skepticism as a poststructuralist "phonophobia," a post-Derridean refusal to privilege speech over writing (3). When in 2005 Peter Middleton mounted a comprehensive defense of the semantics of poetry in performance, it was to these many critiques—by Michel Deguy, Donald Justice, David Wojahn, and Frederick Stern, to name just four others—he turned, making his case that "meaning is extended, complicated, and sometimes transformed by performance" (*Distant* 28).

The resistance to reading to which Middleton is responding has little to do with affiliation to mainstream or avant-garde circles. The year Middleton's book was published, 2005, Donald Hall lodged a complaint against readings in the pages of *American Poetry Review*, targeting not only contemporary performance poetry (e.g., the Nuyorican scene) but contemporary readings in general as putting mistaken emphasis on literal utterance. Making an unusual alliance with Silliman, the more mainstream Hall argued that a poem's truly important sound effects are not literally spoken but rather silent and unheard: "Great sound in a poem," as he put it, "has nothing to do with real performance but with potential performance" (11). The previous year, I encountered similar resistance when describing ideas for this book to the experimental poet Joan Retallack, a friend. She let me know it was a fool's errand to look critically at such ephemera; poems are texts, not instantiations of texts. Yet recent scholarship has either ignored this skepticism or abandoned such legitimating maneuvers as Middleton's by simply charging into the audio archive to begin the work of hard listening. Lesley Wheeler's *Voicing American Poetry* examines the effects of authorial presence, like that of Edna St. Vincent Millay's radio and live performances, along with academic and slam readings; in a 2012 article in *PMLA*, Christopher Grobe describes the confessional movement as a performance genre; and Derek Furr close-listens to the circle of poets around Robert Lowell. Poetry in performance has moved from the periphery of mainstream interest toward its center.[2]

This study focuses on readings by poets most closely associated with page poetry, not performance: Robert Frost, Gwendolyn Brooks, Charles Olson, William Carlos Williams, and Larry Eigner. Though my listening focuses on readings from the midfifties through the sixties and seventies and in some cases later decades, I call this "sixties reading" because the crucible of this skeptical performance mode has its birth in the sixties, a period marked by social rupture on a grand scale. Poets informed by an ethos of sixties reading may well be "sixties readers" later in life, as when Gwendolyn Brooks reads at the Guggenheim Museum in the 1980s, a performance to which I pay close attention. I want to emphasize the dialectic between possibilities of physical presence—often metonymically represented by the human voice—and skepticism about its promises, frustrations over its limits, and fear about its dramatically public nature. That this is a story about the sixties is no coincidence: the period itself was deeply invested in the question of physicality's dividends, the power of "bodies on the line," and the authenticity that a live voice produced. A breathing, visible element of public space—a radical protester declaiming a university administration, a civil rights leader addressing massive crowds, a lone singer with a guitar—took on dramatically new meanings. In *Hearts and Minds* (1996), his book about Vietnam-era protest poetry, Michael Bibby demonstrates how the body in the 1960s was politicized as *the* "source of political identity," one that resonated clearly with the poetry of and after World War II (18). "Throw your *body* into the Movement," said Charles Jones, a member of the Student Nonviolent Coordinating Committee (SNCC), in 1961 (qtd. in Bibby 20, emphasis in the original), a phrase reminiscent of Michael McClure's description above of Ginsberg, whose "human voice and body had been hurled against the harsh wall of America." The editors of the essay collection *The 60s without Apology* (1984)—Sohnya Sayres, Anders Stephanson, Stanley Aronowitz, and Fredric Jameson—begin their introduction to the era with a description of the Italian avant-garde composer Luciano Berio's *Sinfonia* (1970), composed in the late sixties, the third movement of which presents fragments of Mahler and Debussy, bits of speeches from leftist political events in France and the United States in the late sixties, overheard snippets of conversation, and passages from Claude Lévi-Strauss and Samuel Beckett, all commingling in cacophony to conjure an era in which the human voice (recorded, in these cases) carried a weight of political and aesthetic value that could stand on its own "without the mediation of melody" (1). The *Sinfonia*'s previous movement, titled simply "O King," is an homage to the era's foremost orator, Martin Luther King, Jr. Crucial to periodizing the sixties, voice is one of the era's most persistent tropes, and poetry readings participated directly in a larger sense of personal and public visibility, agency, and presence. This story is well established, though this book's argument resists its dominance. Just as readings drew excitement and power from this emerging culture of performance, they also drew back.

So what is the story of sixties reading? It's the story of conflict between orality and authenticity. Orality refers to the meanings that accrue to spoken language, including a sense of presence, authority, and immediacy. Orality is typically conceived in some relationship to print text, sometimes as its opposite but, since Derrida's deconstruction of the writing/speech dichotomy, more commonly as complexly twined. Authenticity is a much more capacious term and refers here to how to value the collapse of distinction between representation and the real, a collapse given particular edge during the sixties. The literature of early postwar America is rife with cosmic questions about the authentic possibilities of daily life. Intense critical investigations were not just written but popular: Herbert Marcuse's *One-Dimensional Man* (1964) was a study of capitalism's destruction of a complex subjective authenticity; R. D. Laing, a progressive and idiosyncratic psychologist and cultural theorist, wrote *The Politics of Experience* (1967), which sought to rescue a spiritually depleted social order from abiding emptiness, "pseudo-events," Marxist "false consciousness," and "being only half alive" (xiii). It's hard to read these books a half-century later without noting a certain critical clumsiness. When Laing claims, "[W]e are bemused and crazed creatures, strangers to our true selves," we get some sense of the rupture that occurred between Laing's book and our own poststructural era, in which claims about a "true self" ring with undertheorized naïveté. And this was not work remote from poetry readings. Ginsberg actually delivered his talk "Consciousness and Practical Action" at a conference in London organized by Laing himself (Schumacher 485).

I suggest above that orality is a trope for authenticity yet also is in "conflict" with it. How is this possible? In many ways, we can still hear how much speech is associated with presence and truth. In our everyday lives, we are told to "speak truth to power," for example, to "tell it like it is," to "testify" to what's real—or at least these phrases circulated decades ago. Yet in fact, in writing from the sixties and afterward, orality and authenticity can be seen indeed as locked in an awkward, unresolved duel. On the one hand, the faith in orality is sacrosanct, with poets like Ginsberg and Olson representing well-staked positions on the value of orality. Walter J. Ong, Marshall McLuhan, and J. L. Austin helped shape a discourse on the primal force of the spoken, arguing for its difference from print and its greater yield of presence. Indeed, this is the primary legacy of sixties reading. Frederick Stern's ethnographic exploration of what he calls "the formal poetry reading" (in distinction to performance-based readings) suggests that "presence" is what still draws audiences to poetry readings, which can often be halting, awkward, low-fidelity affairs: "The presence of the living poet, the sounding of the poet's voice in the present, affirm the reality of life . . . in ways in which the silent and solitary reading cannot" (81). Middleton calls this the "performance of authorship," in which the physical presence of a voice reestablishes the poet as crucial buttress to the clout of speaking subjects, worn down by various effects of modernity—a "subjective crossroads for the enormously complex transactions of institutional legitimation in the contemporary world" ("Contemporary" 269). Voice and authenticity do indeed seem two sides of the same coin.

Despite this fact, however, a subterranean, skeptical resistance to this humanist faith has always been at play, one unsure that speech can achieve its promise of immediacy. As will be demonstrated, speech falls from grace when rendered in performance, which is both the expression of and the swerve away from the promise of presence speech promises. Sixties reading represents this struggle between the presence of the reader and his or her continual beclouding and loss, the presence of the poem and its constant threat to be overwhelmed by technology and institution. This sixties dynamic between faith in, and skepticism of, the authenticity of presence is captured most neatly, perhaps, in Lionel Trilling's book *Sincerity and Authenticity*, a work of cultural criticism urging against uncritical association of liveness with authenticity. Though written in 1971, *Sincerity and Authenticity* meditates on the previous years and even, in a coded way, on Allen Ginsberg himself. Ginsberg was once Trilling's student at Columbia, and they kept in touch through letters through the sixties. Trilling's book is a meditation that reveals the holy, confounding, complicated place authenticity holds in Anglo-American modernity, its many contradictions and paradoxes. Trilling's central argument is that modernity has shifted from a belief in the virtue of "sincerity" toward one of "authenticity," the latter term a complex moral stance society is still coming to terms with. Sincerity is fairly simple: it's a straightforward, moral principle that aligns the individual to society. Remain true to the self, sincerity avers, and you won't dissimulate to others (Trilling 7). This is not mere emotional honesty, Trilling explains, pointing to the errors Donald Davie makes in a 1968 article on the subject ("On Sincerity: From Wordsworth to Ginsberg"), in which Davie laments an "unmediated exhibition of the self, presumably with the intention of being true to it" in so many of his contemporary poets (9). Trilling's idea of sincerity derives instead from *Hamlet*'s Polonius, who in his famous dictum suggests that sincerity of self will lead, ipso facto, to "being true" with others. The two are held in a quaint equilibrium, suggesting a possible balance of personal and social realms (3). However, Trilling argues, this moral simplicity has developed into a mode of authenticity that is "more strenuous" and dialectic, a more capacious and layered formulation that compares the self to a larger cosmic order (11). Authenticity strives to adequately represent one's deeply interrogated essence, to arrive at "personal coherence and purposiveness"—*Being* itself (118). Being authentic is a modern problem, one that requires a full exploration of self and its struggle to find adequate social expression. There's no quick fix.

On authenticity's place in contemporary culture, Trilling's position was that society—represented by "serious art"—is in the midst of a century-long quest for the authentic, something to beware of, as it was in danger of being watered down by popular art, togetherness, and performance. Trilling argues that Rousseau's well-known resistance to the theater emerged from Rousseau's belief that impersonation corrodes performer and spectator alike by generating an "attenuation of selfhood" (64). Rousseau's recommendations for more productive modes of performance sound appropriate to the Age of Aquarius, as Trilling describes them, liberally quoting the French philosopher:

> In the place of "exclusive entertainments which close up a small number of people in melancholy fashion in a gloomy cavern, which keeps them fearful and immobile in silence and inaction," there are to be free and festive gatherings "in the open air, under the sky" at which nothing will be shown. The incidents of these occasions of happy communality will be games and athletic contests, regattas, reviews, and the ceremonies of prize-giving. "Let the spectators become an entertainment to themselves; make them actors themselves; do it so that each one sees and loves himself in others." (65)

Trilling clearly hears Rousseau's language resonating with the sixties popular culture of public gatherings and festivals: "Only a few years ago, the response to Rousseau's view of artistic culture would have been more clearly negative than it is today, when in some quarters it is believed that 'showing' is to be repudiated in favor of participation, exactly to the end of loving ourselves in others" (65). Yet Rousseau's sense that performance is deeply problematic in the way it corrupts spectators through dishonesty, that it is "hostile to the sentiment of one's own existence" (67), indicates his doubt that art is a place for authentic experience. Trilling's surprising conclusion (or not so surprising for those versed in Trilling's weird, revanchist progressivism) is that Rousseau's logic is not as readily dismissible as it first appears. Art is in a stage of crisis in which a *simulated* authenticity is being promoted at every turn—as "participation," as "loving ourselves in others"—yet is simultaneously debased through a lack of authenticity of self. In a brilliant reversal, Trilling suggests that the culture of sixties "participation"—happenings, gatherings, festivals, readings, the carnival atmosphere of public aesthetics—is not, in fact, authentic at all, Ginsberg's ecstatic transmissions be damned.

Peter Berg, a founding member of the radical Diggers group, perfectly articulates the Rousseauian participatory aesthetic Trilling regards so skeptically when he describes "guerilla theater": "It wasn't about putting a play on. The idea was that people who saw the play would actually take part in it. They wouldn't just be an audience, and this production would be a social action to cause or aid the revolution" (144). Direct or "social" action of this sort suggests to Trilling not authenticity or reality—Berg claimed such performance succeeded by presenting "the reality" (144) of social injustices—but rather David Riesman's famous "other-directed" persona, a "reiterated impersonation" of other people based on the very same corporate culture Ginsberg and the Diggers were howling against (66). While Trilling isn't specific about what current figures or movements he may mean, it seems crystal clear: "But serious art, by which we mean such art as stands, overtly or by implication, in an adversary relation to the dominant culture—surely on this ground or nowhere a man can set up the smithy in which to forge his autonomous selfhood? Yet at the present time certain developments in the ecology of art must make us less confident of this than we once were" (67). "Certain developments" are left for us to imagine, but surely they include the mainstreaming of counterculture, the erosion of high and low art, and the like, not the seriousness of Stephen Dedalus's self-improvements. "We understand *a priori*," Trilling says later on, "that the prescriptions of society pervert human existence and destroy its authenticity" (161). He might have added: they do this even when they appear not to.

Trilling had reason to question the culture of presence and performance. In intellectual circles, orality and related terms were growing freighted with associations to presence at a suspicious rate. Marshall McLuhan's *The Gutenberg Galaxy* (1962) equated orality with authenticity and, conversely, print with restrictive enlightenment rationality and the death of voice (Gutenberg's "galaxy" is print capitalism). Movable type, and now media, gave rise to modernity, while orality was cast as authentic, able to be recaptured best through literary experiment: "As the Gutenberg typography filled the world the human voice closed down. People began to read silently and passively as consumers. Architecture and sculpture dried up too. In literature only people from backward oral areas had any resonance to inject into the language—the Yeats, the Synges, the Joyces, Faulkners, and Dylan Thomases" (McLuhan 250).

Walter J. Ong's belief in the ontology of spoken language is equally robust. Ong's book *The Presence of the Word* (1967) examines vocalized speech through a history of presocial orality, print culture, and modern "electronics" and media, interrogating along the way speech's status as a route to religious experience. "Man communicates with his whole body," reads the first sentence, "and yet the word is his primary medium. Communication, like knowledge itself, flowers in speech" (Ong, *Presence* 1). Yet modernity has intruded, Ong says, publicizing and debasing what was once deeply private and close to God (Ong was a Jesuit priest): speech "is now given artificial oral-aural public presence through the electronic media of radio and tapes and loudspeakers. It is projected on television with special visual accompaniment, not only dancing men but also dancing cigarettes and bars of soap. . . . It is towed visibly through the skies behind aircraft and bounced invisibly off satellites" (15–16). Ong argues that humanity's original relationship to the word was deeply spiritual and technology-free, and now that spirit is under attack through what he later calls "secondary orality," the recurrence of spoken voice through new communication technologies like telephones, radio, and recording devices (*Orality* 133–35). According to Ong, the voice of modernity erodes linguistic presence, granted by voice and consubstantial with Being itself. "Presence," Ong says, "does not irrupt *into* voice. One cannot have voice without presence, at least suggested presence. . . . Voice is not inhabited by presence as by something added: it simply conveys presence as nothing else does" (114). In his later *Orality and Literacy* (1982), Ong hopefully aligns such presence with communal possibilities: "Because in its physical constitution as sound, the spoken word proceeds from the human interior and manifests human beings to one another as conscious interiors, as persons, the spoken word forms human beings into close-knit groups. When a speaker is addressing an audience, the members of the audience normally become a unity, with themselves and with the speaker" (73). Ginsberg's notion of "transmission" echoes loudly here. Speech is embodied presence, saturated with authenticity, set against mediated communication. McLuhan's anachronistic modernist primitivism ("backward oral areas") and Ong's faith in orality's communal drive both serve as tropes for orality's association with authenticity. In the 1960s, to speak was to be, a judgment Trilling was reacting to with prescience and force.

Yet for all of orality's promise of presence, the gears grind backward as well. We've seen how "reading across readings" reveals a Ginsberg far less certain of orality's promise than might first be apparent. One way of conceptualizing this schism is to focus on *performance*, a word that calls up an entire field of intellectual practice. This has not gone unremarked by critics invested in the poetry reading. In her recent study of poetry slams, Susan Somers-Willett refers to the form of reception described above as privileging authenticity, a term she explores by reference to key texts in poststructuralist performance studies by J. L. Austin, Judith Butler, Erving Goffman, and Jacques Lacan. Goffman's *The Presentation of Self in Everyday Life* (1959), a seminal text in studies of performance, knocks the struts from causal bridges between physical presence and authenticity. For Goffman, daily life is inevitably shot through with dissimulations at every turn, as in this description of the paradoxes of vocal authenticity that recall (or predict, really) Trilling's discomfort with performance, one captured in the antinomies of Tomás and Adam: "To give a radio talk that will sound genuinely informal, spontaneous, and relaxed, the speaker may have to design his script with painstaking care, testing one phrase after another, in order to follow the content, language, rhythm, and pace of everyday talk" (32). Goffman's skepticism is an opening salvo. He examines the "everyday" behaviors of medical professionals, professional wrestlers, violinists, and suburban "housewives" to suggest the banal normalcy of their artifice.

Performance studies as an academic discipline more largely offers a lens through which to view questions of presence and authenticity in speech and onstage. Accounts of performance by Peggy Phelan and Philip Auslander capture this radical ambivalence regarding the status of performance and its relationship to the real by articulating the status of performance itself. According to Phelan, performance (which includes any kind of staged reading) "implicates the real" by the "presence of living bodies" (148). For Phelan, live bodies onstage attain a kind of ontological veracity and leave behind no copies, or "left-overs," as they radiate pure immediacy, a "maniacally charged present" (148). In this way, recordings of readings—the materials of this study—are just such left-overs, mere traces of what has ineluctably disappeared. "Performance," as Phelan says, "honors the idea that a limited number of people in a specific time/space frame can have an experience of value which leaves no visible trace afterward" (149). This further raises questions about the oral impulse behind poems themselves, which we have seen function as "traces" of Goffman's performances of everyday life. For Phelan, however, these questions are endemic to understanding performance and point to a crucial tension: because the body can't sustain its status as an object of pure presence, the performer actually "disappears" to represent something different, something beyond the performer—the body, the work, the text. As Phelan puts it, performance "uses the body to frame the lack of being promised by and through the body" (151). In performance, something always escapes that we can never fully apprehend or indeed record, though it's always fully and tantalizingly on display. Performance cites, but skirts, the authentic.

Auslander's essay "Liveness" arrives at a similar sense of performance's representational ambivalence and compromised authenticity in a way particularly useful for examining poetry readings. The very idea of "live," Auslander argues, is facilitated by its ability to be recorded; recording creates, paradoxically, a sense of an event's self-similarity and aura; without recording, liveness is impossible (198). This kind of dialectical relationship is commonly echoed by writers on orality itself, as when Ong points out how "writing from the beginning did not reduce orality but enhanced it" by offering an "organizing" technology (*Orality* 9). Yet for Auslander, liveness has indeed become "the realm of the authentic" (207) if for no other reason than it can be *made* inauthentic by way of the distinction between performance and technological reproduction. In this inversion, the live depends upon the recorded, not vice versa. Similar to Phelan's sense of performance's ambivalent relation to the real, liveness balances precariously on its own opposition. In the poet's case, a reader captures immediacy and presence by staging a written text; it's the knowledge of textual existence itself that suffuses a performance with its capacity for authenticity.

In the chapters that follow, I only examine poetry with a textual basis.

There are no "performance poets" per se studied here. Each essay focuses in some way on the distinction between a print text and its performed articulation. This is a crucial point, because this entire argument is predicated upon the distinction between different versions of a poem—its written and spoken instances—and the questions pursued throughout emerge from ones similar to those raised by the writers above. What, if anything, is authentic about these events? How do performances affect a printed poem? Do they increase or reduce a poem's quality of presence? Do they create or deflate a vivid and living encounter with lyric creations? What other meanings get generated by readers as they speak their words aloud, speak around their poems, revise them, chuckle and laugh through them, slip up and misread and mumble? All of these questions put the human voice in tension with the established fact of print. It's a conflict that threads all of the readings discussed below and one deeply enmeshed in the culture and politics of the age.

Speaking Out in the Participatory New Left

"The sheer fact of being there," writes Todd Gitlin of the 1964 antiwar demonstration at D.C.'s Washington Monument, "seemed to be remarkable to begin with" (184). Being physically at hand, visible, and active was a part of a culture of participation—presence of a quite literal kind—that formed the crucible of what we now know as the New Left and, more generally, the civil rights movement that preceded it. "Being there" by putting your body on the line had become immensely important to the mostly black civil rights movement, the mostly white New Left student movement, and the counterculture itself. One can hear the emphasis on participation in this leaflet from the Students for a Democratic Society (SDS), which calls for "a domestic social movement" to end the war in Vietnam by asking for numerically quantifiable presence: "This movement showed its potential when 25,000 people—students, the poverty-stricken, ministers, faculty, unionists, and others—marched on Washington last April. . . . SDS urges everyone who believes that our warmaking must be ended and our democracy-building must begin, to join in a March on Washington on November 27, at 11 A.M. in front of the White House" ("SDS Calls" 192). Attendance generated legitimacy; mass physical presence on public land was a sign of political authenticity, often in the form of public spectacle that drew on a developing iconography of meaning.

The civil rights historian William H. Chafe details the early movement in Greensboro, North Carolina, which was characterized by a persistent push toward direct action due to demonstrators' impatience with "petition and patient verbal protest" and thus saw the origins of the sit-in movement (151). Merely by sitting at a lunch counter, black (and subsequently white) protesters could drive social change with their own bodies. "The sit-ins represented a new language," argues Chafe, a language that "communicated a message different from that which had been heard before. A direct connection existed between style and content" (99). This "style" was communicated nonverbally—"the silence of people sitting with dignity at a lunch counter demanding their rights" (99)—and, to tweak McLuhan's well-known formulation, the style was the message: we deserve rights. Discussing the March on Washington on August 28, 1963, Gitlin emphasizes the lucidity of this new semiotic palette: "[T]he nearly quarter of a million people who came to the Lincoln Memorial . . . were a walking advertisement for racial integration" (144–45). Physical presence was highly politicized and could be read with developing ease.

One manifestation of this new culture of visible presence is captured by the role of public speaking, which I want to argue resonated with poetry readings due to a subdued speaking style that simultaneously foregrounded and undercut authenticity. There is perhaps no greater symbol of the period's public speaking than Mario Savio, the prominent Free Speech Movement (FSM) activist who captures the antinomies of sixties reading well. Savio is best remembered for his 1964 declamation from the steps of Berkeley's Sproul Hall, in which he condemns the bureaucracy of the University of California for barring access to public space for student protest. It's an arresting and affecting speech. Savio stands before a huge crowd and speaks in a pleading, angry voice that becomes emblematic of the New Left's social activist stance: "There's a time when the operation of the machine becomes so odious—makes you so sick at heart—that you can't take part. You can't even passively take part. And you've got to put your bodies upon the gears and upon the wheels, upon the levers, upon all the apparatus, and you've got to make it stop. And you've got to indicate to the people who run it, to the people who own it, that unless you're free, the machine will be prevented from working at all" (qtd. in Lustig 216).

Savio's image of bodies draped across gear-works is striking and recalls McClure's description cited above of Ginsberg's Six Gallery reading as "a human voice and body" being "hurled against the harsh wall of America and its supporting armies and navies and academies and institutions." Moreover, Savio directs the assembled crowd to acknowledge the possibilities of its own presence at that spot. Being on those campus steps was transformed into an act of politically effective accountability. Literally, "being there" in the FSM itself—which, as in black civil rights struggles elsewhere, included fire hoses and bayonets pointed at protesters (Martin 91)—had a special status, and Savio's fiery address captures the wrought, emotional pitch that made him, as historian Doug Rossinow puts it, the "hot-eyed spokesman" of the student movement, the "angry, eloquent" sixties "icon of public consumption" (536). Footage of Savio's exhortations at the microphone, with the reporters' oblong tape recorders perched dispassionately near his mouth, is indeed affecting. Michael Rossman, himself a part of the FSM, recalled that Savio had the kind of "authenticity" that ensured his words would be heard (qtd. in Rossinow 533). Wendy Lesser, who drew Savio's work into the literary journal the *Threepenny Review* by publishing one of his speeches in 1995, associates Savio's authentic presence with spoken language: "He was the last American, perhaps, who believed that civil, expressive, precisely worded, emotionally truthful exhortation could bring about significant change.... The irony is that his power lay entirely in the spoken word, so that what he said on any given occasion could never quite be captured in print" (563). As an icon of sixties speaking, Savio seems to represent the power of the lone body radiating truth, summoning into being forces ungovernable and real. It's perhaps no surprise that Rossinow ends his essay on Savio by suggesting he was truly prophetic and shamanistic, divinely inspired when he spoke, "in a religious state. He trembled and his eyes burned" (548).

Despite this iconographic presence and declamatory style, much of Savio's public persona conflicts with his private image and chimes with the antinomies of sixties reading. As a flood of biographical and critical sources attest, Savio in fact was demurring of recognition, emotionally removed, and skeptical of the aura of heroic individualism his presence seemed to announce. Describing Savio's earlier work with voter registration drives in Jackson, Mississippi, Berkeley historian Waldo Martin characterizes Savio as "shy" (the most frequent word used in such remembrances) and totally absorbed not in the performance of authorship but in "concerted social action" (94). Martin's fellow historian Ruth Rosen defined Savio's style as "reluctant leadership" (qtd.

in Martin 95). Rossinow suggests that Savio was "astonishingly different" in private from his public image, "not self-aggrandizing as his melodramatic public style might suggest" (535) but rather "gentle, inarticulate" (536). This inarticulate quality was captured in his actual speaking voice, which, though powerful, Savio worked hard to develop due to a speech impediment in his youth (535). This self-abnegating streak wasn't modesty so much as a resistance to individualism over collective action. When a reporter from the *New York Times* flew to California to interview the Berkeley student leader about the FSM, Savio refused, saying he didn't wish to be cast as the movement's leader (534). "Savio did indeed project a sense of authenticity to his fellow students in 1964," concludes Rossinow, "but it was a different kind of authenticity whose character is not easy to recapture today" (548). This "different" authenticity did not rely on full-frontal self-exposure, or a squaring of the private self with the public weal—what Trilling would call "sincerity." Rather, it was a conditioned vulnerability, a desire to effect change but not be its sole agent, a donning and doffing of the leader's mantle. It was a struggle borne out in his voice itself, which recognized, as did those Greensboro protesters, the correspondence of form and content. Wendy Lesser's "Elegy for Mario Savio," written on the occasion of his death in 1996, attributed Savio's "power" "entirely in the spoken word" (563). "His voice—the very sound of it, its accent and emphasis and pitch—was physically a part of the meaning of his words" (563).

Public speaking, voice, and "stage presence" were thus fundamental not just to political language but also to the language of the Left, white and black. The civil rights movement is of course dominated by the figure of King and his nuclear oratory, yet the less celebrated figure of Bob Moses was also a notable speaker, one who drew upon the ironically "reluctant" tones of a Mario Savio. Moses was Savio's contemporary and worked for the SNCC, "its foremost saint," as Gitlin says (148). Like Savio, Moses's voice was crucial to his appeal. "In voice and gesture," writes Gitlin, "Moses did more than anyone else to create the premium movement style: diffidence over bravado; quiet assertion rather than driving crescendos; plain, halting speech rather than rolling phrases" (148). His speaking style led to what Gitlin calls "a cultivation of the inarticulate" in the civil rights movement, one that spread outward to the SDS and beyond (149). To speak softly, as Moses did, was to recognize the voice's extraordinary value in the semantics of style, and leaders like

Moses and Savio (who actually worked with Moses in Mississippi prior to his better-known activities in Berkeley) were attuned to the authentic presence their voices commanded. Yet by no means did softness equate to lack of leadership—quite the opposite, argues Gitlin, who maintains that self-muffling and deflection "didn't eliminate leadership, only disguised it" (149). Voice had been made semiotically labile.

I TAKE THIS political detour through the lives of Mario Savio and Bob Moses, through the civil rights movement and the New Left, because poetry readings were so deeply enmeshed in this culture of public speaking and presence. If poetry readers were operating within the humanist-skeptical dialectic, so were speakers like Savio and Moses for whom authenticity was an equally complicated, crisscrossing affair of self-revelation and vocal evasion. Many poets made easy alliance between these larger social movements and their art. "I was always interested in Surrealism and Expressionism, and I think the reason was to really try to get below the surface of things," Amiri Baraka has claimed. "The Civil Rights Movement, it's the same thing essentially, trying to get below the surface of things, trying to get below the norm, the everyday, the status quo, which was finally unacceptable, just unacceptable" (qtd. in Kane 13). A quite literal crossroads providing such a place-specific link between public and poetic forms of declamation was the college campus. The campus, a site for both activism and poetry in performance, shows how readings functioned in often contradictory ways. For the political Left, the campus was ground zero for protest, occupations of administrative buildings occurring in Frankfurt, London, Berkeley, and New York City (Sayres et al. 2). Yet the campus was also the place where so many poets read their work. Sometimes, social activism and poetry reading neatly dovetailed, as when Gwendolyn Brooks read in 1967 at Fisk University, an event that effectively politicized her. Other readings were not overtly political. Ginsberg frequently appeared on campuses to read. Two of his infrequent full readings of *Kaddish* took place at Brandeis and Harvard, and he actively participated in campus-based demonstrations, notably in Berkeley (Ginsberg, *Deliberate* 235). In his miniprimer "Demonstration or Spectacle as Example, as Communication or How to Make a March/Spectacle," Ginsberg offers advice to a planning committee on how to create a "spectacle" at a Berkeley antiwar march planned for November 1965, a march in which Ginsberg himself was to participate. The list is a weird blend of counterculture trippiness, serious concern for marchers' safety (the Hell's Angels were threatening violence), and political conviction. Here are some sample ideas, listed by their numbers:

> 4. Marchers who use American flags should bring those: at least one front row of American flags and myriad in the spectacle.
>
> 9. Candy bars carried by marchers to offer Hell's Angels and police.
>
> 16: At first sign of disturbance, public address systems swing into vast sound to loud *Beatles* "I Wanna Hold Your Hand" and marchers instructed to dance (if not doing calisthenics or Lord's prayer). (Ginsberg, *Deliberate* 11–12)

Like Savio, Ginsberg's sense of his relationship to university institutions could be oppositional. About the Harvard *Kaddish* reading, Ginsberg is sure to point out that he was later ejected from Lowell House after he and Peter Orlovsky were charged with conducting "sex experiments" and "chanting Buddhist prayers," events "too confusing to the Academy" (*Deliberate* 235). In "Notes on Finally Recording 'Howl,'" Ginsberg addresses "the Academies," saying, "[P]oetry has been attacked by an ignorant and frightened bunch of bores who don't understand how it's made, and the trouble with these creeps is they wouldn't know poetry if it came up and buggered them in broad daylight" (83).

Ginsberg's frustrations do indeed concern the tweed-jacketed "bores" themselves, a sentiment shared by other poets. As Gwendolyn Brooks told an interviewer, "[Y]ou and I know that many a Dr. Puffanblow writes a duller piece than does Susie Butterball, the high school sophomore" (*Conversations* 25). Yet the larger context was that the battle lines over the sixties culture of protest were drawn straight through campus quads. Big universities in the postwar era were indeed transforming themselves from communities of humanist and scientific research and liberal arts into larger, organized research institutions that held clear similarities to the managerial, administrative, corporate culture of productivity against which the intellectual counterculture established itself. In a chronology of key sixties events between 1957 and 1976 compiled by Sohnya Sayres, Anders Stephanson, Stanley Aronowitz, and Fredric Jameson, student movements on college campuses appear frequently, including the student sit-in at Shaw College (which was the origin of the SNCC); the formation of the SDS at Columbia University and the FSM in Berkeley; the first University of Michigan "teach-in"; and student rebellions in Warsaw, Poland, and Mexico City (187). The college campus performed as a microcosm of larger national forces in the struggle between "the system" and those who opposed it.

In this regard, the first half of Savio's speech quoted above is worth mentioning, as it refers to the president of the University of California system itself, Clark Kerr, a towering figure in the history of American university education due to his recognition of the corporatizing university. Savio's speech on the steps of Sproul Hall was given directly following a meeting with Kerr, who framed his refusal to publicly acknowledge putting pressure on the board of regents as a rhetorical question: "[W]ould you ever imagine the manager of a firm making a statement publicly in opposition to his board of directors?" Savio addresses the crowd: "Well, I ask you to consider," he begins,

> if this is a firm, and if the board of regents are the board of directors, and if President Kerr in fact is the manager, then I'll tell you something. The faculty are a bunch of employees, and we're the raw material! But we're a bunch of raw materials that don't mean to be—have any process upon us. Don't mean to be made into any product. Don't mean . . . [d]on't mean to end up being bought by some clients of the University, be they the government, be they industry, be they organized labor, be they anyone! We're human beings! (qtd. in Lustig 217)

That Savio casts the university's administration in corporate terms is no accident. Kerr's book *The Uses of the University* (1963) paints a picture of the modern research institution as a "multiversity," a many-tiered, sprawling place juggling undergraduate, graduate, and professional education programs, the professoriate, nonacademic staff and workers, the administration itself, alumni, politicians, and the business community (14). Kerr calls it a "mechanism held together by administrative rules and powered by money" (15). "The managerial revolution" railed against by leftist intellectuals from the previous decade, like C. Wright Mills in *White Collar* (1951) and David Riesman in *The Lonely Crowd* (1950), "has been going on also in the university" (Kerr 22). Savio's cry is against this managerial elite, embodied by the University of California itself.

To be sure, most campus readings were not oppositional at all. Robert Frost toured colleges on a virtual circuit. David Shribman, who transcribed and edited a series of Frost's campus appearances, claims Frost's campus readings were "those he liked best" (Frost, *Robert Frost* x), though Frost did cast the university in the role of modern-day patron in the absence of other options. It may be useful, again, to examine Ginsberg in this regard. In a well-known essay, Diana Trilling describes one of Ginsberg's readings, held at Columbia University in 1959. Trilling, the wife of Ginsberg's former professor Lionel, attended and wrote a reflective, sometimes arch, often condescending description of the reading that, if it can be trusted at least in its basic outlines, reveals not only what happened but also how a contemporary listener received it. For Trilling, Ginsberg's reading at Columbia marked his return to "respectability," as well as a supplication to the authority of her husband, whom Ginsberg's work had not pleased in the past. (Trilling, in a letter to Ginsberg after reading an early draft of *Howl* and other poems, wrote: "[P]erhaps you will believe that I am being sincere when I say they are dull" [Ginsberg, *Howl Facsimile* 156].) Her supercilious gaze and utter lack of hipness can jar a modern reader, but she registers how the reading at Columbia was dramatically different from, say, the Six Gallery performance: its anarchic elements have cooled, Ginsberg is "touching" in his earnest desire to appeal, he had a "sweetness in his face and to his sweet smile" (D. Trilling 169), and—a point Trilling makes with some emphasis—he was clean-shaven and "neat" (166). More importantly, though, the "poet-rebel-poet," as she put it, was *performing* differently:

> For the fact was that Ginsberg, reading his verse, had naturally given it the iambic beat: after all, it is the traditional beat of English poetry where it deals with serious subjects, as Ginsberg's poems so often do. A poet, one thought—and it was a poignant thought because it came so immediately and humanly rather than as an abstraction—may choose to walk whatever zany path in his life as a man; but, when it comes to mourning and mothers and such, he will be drawn into the line of tradition; at least in this far he is always drawn toward "respectability." (D. Trilling 172)

Sometimes Trilling sounds precisely like the kind of frightened bore Ginsberg mocked. Robert Bly indeed parodies Trilling's boringness in his response, "The Other Night in Heaven," which begins: "My name is Diana Tilling [*sic*] and I am very important" (qtd. in Ginsberg, "Notes" 75). And yet here, Trilling characterizes Ginsberg as seeking approval from the Ivy League intelligentsia. The "poignant" quality was this struggle between a poem composed in long, guttural, unmetered lines and his vocal performance of it, which "neatened" it into traditional form. Was it the presence of Columbia itself that caused this rhythmic groveling? Did it even occur? It's hard to say for certain, though when she refers to the poet's recent readings Trilling recognizes, as very few commentators on Ginsberg seem to, that Ginsberg modulated his performance for the occasion: "Ginsberg at Columbia on Thursday night was not Ginsberg at Chicago . . . or Ginsberg at Hunter either, where Kerouac ran the show" (D. Trilling 157). The Columbia reading reveals again the antinomies of sixties reading and the importance of campuses in establishing them. In the following chapters, college campuses play an important role for Frost, Brooks, Olson, Williams, and Eigner as readers.

Furthermore, this emphasis on campus reading and the ramifications of political rhetoric adds to what is often imagined as a legacy of much early forms of public speech. One version of this history emphasizes, for example, how poetry readings still draw from the kind of advice to readers given in an elocution manual published by J. E. Carpenter in 1906.

> It is, perhaps, not saying too much to aver that only a poet can read poetry properly: at any rate only those who are perfectly imbued with the poetic feeling can do so. Given all these qualifications, and action, voice, and gesture will follow naturally and spontaneously; the electric fire will flash from the speaker to his audience, enthusiasm will be kindled, and a result that only true genius can achieve will be accomplished. . . . To the hearers it should be as though the speaker were giving the utterances of his own heart, and his own brain, an impulsive and involuntary outpouring excited by existing and surrounding circumstances. (qtd. in Middleton, *Distant* 86)

Peter Middleton suggests that poets still read "as if they were uttering the lines for the first time in 'an impulsive and involuntary outpouring,'" and it is indeed surprising how much a how-to instruction book can prefigure a great postmodern stentor like Charles Olson, with whom Middleton compares such a gesture. Yet it's also true that such ideas get reborn. Campuses were not the first place to see fiery oratory, nor were poetry readings in the sixties sui generis affairs, drawing as they did on histories of elocution, recitation, public ceremonies, and schoolroom pedagogy.[3] These things were reanimated and warped in new ways as they found traction in the culture of sixties reading.

The Ontology of the Poem

What are poems? I'm arguing that this question haunted poetry readings in the sixties, generating an urgent performance of presence that occluded its own anxiety. If the sixties "culture of spontaneity," as Daniel Belgrad terms it (216)—a physically immediate, kinesthetic "poetics of presence" that radiated through and past virtually all postwar avant-gardes—positioned the body and voice as its metonymic sign, at the center of cultural meaning and value, poetry went through a similar trajectory, and it is for this reason that I've been tracing larger orbits of cultural value. Poetry's new life on the stage and platform was a dramatization of poetry's shifting status, from a rhetorically stable object of critical examination to a textual form responsive to history. Readings uprooted poems from the white space surrounding them, repositioned them in various and varying lights, replanted and pruned them, all the while suggesting that poems may not be the stable, substantial objects they had been. Was poetry abstract or concrete? Mystical or political? Spiritual or physical? Ideal or Real? Present or endlessly articulated? Sixties readings investigated these questions. We've seen already how, for all of Ginsberg's claims to and demonstrations of bop prosody and live spark, there's a different, somewhat historically obscured side of this aesthetic—reserved, diffident, disenchanted with the immediate effects of liveness, even nostalgic for the strophes of traditional meter. Next we'll see how Robert Frost's own management of this dialectic produced reading after reading of cautious, canny performance that became emblematic of the age.

One reason for this new sensibility was that poetry itself was radiating in dramatically new directions due, in part, to technological innovation. In print, the mimeograph machine facilitated an explosion of literary journals, and with the advent of photo-offset printing a new kind of nimble, responsive small press could answer quickly to current events via pamphlets, chapbooks, broadsides, and actual volumes of poetry. In the pages to come, such publications appear frequently, as when Charles Olson describes in detail one of his poems featured in *Floating Bear*, the influential newsletter edited by Diane di Prima and LeRoi Jones. The creation by Dudley Randall of the Broadside Press is another prime example of how poets could counter problems of literary self-determination: Randall founded Broadside to secure rights over his "Ballad of Birmingham," which the singer Jerry Lewis wanted to use for song lyrics (Kent 192). Because it provided an outlet for black writers in need of sympathetic editors, Broadside took off, eventually becoming the home press of Gwendolyn Brooks for close to a decade. This world of print was often clearly implicated in readings themselves, which acted in concert with such responsive forms of material publication. And alongside this boom in small presses, now widely available microphones and speakers aided mass readings, and on cheap magnetic tape and glossy black vinyl the sacred voice of the poet was constantly being "captured"—the very word suggests restriction and confinement—and sold in far-off places for years to come. What did poets think of these developments? Did they affect their poems? How was the relationship between poet and poem changing? In short, was the ontology of poetry in flux?[4]

The short answer is: yes. For contrast, one could focus on the preceding orthodoxies of the New Criticism, which treated the poem as an object imbued with ontological grace. The story of the New Critics is arguably the master narrative of twentieth-century Anglo-American literary study, so there is no need to sketch its broad outlines here, though it's worth pausing briefly over the New Critics' sense of lyric ontology as a way to frame what followed it. John Crowe Ransom's "Poetry: A Note on Ontology" (1938) is one of a number of formalist arguments that make the case for poetry's objective existence. "Metaphysical poetry," Ransom argues, is distinct from "physical poetry," the poetry of the imagists, like Amy Lowell, and from George Moore's "pure poetry," which Ransom calls "Physical Poetry" (117). On the other hand is "Platonic poetry"—abstract, idea-oriented lyrical form, decidedly "bogus" in its tendency to "illustrate" ideas with things rather than to embody them (128). Metaphysical poetry, however, travels a *via media* between these two extremes. It's a poetry that welds concretions to thought in what Ransom calls "miraculism," which occurs "when the poet discovers by analogy an identity between objects" (139) and makes them apparent in language. This poetry is ontologically coherent, having in it a quality of truth telling that is unshakable, a larger tenet of New Critical formalism audible in its language of visibility and presence. W. K. Wimsatt's *The Verbal Icon* (1954) and Cleanth Brooks's *The Well-Wrought Urn* (1947) are two major New Critical works that even in their titles figure the poem as a coherent, organically whole and self-sufficient craft object. This criticism has meant, as Brooks put it, "cutting [literature] loose from its author and from his life as a man," "severing it from those who actually read it" (G. Davis 85). William Logan points out that the New Criticism grew up around modernism in part to "justify" modernism's confounding difficulties (G. Davis xii), though the practice of close reading—which depends upon the formal coherence of literary content—is still very much with us in classrooms despite its waning importance in actual scholarship. This may indicate how historically implicated such a dehistoricizing methodology actually was, yet the fact remains: the poetics that preceded postwar American poetry valued a complex, page-based poet of formal exactitude. The poem was present, and it was present there on the page.[5]

Bodies on the Line argues that the 1960s saw poets questioning poetry's transformations into materialities of performance—endless readings, endless public performances—alongside technological forms like recording and video in ways that go roots-deep into lyric ontology. The anxieties and tensions explored in the subsequent chapters—Frost's evasions of presence, Olson's resistance to orality, Brooks's queasiness at public poetry—derive in part from this sense of seismic change to lyric itself. One such significant mediating force, for example, was sound reproduction and amplification technology, which had already been reshaping public attitudes toward the reality of language itself. In *The Audible Past*, Jonathan Sterne argues that technological reproduction of sound had been based on a series of paradoxical and interdependent relationships since the inception of recording in the nineteenth century. Sterne points out that conventional understanding of "original" and "copy" dominated sound recording from the first recordings by Edison, and that loss of aura and authenticity was a by-product of mediation. "The human voice *is* the human on the New Orthophonic Victrola," declares one ad for an early phonograph reproduced in Sterne's book, suggesting that the relationship between voice and its recording is to be measured by what Sterne calls "fidelity" of copy to source, "a measurable correspondence between two different sounds" (222). That ad reveals a clear anxiety: that the reproduction won't measure up to the "real" thing. Yet Sterne suggests, in ways similar to Auslander above, that "original" and "copy" feed off each other in a hermeneutic circle. Walter Benjamin's well-known argument on loss of aura due to mechanical reproduction, says Sterne, registers a counterclaim, too—that aura is "an artifact of reproducibility, rather than a side effect or an inherent quality of self-presence" (220). To create aura, an inauthentic copy is necessary, as "authenticity and presence become issues only when there is something to which we can compare them" (220).

It's fascinating to see how poets' attitudes toward sound recording were still coming into being in the postwar years and how different Sterne's sense of authenticity is from the optimistic, celebratory swell of excitement around "breath" and the live body poets were beginning to display and then distrust. Ginsberg's writing, for example, repeatedly positions the body and breath as the starting line for poetry. He refers to the "breath groups" of "American speech" in *Howl* in his essay on recording that poem (*Deliberate* 229) and suggests there that the genesis of writing is in speech when describing the "Moloch Moloch" opening of part 2 as deriving from his "muttering" those words while high and walking the streets of San Francisco. *Kaddish* is likewise depicted as beginning in an all-night talk with a friend, reading from the actual Hebrew text (*Deliberate* 233). In his long essay "On Walt Whitman, Composed on the Tongue," Ginsberg approximates the speaking voice in his prose style: "Then there's this very famous poem where he realizes, yeah, sure, but all that's transitory, it's going, there's not much, you know, like 20 years, 50 years; then zap it's gone" (*Deliberate* 307). Inscribed in poems and structuring them through composition, the human breath comes spilling from Ginsberg's mouth and gets poems going.

Or does it? Ginsberg also displays a competing and contradictory fascination with technological mediation, one that seems not to recognize the interplay between presence and absence described by Sterne. While in his prefatory remarks to recording *Howl* (cited above) Ginsberg is clearly skeptical of the limitations a recording puts on presence, elsewhere recording technologies aid his composition through their ability to capture liveness. In "Abstraction in Poetry," Ginsberg celebrates Kerouac's exploitation of machinery in reduplicating spontaneity, explaining that he was "copying actual recorded tape conversations of his hero and then imitating it in ideal dream-conversation prose" (*Deliberate* 243). Tyler Hoffman quotes Ginsberg's use of the tape recorder, which offered him the immediacy of dictation, in composing "The Fall of America" (*American Poetry* 140) and points out how Ginsberg's own tape recorder functions as a kind of personalized counterstatement to the machineries of war and "commercialized mass vocalism" (141). How are we to understand Ginsberg's attitude toward technological reproduction? Hostility gives way to embrace; what once eroded the aura of immediacy now assists it. Moreover, Ginsberg's paradoxical attitude toward technological mediation dramatizes a more general confusion about poetry's ontological status in an era of amplification, recording, and public performance.

If readings were liberating and celebratory, they also tugged at poets' sense of what was happening to poems themselves. All poets discussed in this book are formalists of a sort, and all are deeply committed to poetry of the page; each one was also invested in reading poems aloud. How do tensions between poems as performed and as more stable things play out? In a larger way, this is a question for theories of the lyric, which inquire into the limits of a "bounded" lyric form. Sharon Cameron's book on Emily Dickinson's fascicles, *Choosing Not Choosing* (1992), argues that the fascicles Dickinson created out of (or as?) her poems—small, hand-sewn booklets of holographs full of variants and a range of textual marks—raise "a question about what constitutes the identity of the poem" (4). These books, Cameron says, "*embody* the problem of identity" (4, emphasis in original). Cameron quotes Allen Grossman's reflections on bounded lyric in *Summa Lyrica*, in which Grossman defines a "closural frame" for poems: "The quality of singularity manifested in each instant of utterance is in each case of manifestation, syllable by syllable, the frame of the poem (that is, its closure)" (5). If fascicles test lyric closure or boundedness, readings test and retest it. What kind of "closural frame" does a poem like *Howl* have, composed, performed, revised, and reiterated more than once before seeing its first day in print? The story of poetry readings I tell here is not that they are the place of authentic presence. It's that they're sites for interrogating the very idea of presence, the idea of authenticity, and the ontology of the lyric itself.

BODIES ON THE LINE. The title of this book sounds a clarion call of the 1960s itself, signifying political commitment. The phrase shows up across generations. In a 1967 interview with Paul Angle, Gwendolyn Brooks said, with some frustration, that "the thing that is stressed by the people who have their hearts and bodies on the line is that progress, a little bit more each year, is not enough" (*Conversations* 17). In a recent interview, reflecting on "her generation" of the sixties, the experimental poet Ann Waldman articulated an unchanged sense of the term:

> For me and members (old and young) of my generation (if I may be bold to speak for some of them) the "real work" means reclaiming poetry as a present art and act, as "news that stays news" (in Ezra Pound's sense), and as proclamation and transmission, with a sense of speech and the word being sacred, not just a euphemism from the thugs in the White House. It is the word moving on and off the page and out of an empathetic imagination. That relates to the inter-connectedness of the larger world community. Literally putting your words and bodies on the line in a struggle for greater sanity and justice in the world. (Pearlman)

Clearly, the phrase "bodies on the line" is synonymous with physical visibility, actual presence, social justice, and a certain amount of personal risk. And yet in this study, the preposition "on" accrues multivalent meanings. If I'm right that poets were entering political life as readers of poetry, then they were indeed "on" the line. Yet is this a positive stance—as if to say, as a musician would, that a horn player is "on" tonight? That poet and line fall in syncopated grace? Or does "on" signify an imposition: "You're sitting on my coat!" Or is it just a showbiz encouragement: "You're on!" Behind the resounding heroics the phrase suggests, it also contains a less certain note. Are poets reading poems *sitting on*—suffocating—the lines of lyric? The word "line" neatly links the aesthetic and political: poets standing on the physical lines of protest and activism were also working with lines of written text—the line of the poem. Did poets see this as a good thing? Does the phrase "on the line" imply a kind of lumbering imposition behind the aggressive acquisition of poetic effect? Poets were putting themselves "on the line" by speaking out in front of audiences, and yet they were also putting their bodies on the line of the poem itself. Was that liberating or dampening? Such questions are ultimately unanswerable. Poets' belief, excitement, fear, frustration, and confusions about this new verbal style are the subject of this book.

CHAPTER 2 OFFERS the first full-scale critical account of Robert Frost as a reader. While Frost had a long career, I examine recordings made primarily in the mid-1950s up to the time of his death in 1963. Frost's readings reveal a poet straddling the line between humanist expression and skeptical distance, poetic ontology and its deflection, and the sacrosanct embodiment of lyric authenticity and its performative multiplicity.

Chapter 3 listens in to two important and very different readings by Charles Olson, arguing that while Olson is seen either as a poet of breath or a poet of what one critic calls "graphicity," or writing, in fact his readings reveal his confused relation to live voice. Speaking at two different college campuses—Berkeley in California, Goddard College in Vermont—Olson reads in dramatically different fashions, demonstrating nostalgia for textual certainty despite reeling professions of the anarchic possibilities of voice.

Chapter 4 claims that Gwendolyn Brooks's voice in recordings and at poetry readings dramatizes the slow, often contradictory, and ultimately incomplete transformation Brooks made from a private to a public poet. Voicings of poems show Brooks as a public poet straining for expression in early private poems and, later, as a private poet nostalgic for the lost interiority in public, even declamatory poems. My reading, which is based on a diverse set of materials—an episode of a radio show, recordings of poetry readings, a vinyl LP, and a short documentary film, along with a host of archival materials—intervenes into a long-standing critical debate about Brooks's poetic career, which was seen as either bifurcated or not by the Second Black Writers' Conference at Fisk University in 1967.

Chapter 5 refracts the book's entire argument by listening to two readers with disabilities. William Carlos Williams has never been read as a poet of disability, but in fact he experienced increasingly severe expressive aphasia from the early 1950s onward due to three powerful strokes. Larry Eigner's cerebral palsy limited his speaking voice to a barely comprehensible approximation of standard speech. I argue that both Williams and Eigner limn the poles of "cripped" and normal speech to reveal the ways the speaking voice can upset expectations of normalcy and produce as a result new forms of presence. In the larger terms of this study, disabled reading torques the humanist/skeptical dialectic: Williams reading onstage performs a (failed) simulation of a "normal" humanist reader; reading aloud, Eigner "untypes" his poems, which were generated by slow and methodical punching with his right index finger of typewriter keys. Both poets speak in relationship to a perceived standard of postwar normalcy, one that generates new attitudes to literary form, shifts our sense of how we should understand the nature of disability, and establishes both as deeply invested in the aesthetics of performance.

A Note on Sources

The performances studied in this book are drawn from diverse sources. Some chapters rely almost entirely upon archival recordings, inaccessible to listeners outside the holding library. Chapter 2, for example, draws primarily upon tape recordings housed in the Woodberry Poetry Room in Harvard's Lamont Library as well as the Recorded Sound Reference Center at the Library of Congress. Many of these recordings are simply raw, unedited tape of Frost reading, introduced by a faculty member, interrupted by coughs and sirens and scuffing chairs and misplaced spectacles and creaking doors. For my chapter on Gwendolyn Brooks I drew material from the Schomburg Center in Harlem and the New York Public Library for the Performing Arts. Sometimes such material is simply a commercial recording, like the vinyl LPs made by Frost and Brooks on the Caedmon label, or a radio program, TV documentary, or other rare item. Outside of libraries and special collections, I've drawn heavily upon Web-based resources, which have grown considerably during the process of writing this book (see the appendix). When I began my research at Harvard, for example, I listened to cassette tapes on a small playback machine that perched on my lap. Since that time these recordings have been digitized, though due to copyright restrictions such files are available only to affiliates of Harvard University. It's hard to believe, in fact, that until very recently many of the Frost recordings I refer to in this book existed solely in a few very fragile and erasable spools of magnetic tape.

Many more resources discussed here are easily accessible and in the public domain. I have worked from the Website PennSound, which since its launch in 2005 has become the most robust resource on the Web for free and freely available sound files of poetry readings. While PennSound focuses on contemporary writing, there are essential recordings from earlier decades too, and I listened to their digitized materials for my discussions of Ginsberg, Ashbery, Olson, Williams, and Eigner. Sometimes, versions of these recordings overlap with archival or other provenances, as when I found a rare Eigner cassette tape in his papers in the Thomas J. Dodd Research Center at the University of Connecticut that was, conveniently, already digitized on PennSound. Sites like PennSound (and its cousin UbuWeb, dedicated to avant-garde recordings) aren't simply making these materials more easily accessible; by doing so, they're shifting the bank of primary materials students and scholars can study away from solely print-based ones. While it's important to work from archival sources when necessary, there is great value in drawing upon accessible materials. This way a reader of my chapter on disability poetics, for example, can easily listen along to my analysis of Williams or Eigner. This is not simply convenient. It is also driven by a preservationist impulse and has enormous pedagogical implications.[6]

As mentioned, however, the bulk of these recordings are of more recent and typically avant-garde poetries. Modernist poets obviously recorded less frequently than their middle generation and later successors, but there's more to the problem than that. As Derek Furr points out, more recent poets conduct "experiments in sound, or sound and technology, deconstruct presence and redefine the boundaries of the poetical" (9), making recording more apparently essential to their work. Michael Davidson's comments cited earlier about postwar poetry's "new oral impulse" meant that reading and orality were essential aspects of these poets' work (97). For many such figures, recording (and the "oral impulse" that drives it) has become more than a means toward preservation or reproduction; through its use in the process of composition, it has become part of the work itself. The avant-garde poet David Antin tapes his own spontaneous "talking" and then transcribes and lineates the recording, making the poem's existence an interplay of speaking, technological reproduction, and writing.[7] Antin may provide a poetic that is radically different from Frost's, but even scanning the contents of two major essay collections on recorded poetries—*Sound States: Innovative Poetics and Acoustical Technologies*, edited by Adalaide Morris (1997), and *Close Listening: Poetry and the Per-*

formed Word, edited by Charles Bernstein (1998)—suggests an emphasis on contemporaneity, experiment, and performance. Subjects considered in these books include John Cage, Caribbean performance, poetry slams, Black Arts reading, and Hawaiian pidgin literature (though two essays on modernists do appear in Morris's volume, one on Joyce and the other on H.D.).[8] I hope that *Bodies on the Line* adds to these discussions a series of poets rarely, if ever, included in discussions of recorded poetry.

2

Robert Frost, Live

But all the fun's in how you say a thing.
—Robert Frost, "The Mountain"

The most famous poetry reading in American history occurred on Friday, January 20, 1961. On that bright and chilly morning, Robert Frost stood before a vast crowd assembled at the Capitol in Washington, D.C., to recite "The Gift Outright" as part of President John F. Kennedy's inauguration ceremony. Frost had planned to say two poems that morning. The first, "Dedication" (subsequently titled "For John F. Kennedy His Inauguration"), Frost couldn't complete because the sharp sun blinded his failing eyes, despite his having had the poem typed on an oversized-character typewriter once used by President Eisenhower. After fumbling through the first few lines of "Dedication" Frost abandoned it altogether, telling the crowd, to their roaring approval, that it was merely "a preface to the poem I can say to you without seeing it" (Thompson and Winnick 281). He then intoned "The Gift Outright" in a voice that Frost's biographer Lawrance Thompson calls "firm and unfaltering" and a reporter for the *Washington Post* termed "natural" (qtd. in Thompson and Winnick 282), though he dramatically revised the poem's final line, "Such as she was, such as she would become." Thompson describes the scene as Frost reached the end of his poem: "Here he paused, and in slow, accentuated tones, gave his altered version of the last line: 'Such as she was, such as she *would* become, *has* become, and I—and for this occasion let me change that to—what she *will* become.' Without pausing, he continued to speak. '... and this poem—what I was leading up to—was a dedication of the poem to the President-elect Mr. John Finley'" (281). In fact, this was a prosy improvisation on a previously agreed-upon revision to just one word in the final line. At Kennedy's request, Frost had allowed a substitution ("if only for a day," Kennedy had said) of "would" to "will"—the final words would read "such as she *will* become"—which the president thought "more positive-sounding" (278). And apparently, no one caught Frost's embarrassing blunder. John Huston Finley, Jr., was a Harvard professor of classics; it appears Frost simply confused their names. In any case, the great poet left the rostrum to applause, and Kennedy was administered his oath of office.

This uncharacteristically brief live poetry reading reveals that, for Frost, a poem is not a steady thing. It can be revised, sometimes quite willingly, for an occasion. (It can also be the site of unadulterated error, something different from revision.) One implication of this is that Frost's poems can be understood in dramatically different ways according to their spoken contexts. As Marit MacArthur points out, following the Kennedy reading, "The Gift Outright" has been interpreted as endorsing "triumphant nationalism" and "a celebration of colonialism" (63). It's true that this reading corresponds to Frost's own gloss of the poem around this time as being "about the Revolutionary War," as he put it in a November 29, 1960, talk at Dartmouth College (Frost, *Robert Frost* 137). Pushing this reading even further, Frost says the poem depicts a "conflict of good and good not good and bad. . . . The British colonial system was a good thing, but we got going ourselves" (137). Some have followed Frost's self-analysis. Reading the poem as an apology for colonialism, Tyler Hoffman wonders at Frost's "blindness" to "the abuses and systematic oppression of native peoples" and quotes the Irish writer Tom Paulin, who critiques the poem's claim to Manifest Destiny and what Hoffman refers to as "Frost's dismissal of American Indian culture" (*Robert Frost* 207).

Yet without the framing device of a presidential inauguration to guide such an interpretation (indeed, Hoffman situates the poem in just that context), MacArthur shows through close reading of Frost's notebooks, letters, and the poem's ambiguous final lines that "The Gift Outright" was originally a response to New Deal policies (it was written in 1935 though not published until 1942), which Frost notoriously despised, and the "careless attitude of the American people toward the American landscape" and native populations (67). In fact, says MacArthur, this poem displays "measured contempt" for the "we" of the poem—colonials ourselves, no doubt (69). Further complicating matters, the poem's original publication, in a 1942 issue of *Virginia Quarterly Review* on the progress of the war, suggests what MacArthur calls "uncertainty" about that event rather than sure-footed patriotism (63). Perhaps Kennedy should have asked for more tweaking.

So what does this tell us about Robert Frost and live reading? One answer is that readings insured Frost's poems would remain interpretively labile; poems written decades earlier could become, simply by voicing them in a new context, relevant to changing social and political circumstances. Another example: at a Harvard reading on December 2, 1962, after he had returned from a well-publicized trip to the Soviet Union, Frost acknowledges after being asked to read "Mending Wall" that "it didn't have any politics in it when I wrote it." He clearly gauged the social dynamics that had transformed his 1914 poem, about two neighbors locked in a fearsome ritual of border maintenance, into a Cold War allegory—a process expertly detailed by George Monteiro—and willingly acknowledged and even exploited them.[1] Just as "The Gift Outright" absorbs and recirculates timely inflections at Kennedy's inauguration, so "Mending Wall" is yoked into postwar politics at Harvard. This process suggests how much Frost treated readings as opportunities to politicize his poems in response to particular audiences. To Harvard dons, Frost admits the newfound politics of the poem as he relates what he told Khrushchev in their brief meeting in Moscow: "You eased down from the harshness of some of, some of your doctrines to somewhere near socialism, I suppose, and we're straining upward, over my dead body, straining upward through phases of the welfare statism [*sic*], a kind of socialism too, and now we must be so close together in socialism that we should be sociable." In Frost's facetious manner, the joke scolds a politically liberal Harvard audience by suggesting that "our side" is slipping dangerously close to Soviet socialism. From this vantage, "Mending Wall" updates an earlier work into current contextual terms for the sake of a coterie he may well wish to admonish.

It would be a mistake to take away from these examples merely that Frost was a contextual opportunist who drafted audiences and occasions to the work of reimagining his poems. In fact, in this chapter I argue something far more ambitious: that poetry readings offered Frost a site for questioning the very identity of lyric poetry itself. What is a written poem's relationship to the voice? How do writing and speaking correspond in a poem? From where does a poem's authentic voice derive? Experienced readers of Frost know these questions to be among the poet's most fundamental literary concerns, and the live poetry reading offers him an occasion to work them out, often with paradoxical results. The above episodes reveal that readings could mold a poem's reception with the mere use of occasion, and Frost employed numerous strategies—including contrasting vocal tones, sequence and commentary within and across readings, and intersplicing poems with paratexts and asides extraneous to the poems themselves—to destabilize the ideal of coherent, self-enclosed lyric unity.

And yet I also describe an opposing agency in Frost's work, arguing that the sound of voice—Frost's inflections and rhythms when reading aloud in a style that I will follow Frost in calling "humanist"—imagines that readings summon into being the original forces that created the poem. The humanist voice claims creative authenticity and endurance by reuniting the poet with the moment of his *poesis*, returning him to the poem's ontological source. In "The Figure a Poem Makes," Frost describes this humanist permanence of creative genesis: "A poem may be worked over once it is in being, but may not be worried into being. Its most precious quality will remain its having run itself and carried away the poet with it. Read it a hundred times: it will forever keep its freshness as metal keeps its fragrance. It can never lose its sense of a meaning that once unfolded by surprise as it went" (*Prose* 133). Frost's language bestows upon the poem a definite pronoun—"it"—and stakes its claim for changeless endurance, even though it's one that emerged spontaneously "by surprise." His readings capture this friction between incorruptible "freshness" and opportunistic change, and in this dialectic they functioned as dramatizations of this condition, of poetry itself caught in the crosscurrents of sixties reading. As spoken performances of written texts, readings allowed Frost not to solve this problem but to work it through at a time when reading was becoming essential to the life of poets much younger and aesthetically progressive.

This chapter is a significant addition to Frost studies and to the burgeoning study of performance and sound recording. Regarding the critical discussion on Robert Frost: the fact is that while some of the recordings I discuss have been heard before and even mentioned in biographies and critical works, none has actually been taken as a primary focus of analysis until now. One reason for this is a simple limitation of access: as mentioned in the introduction, most of the Frost recordings discussed here have been gathered from archived recordings that require a site visit to experience. I listened to these on audiotape cassettes housed in the Woodberry Poetry Room in Harvard's Lamont Library and others in the Library of Congress's Recorded Sound Reference Center. (Some tapes contained specific information regarding date, audience, and/or event, e.g., "Robert Frost Reading His Poems for a Joint Meeting of the Chesapeake Chapter of the American Studies Association, March 31 1959," while others offered almost nothing, e.g., "Robert Frost 1955." I also make reference to some of Frost's commercially available recordings, though they're of less concern in this essay, which takes as its focus live encounters. When possible, I've tried to suggest how Frost may have been responding to particularities of his audience or historical contexts, though sometimes this has been difficult to do.) Unless one actually travels to such archives, access to Frost's recordings is limited because his estate will not allow online clips to be published, except in the case of a university making files available to its own students (such is the case at Harvard). This creates somewhat of a disjunction: Frost has an enormous audio archive, possibly one of the largest of any modernist or early twentieth-century poet, and yet it is more restricted than virtually any other.

Another reason Frost's recordings have received little attention is also described in chapter 1, namely, what Garrett Stewart refers to as a "'phonophobia' generated in the wake of the Derridean attack on the Logos" (3). Robert Frost aside, performance has only recently been taken as a serious modality for analysis. And yet I hope to demonstrate here not only that Frost's identity as a performer has been overlooked but also that this dearth of critical attention is doubly odd, as his readings so clearly dramatize ideas central to his self-descriptions as a poet.[2] In fact, I place Frost rather than Ginsberg as the key figure inaugurating public poetry reading in the 1960s. Frost? I can hear you, Reader, snickering from here. Frost, mocking progressive New Deal policies? Frost, the rural modernist? And yet it was Frost who eventually became such an iconic stage reader of poetry that the middle generation's own premier declaimer, Allen Ginsberg, called him one of poetry's "original entrepreneurs" of live reading (qtd. in Parini 319). And it was Frost who first made a career out of traveling from campus to campus to read, lecture, and crack wise at the microphone in exchange for a living wage. It wouldn't be an overstatement to say that Frost virtually invented the career of the poet on tour. It was a career Gwendolyn Brooks would pattern her own upon, as would William Carlos Williams in his later years. Brooks's paean to Frost, "Of Robert Frost," captures Frost in his later years, a grizzled veteran, with notable eyebrows and "iron at the mouth," and, as if before the podium, with "a place to stand" (*Selected Poems* 122). Moreover, it's Frost who most deftly captures the antinomies of live reading in the 1960s, when he was still, despite his age, a vital reader, one who revealed reading's promises and pitfalls, emotive possibilities and opportunities for deception. Every poet in this study contends with the selfsame forces. If Ginsberg found himself able and ready at the mike, it's because of Frost's "entrepreneurial" example, which Ginsberg eagerly imitated. And if Ginsberg wished to shuffle off his performative mantle as time went by, that too was related to Frost's telegraphic ambivalence. For this reason, I wish to claim that Frost was a *pivotal* figure in the history of poetry in performance, turning from earlier traditions of live reading toward modern ones. In what follows, I'll describe that pivot in detail, starting by referring back to the histories of poetry reading that Frost knew and transformed through his canny performance style.

Frost and the Spoken Voice

Before moving on to the recordings themselves, I want to emphasize how important spoken language was for Frost. When Frost was a child, his mother, Belle, often read to him from the Bible, Walter Scott's *Tales of a Grandfather*, *The Poems of Ossian*, and Thomas Hughes's 1857 novel *Tom Brown's Schooldays*, one of Frost's childhood favorites that Belle reread aloud often (Thompson, *Early Years* 69). In fact, Frost's mother read so much that Frost claimed he didn't silently read an entire book by himself until age fourteen (72). All of this reading had some odd consequences. Frost recorded experiences of "second hearing," or hearing voices in his head, an imaginative experience likely suggested by his mother's love of the Scottish fabulist George MacDonald's dreamlike stories of fairies and the spirit world (36). This stress on reading or speaking aloud at home was also reinforced at school for much of Frost's life, though he wasn't always comfortable speaking aloud. Studying classics at the Lawrence, Massachusetts, high school entailed frequent "recitations" before the whole class, events that set his nerves on edge (79). And though Frost was also an enthusiastic member of the Debating Union, his first important speaking engagement—giving the valedictory speech at his high school's graduation ceremony—sent him into such agonies of nervous consternation that when he arrived onstage he fumbled awkwardly through his well-prepared homily (130), prompting the *Lawrence Eagle-Tribune* to remark that "its merits might have been shown to better advantage in a more natural delivery" (qtd. in Thompson, *Early Years* 132). As Frost's career unfolded, his poetry would often quite literally inscribe voice into poems, from the dialogues in *North of Boston* (1914) to the late *A Masque of Reason* (1945). He would also take a particular interest in Shakespeare's dramatic works, and drama in general, as a teacher at Pinkerton Academy in Derry, New Hampshire, where he helped students stage plays and masques by Marlowe, Milton, Sheridan, and Yeats (Frost, *Prose* 75). And of course, he would compose influential statements about writing and speaking in letters and other prose about "the sound of sense" and "sentence sounds" (discussed below).

That such engagement with spoken language constituted repeated and important literary experiences for Frost is not a mere peculiarity of his biography. Live reading was a crucial part of American culture in the late nineteenth century, especially in the Northeast, where it was typically employed as a pedagogical tool for moral guidance. Lesley Wheeler points to conventions of reading poems aloud in a variety of social institutions, including "drawing rooms and salons, clubs, churches, cabarets and cafés, universities and schools of all levels, libraries, bookshops, and concert halls" (*Voicing* 4). Joan Shelley Rubin's *Songs of Ourselves* (2007), a social history of poetry in America, describes the schoolroom during this period as "the most consistent and predictable" venue for reading verse aloud, though a variety of occasions—including holiday celebrations, commencement events, elocution contests, and pageants—kept reading aloud at the center of American life (107). These readings often came with clear moral instructions. One popular idea at the time was the metaphor of a "memory gem"—a passage of poetry or prose that students could commit to memory and then rely upon for moral guidance (110). Students would memorize and recite Holmes's "The Chambered Nautilus" or Bryant's "Thanatopsis" to derive clear "lessons of the text" (114). This model, which implies that poems contain incorruptible and stable ethical formulae, persisted for decades into the twentieth century, when it shifted from an emphasis on moral instruction per se to what the Deweyan educator Sterling Andrus Leonard described as "true, and significant experience" and a process redolent of humanist authenticity called "re-enactment" between reader and writer (qtd. in Rubin 129). A passage from a 1934 pedagogy textbook links the reader to the writer in terms of a shared encounter: "Only when the teacher learns that poetry and prose were written chiefly to be re-experienced or relived by the reader can we begin to hope that children will learn to like to read excellent things" (129). Both examples imply that poetry contains something stable at the core; the literary ambiguity New Critics would begin to champion in the following decades had no place in these events. Frost would continue to work within this paradigm over the course of his life, maintaining in some way, however compromised and complicated, a sense of a poem's unshakable identity of meaning.

Outside of the schoolroom, orality was likewise privileged over the material text. Ingrid Satelmajer describes oral poetry during Frost's childhood years and later as holding a "constant and prominent role at public events" (205), with printed matter—magazines, newspapers, and periodicals—typically providing a "performance text" (207) to be voiced by readers. Likewise, Joan Newlon Radner describes the lyceums of northern New England at midcentury as places where orality dominated literacy and reading functioned as a form of social cohesion, or "improvement" (176). During lyceum events, participants would hand-write a "newspaper" full of real and fabricated news, poems, stories, and other items, then read and discuss them aloud. These events included "declamations, recitations, dialogues, essays, lectures, mock trials, public critiques of the presentations, and oral performances" (177). While it's impossible to know exactly what remainders of this cultural emphasis on reading and orality Frost imbibed during his childhood, his lifelong emphasis on reading and internalizing poems is of a piece with this New England orality. The crowd's cheering at Frost's abandonment of the material text at Kennedy's inaugural in favor of a "poem I can say to you without seeing it" suggests the cultural durability of such scenes for all involved.

As Frost developed as a poet he read often, despite debilitating nervousness and stage fright. In fact, as he matured, readings and talks became a regular part of his life and a reliable source of his personal income. By 1920 he was earning between $50 and $100 per appearance, not a small sum at the time, and that rate would steadily increase over his lifetime (Thompson, *Triumph* 150). Yet for Frost, readings were never simply recitations or vocalizations of a series of poems, as we might expect from either his schoolroom experiences or readings by poets today. As Lorenzo Thomas has argued, poetry readings need to be carefully historicized based on the implicit social conventions that guide their procedures (301). Thomas argues that Frost's reading style is most closely associated with the "poet-performer movement" described by Paul H. Gray, in which poets like James Whitcomb Riley, Edna Wheeler Wilcox, and Vachel Lindsay read a "petit-bourgeois" style of platform poetry mostly to "farmers, merchants, salesmen, and housewives" centered on the dramatic performance of the poems themselves, as well as the bucolic population they represented (301).[3] If one listens to Frost's many recordings and reads the twenty-seven transcriptions of readings and excerpts of readings recently collected in *Robert Frost: Speaking on Campus* (2009), it's easy to hear how Frost drew upon this platform tradition, what Wheeler describes as "lecture-recitals" and "reading-lectures," typical of "popular lecture tours of the nineteenth century" (*Voicing* 9). In the introduction to *Speaking on Campus*, which transcribes just some of the hundreds of campus readings Frost gave, David Shribman describes Frost as a "'performance artist' before the term existed," though in truth his talks were fairly predictable in form (xx). They featured the poet standing at a lectern and speaking into a microphone, usually on a particular theme, and intermittently reading poems (e.g., at the Rocky Mountain Writers' Conference it was "What Poetry Thinks of Our Age" [Thompson, *Triumph* 424]; at the Winter Institute of Literature at the University of Miami, "The Uses of Ambiguity" [434]; for the Charles Eliot Norton lectures at Harvard in 1936, "The Renewal of Words" [444]). This style ensures that Frost will begin offering some kind of framing as he moves along, a structure that leads almost inevitably toward the interpretive malleability described above.

Yet Frost's ideas about voice and lyric suggest not malleability but rootedness in the fundament of authentically spoken language, making simple claims about contextual framing and reframing difficult. As Frost writes in a letter to Sidney Cox, the "living part of a poem is the intonation entangled somehow in the syntax idiom and meaning of a sentence. It is only there for those who have heard it previously in conversation" (*Letters* 107). For Frost, speaking always comes first, and the figure of the writer is a kind of textual shaman, locating, absorbing, and alienating the immediate idiom into the symbolic order:

> I say you cant [*sic*] read a single good sentence with the salt in it unless you have previously heard it spoken. Neither can you with the help of all the characters and diacritical marks pronounce a single word unless you have previously heard it actually pronounced. Words exist in the mouth not in books. You can't fix them and you dont [*sic*] want to fix them. You want them to adapt their sounds to persons and places and times. You want them to change and be different. I shall be sorry when everybody is so public-schooled that nobody will dare to say Haow for What. It pleases me to contemplate the word Sosieti that the reformers sport on their door plate in a street in London. The two i's are bad enough. But the o is what I love. (*Letters* 108)

In Frost's orality, the spoken voice represents a connection to "persons and places and times" that print loses without periodic retuning. Above, the solecism "Sosieti" has the virtue of the insistent /o/ inflected, presumably, by a middle-class speaker (as opposed to "real" society member).

Yet even these "sentence sounds" (*Letters* 111) and "sound-posture" (qtd. in Newdick 4), as Frost calls them—which posit that tone and vocal inflection in spoken language must be captured in writing to give it "life"—are fringed with cautionary distance and can be heard to express a basic tension between writing and speech. For example, who is writing the words Frost records? When Frost says a "man is all a writer if *all* his words are strung on definite recognizable sentence sounds," the writer is figured as a cultural elite who transforms (rather than inhabits) these sounds "fresh from talk, where they grow spontaneously" (*Letters* 111). Thus the very idea of sentence sounds already situates the writer of them at a remove; sentence sounds sound to the *writer*, not the talker—after all, for the talker, this would all be beside the point.[4] Writing to Lincoln MacVeagh, Frost plays this role of linguistic anthropologist by phonetically translating the "sentence sounds" of New Orleans, where he had recently been, in a way that clearly reveals this status of the outsider: "When I suppose I felt coming on was the dengue (pronounced dang you) fever from a mosquito bite I got on my first day at New Orleans (pronounced differently from the way I was accustomed to pronounce it)" (Thompson, *Triumph* 213). So "sentence-sounds are very definite entities," as Frost wrote to John Bartlett. "They are apprehended by the ear. They are gathered by the ear from the vernacular and brought into books" (*Letters* 111). And yet they are also in need of the writer's aid and assistance. In this way, Frost's readings follow a particular three-step process: (1) Frost draws on "definite" sounds "gathered by the ear"; (2) Frost creates written texts that end up dead or dying in print; (3) Frost then breathes them back into life through his voice. Reading is a work of reanimation that captures Frost's nuanced sense of talk and text.

Humanist Reading and Performance

One way of accounting for this quality in Frost's reading of presence and absence, identity and deconstruction, is to conceive of reading as performance, a term that captures the double nature of Frost's acts of "reanimation" described above. As described in chapter 1, performance theory complicates popular and critical assumptions that spoken voice is saturated with authenticity and resists its material condition—or what I am here calling *humanist* reading. I'll outline this humanist style in greater detail as it pertains to Frost before articulating Frost's performative mode.

In humanist reading, voice is coextensive with self, and the speaking of writing reanimates language with the original creative impulsion that generated it. This is similar to what the critic Maria Damon calls the "relatively recent (i.e., post-Romantic) inner-directed lyric tradition," in which fusing, or fusing once again, a written poem and the speaking of that poem is a reading's central function (332). Another way of saying this is that humanist reading imagines that poet and poem cohere in a speech act that itself reconstructs the original moment of *poesis*, the "voicing" of truth. This is perhaps the best-represented mainstream attitude toward the value of poetry readings, an attitude John Glassco dismisses as the "naïve listener's belief that he is getting 'closer' to a poem by hearing it from the poet himself" (qtd. in Middleton, "Contemporary" 263). Bernard Richards calls the equation of recorded voice with authenticity the "phonographic fallacy" (qtd. in Prins 47). I am calling it the "humanist voice" because it seeks to reunite poem and human subject-speaker, to reanimate the dead letter of text.

"Orality" is a similar term that should be distinguished here. Walter J. Ong's description of orality as prior to writing pictures a linear progression: "primary" orality is the universal condition of language, and alphabetic literacy is a development of it, in which the written becomes a "residue" of speech (*Orality* 11). For Ong, an oral utterance is historically prior to written text, even though—like Frost's description of the cultural elite capturing sentence sounds—literacy "enhanced" the spoken by allowing it to be ordered, studied, objectified, and developed in complexity (9). When critics reflexively use the term "orality," they mean something like what Ong describes. Jacques Roubaud's "Prelude: Poetry and Orality," for example, argues that the printing press created a "breaking of the bond between word and sound" so profound that it "brought about a new double form called poetry" that ensured the "indissociable" nature of speech and writing (18). Roubaud imagines the poet as a preservationist of primary orality. Humanist reading, however, is more concerned with the notion of recapture or reanimation described above rather than the simple fact of oral primacy.

To be sure, these ideas are closely knitted. Frost himself equates humanism with orality in his essay "The Figure a Poem Makes," calling the "humanist" one who can write sentence sounds—one "who cares how sound a poem is if it is only *a* sound" (*Prose* 131, emphasis in original).[5] Poetic genesis relies upon the act as an imitable moment, one that "can never lose its sense of a meaning that once unfolded by surprise as it went," in the famous formulation cited above. The essential word here is "once"—at the moment of poetic generation the poet "snatches a thing" from time and captures it (133). This marks the poem as fossilized inspiration, and so to read a poem aloud is to make it a living, fleshly thing again. This humanist assumption of poetic durability is easily visible today as part of the machinery of reception surrounding Frost's marketed recordings, making it an uncritical assumption doubly important to challenge. Here, for example, is a blurb written by Billy Collins for the back of Frost's CD for the Voice of the Poet series, in which Collins prepares thousands of contemporary listeners to receive Frost's words in just this humanist manner. Drawing on the very same language of "reenactment" used by the Deweyan educator Sterling Andrus Leonard, Collins claims: "To hear a poem spoken in the voice of the person who wrote it is not only to witness the rising of words off the page and into the air, but to experience an aural reenactment of exactly what the poet must have heard, if only internally, during the act of composition." One couldn't find a more succinct description of humanist reading than Collins's phrase "aural reenactment." Embedded in Collins's logic is the idea of the prelinguistic, rhapsodic voice as described by Plato's *Ion*, trapped in the nets of the poem and released again when voiced.

It isn't quite as tidy as that for Frost. In fact, Frost's reading recalls this idea's virtual opposite: Derrida's ideas about linguistic absence. For Derrida, Ong's oralist hierarchy of speech/writing displayed above is problematically stable. True, what "disappears" in writing, as Derrida argues, "is the self-identity of the origin, the self-presence of so-called living speech" (296). And yet, he points out, "[i]s not the center, the absence of play and différance, another name for death? The death which reassures and appeases, but also, with its hole, creates anguish and puts at stake?" (297). Paradoxically for Derrida, the absence of a voice *legitimates* writing by acknowledging writing's remoteness from speaking presence but celebrating it for that very fidelity to the true condition of speech itself—which is absence, what Derrida calls *différance*. As seen above, Frost considers voice as a fabled precursor to written language, which can only approximate speech in its inevitable absence from the page. In this way, Frost's celebrated concern for the "sound of sense" in poetry actually evades or even represses the presence of a speaker in favor of the text that will "speak" in its absence, the text that will be authenticated by the supposed reproduction of its own primacy. This is why the figure of the writer is important in Frost's description above—the poet gathers the sentence sounds and vouches for their authenticity but inevitably muffles them in the process of writing them down. So as Frost tantalizingly posits voice as the dead center and "absence of play," he swerves toward that voice's distribution into devoiced, printed poem. This connection between Frost and Derrida is not meant to turn Frost into a poststructuralist, but it suggests that Derrida's critique of the speech/text dichotomy serves to complicate too easy an assumption about humanist vocal "reenactment."

Historically speaking, however, listeners have consistently perceived Frost's spoken poems as redolent with authenticity; Frost is typically received in these humanist terms as "natural," "spontaneous," "sincere," and "informal," all terms suggesting the immediacy and presence of the poet (as did the *Washington Post* reporter quoted above, who referred to Frost's reading at the Kennedy inaugural as "natural"). Reginald Cook's 1956 article "Notes on Frost the Lecturer," for example, refers to Frost's "human aspects" and "natural presence" (qtd. in Shribman xx). After a 1920 reading in Arlington, Vermont, that town's *Banner* newspaper described Frost's "utter quiet sincerity" and recalled that to "the large and breathlessly attentive audience which gathered at Mrs. Gilchrist's house to hear him, he read poem after poem as though he were that moment composing them; as though they were as new to him as to anyone" (qtd. in Thompson, *Triumph* 147). Sometimes this humanist reception is coded as "informality," as in an article in the *Michigan Daily* that appeared after Frost read at the University of Michigan in 1921. Twice in one paragraph, the article employed the phrase "complete informality" (qtd. in Thompson, *Triumph* 177). A 1935 reading at Amherst crystallized Collins's humanistic sentiment. A student wrote in the college paper of Frost's talk that the poet "gives us the feeling that we are attendant at the process of creation" itself (qtd. in Thompson, *Triumph* 417).

Conceiving of Frost's poems in terms of "performance," however, offers a helpful corrective to humanist listening and captures Frost's sense of cramped ambivalence about his lyric voice—is it authentic and humanist, or is it not? Can speech be faithfully represented, or is it warped by shamanistic reanimation? Are we hearing authentic sentence sounds, or is reading opportunistic lyric refashioning? Joseph Roach has argued recently in the pages of *PMLA* that performance is "Orphic," always glancing back as it moves forward, "authorized by something prior, even when it isn't" (1078). By this Roach means that performance is based on a tension between embodiment and change, material substance and transformation. Frost is an Orphic performer in this sense: he looks toward the immediacy of the stage and, simultaneously, back to the erstwhile creation of the poem. His readings are reconstructions of this precise friction between humanistic reading—in which a poem is "reenacted" as a bodily presence—and skeptical deconstruction—in which, as Roach puts it, poetry becomes a "figural substitution" of the real (1085).

How this friction heats up in actual performances is the focus of the remainder of this chapter. In what follows, I describe how Frost's archival readings may be understood as themselves negotiating this Orphic tension between humanist orality and conceptualizations of voice damningly aware of their performed condition. On the one hand, through writings, staged phrasings, and performances of authenticity, Frost invokes a humanism of voice. Yet he also reverses this equation by destabilizing the centrality and singularity of the voice itself in the performance of poetic inflection, sequence, commentary, and interruption. If Frost has generally presented himself and been received as a humanist reader, I hope to show that this style is constantly undermined—or dramatically complicated—by his own tendency to challenge the orthodoxy and boundary of his lyric productions. In proposing to read Frost's vocal accent, inflection, and associations against his humanist style, I am suggesting something analogous to what Jerome McGann has termed the "bibliographic code" (16), his name for the semiotics of text. Perhaps this semiotic environment surrounding—and produced by—a voiced poem could be called the poem's audiographic code.

Robert Frost, Live

What does Frost's humanist reading actually sound like? For one thing, it is never produced without a clear sense of an opposing, skeptical tension. Deep listening to Frost's recordings reveals that one of his habitual cadences is to play two central accentual strategies of voice against each other. What I call "sighing" functions as a trope for humanist expression. The other, what I call "tumbledown" phrasing, runs against the grain of sighing by self-consciously citing its own discomfort with literariness. Together, they sound as an audible allegory of Frost's persistent tension between the authentic and the staged.

"Sighing" is the raising of vocal pitch, elongation of vowels, and what can sound like a singing of the syllables being sighed; like an actual sigh, the breath leaves the throat in an easy, mournful release. Frost's most notable sigh, one he can be heard to perform in virtually every recording of the poem, is found in the line from "The Road Not Taken," "all the difference." As he approaches the word "all," Frost raises his voice, pinches his larynx tight, and quivers the line of the word, seeming for a moment to almost sing it. The trope of sighing likely derives from Victorian lyric conventions of reading that suggested the emotive expressivity of poetic language that speaks from the oracular impulse. Citing early recordings of Tennyson, Jed Rasula calls this style "chanted not spoken, an incantation not a recital," and notes the phenomenon of the "vowel drone" (235). He quotes Ford Maddox Ford in what is an exemplary description of Victorian reading, remembered from Ford's childhood: "Mournfully, then, up and down the staircases, there would flow two hollow sounds. For, in those days, it was the habit of all poets and poetesses to read aloud upon every possible occasion, and whenever they read aloud to employ an imitation of the voice invented by the late Lord Tennyson, and known, in those days, as the *ore rotundo*—'with the round mouth mouthing out their hollow o's and a's'" (236). The sigh evokes this mournful, elegiac Victorian sound and serves, for Frost, as a signifier of intense emotional authenticity and pitch. (Of course, its repeated use and possibly Victorian origins suggest the sigh is already a *trope* of humanist reading.) Richard Poirier's description of Frost's "extravagance" of meaning is also a useful comparison here. Extravagance, for Poirier, is "the enactment of any search for possibilities other than those already domesticated," literally the "walking beyond" or extension of ordinary into unexpected and revelatory (*Knowing* 89). Extravagance echoes Frost's vocal dialectic between ordinary and enriched spoken vocabularies. "With what seems to me an admirable evidence of human sympathy and poetic daring," Poirier says, "'extravagance' in Frost can be made to reside often in the most quiet of those idiomatic phrases by which, in ordinary speech, we unknowingly talk in visionary language" (91). Frost's sighs often walk language beyond itself to create an aural seme of what Poirier suggests is merely inherent in words alone.

Diametric to the sigh is "tumbledown" phrasing: rushed, quick, flat, and impatient to achieve its end. Tumbledown is the opposite of sighing, shortening caesuras and gaps between words, obliterating effects of enjambment and meter, and pragmatically seeking to finish as quickly as possible. Tumbledown speaks as if time were money. As counterpoint to the sigh, which extends and caresses, tumbledown eradicates what Nick Piombino calls the "aural ellipsis" of spoken language, in which the listener is granted affective agency by being able to "weave into any elliptical speech act certain elements of his or her internal experience" (54). Disdainful of such pausing, tumbledown is the voice of auction, barter, and transaction. If the sigh signifies through its watermarking of aural ellipsis the poignancy and connotative capacity of words that carry more weight than in everyday speech, tumbledown strips words of their plangent qualities. Where the sigh embarrasses words with extravagance, tumbledown divests them of it.

Three readings of "The Road Not Taken" reveal how Frost plays these two phrasings against each other, the one insisting on literary emotiveness, the other dismissing it with a shrug.[6] At a March 13, 1962, reading at Harvard, less than a year before his death, Frost says after being asked to read "Stopping by Woods on a Snowy Evening" and "The Road Not Taken": "I know what you're thinking, and I'm thinking it too. Can a poem get too [pause] worn, you know, too much read?" He then compares himself to Longfellow, a poet overshadowed by his own popular success, and ends with an appeal: "Anyway, I'm going to say those poems, have mercy upon them, be merciful. Don't get tired of them, please." In this reading, tumbledown appears to signify this prefigured impatience (performed or genuine) with the burden of these poems, while the sigh honors the audience's desire to hear them; it is as if Frost is denying in one line what he willingly grants in the next. This is especially important for Frost to stress at a Harvard reading, where he can be sure most of his audience not only knows this poem but his other poems well. During a reading of "The Road Not Taken" later that same year (on December 2), Frost sighs the words "fair" in line 6, "really about the same" in line 10, "kept the first" in line 13, and "wood, and I— / I" in lines 18 and 19. The rest of the poem flashes by with tumbledown speed, except for the final line's "all," which Frost attenuates into a long, quavering, emphatic admonition. A few years earlier, in 1955, Frost again sighs "just as fair" in line 6, "I kept the first" in line 13, and "I shall be telling this" in line 16. So while precisely the same words within "The Road Not Taken" aren't always read sigh or tumbledown, these two registers contend for the speaker's mood. In this poem in particular, tonal indecisiveness stands in distinction to the speaker's seeming clarity of choice about the road not taken. The voiced poem is dialogically ambivalent about its own willingness to afford this event the meaning it seems to more reliably elicit in print. That is, is Frost really so certain of the road not taken? This all has clear implications for a critical understanding of the poem. For example, Tyler Hoffman reads "The Road Not Taken" as full of "intonational ambiguity" from the start, especially in the final lines:

> If we hear the final statement ["I took the road less traveled by, / And that has made all the difference"] as heartfelt, absent a moralizing strain, we probably regard the speaker with some sympathy, as symbolic of the human propensity to construct fictions to justify choices made in clouded circumstances. But if it strikes our ear as sententious, we are more likely to laugh at his expense, to mock his pretentiousness. Frost permits us to hear the final statement in at least these two ways, perhaps at different stages of our life, even as we register its irony, and so encourages us to come to terms with our vexed attitudes about what it means to fashion a personal history. (*Politics* 113)

While this is an astute reading of the poem's essential "intonational ambiguity," it's hard not to be swayed by Frost's sighing "all" when he sighs it, hard not to be pulled more closely toward a laugh at the speaker's expense—if only for that reading and at that moment.

"Birches," another poem Frost was often asked to say at readings, is also one he repeatedly bifurcated into sigh and tumbledown, as the March 13, 1962, reading demonstrates. This reading shows Frost deploying these two phonal registers not only against each other but also against the presence or absence of tropes in the poem. This means that metaphor is read tumbledown, and flatter, expository writing is read sigh, creating another form of counterpoint in the poem: figurative language and poetic affect are both admitted into the inflective repertoire but denied their full authority as modes of speech. Reliably vacillating between sigh phrasing and tumbledown, Frost signifies the tensions between extravagant poet and pragmatic farmer. Thus "stay" at the end of line 4 and "themselves" at the end of line 7 are sighed, and then, as if to atone for this emotive double punch, he burns through line 13, an insistently metaphoric line that suffocates, in this reading, from speed and compression. This tendency to countermand metaphor with rushed sound is also apparent in the striking simile "Like girls on hand and knees that throw their hair / Before them over their heads to dry in the sun," which Frost speeds through mightily, as if to deny the lines' affective heft. Yet the relatively quiescent "boy" in line 23 and "all there was" in line 32 are sighed. These are innocuous, almost banal places for Frost's inflection to instantiate extravagance, and so he deploys dramatic inflection only when its semantic qualities are most muted.

This self-inoculating pattern continues through the rest of the poem until line 53, when Frost slows his pace to signal the poem's ending (something he does in many readings of the shorter lyrics).[7] In the end, however, sigh and tumbledown phrasing work dialectically to signify extravagance in muted language. They play restraint against trope, humanism against occasion.

Contemporary listeners to Frost have often observed this effect of vocal tone playing dialectically against speaking subjects. For some, Frost's voice was distinctly modern in its rejection of fey Victorian aestheticism, the kind of Tennysonian *ore rotundo* mentioned above. Elizabeth Shepley Sergeant notes that Frost "enunciates in his dry, sly, halting way" so "different from the glib aestheticism his students might expect of a poet" (qtd. in Parini 450). Yet Sergeant's reading of Frost's voice is laden with belief in its authenticity and air of reality, clearly the product of her own readerly humanism. Her ear requires familiarity with conventions of reading, suggesting that Frost's voice is carefully modulated to construct for itself a new speaking persona distinct from the associations with what "poetry" often sounds like. This comparative kind of listening, which hears something new and divergent in Frost's vocal accent, appears often in reactions to Frost's voice. Stanley Burnshaw recalls "that deep grainy voice—a voice that made other voices sound thin or abstract" (qtd. in Parini 455). In 1937 Reginald Cook described Frost's voice in such capacious terms that he sounds like Emerson's representative man, marrying the low ("Irish speech tones") and the high ("Miltonic eloquence") with democratic ease, his voice a casebook of jarring, dialogic self-styling: "Frost's voice is medium in pitch, rather low than high, but not guttural; and it registers sensitively shades of feeling—elation or scorn, exultance or sadness. It is the voice of a man whose ear is in key, reproducing at will Irish speech tones or nuances in colloquial idiom or the blank-verse paragraphs of Miltonic eloquence. It is a voice easy to listen to all day long" (qtd. in Parini 352). Listening to the BBC archive of Frost's radio talks in England, the English critic B. J. Sokol finds that Frost's occasional "growling tone of voice" was "premonitory to joshing lies," suggesting through mere tone the doubtfulness of his own self-representations as a "simple 'farmer' in 1914 Gloucestershire" (401). As listeners like Sergeant, Burnshaw, and Sokol attest, responses to Frost's voice are intense while also deft in drawing comparisons to a range of vocal speaking styles against which Frost's rhythms jibe. This accentuation of voice pluralizes the singularity of the lyric speaker, often introducing into the poem a baseline of irony.

Yet at many other times, Frost can be heard laying bare the machinery of tonal strategies for his audience in paratextual commentary, belying the humanist voice in a different way. This is particularly noticeable during readings at Harvard and the Library of Congress, where he could count upon an audience being literary and thus requiring him to accentuate distance between himself and them. Referring to a just-completed reading of "Lines Written in Dejection on the Eve of Great Success" during the December 2, 1962, reading, Frost informs his Harvard audience that the poem was really "countrified": "[Y]ou probably didn't notice, but in my ear I said 'cow' like a Vermonter." The phrase "like a Vermonter," with its reliance on simile, suggests how staged Frost imagines his accent to be. At a reading in the Library of Congress on October 24, 1955, Frost says after line 11 of "The Star-Splitter," "see, that's the New England accent," referring both to the line's halting, interrupted syntax ("Has a man, I should like to ask, no rights") and to his own tonal inflection. Frost often plays lecturer, pointing to the deliberate effects of his rhyming patterns. One particularly sharp episode comes from a talk in the Coolidge Auditorium of the Library of Congress to high school honors students, an audience for which he acts the role of educator more than in other venues, presumably because he's talking to students. He says, "[S]ee, I'm gonna emphasize the rhymes" during a reading of "Departmental" and goes on to move through the poem leaning on each end rhyme with a hammy insistence on the rhymes' comedic effects. Such moments serve not to establish his authenticity as a reader or to dramatize (and it would be a dramatization) Leonard's "reenactment" but to play with tropes in audiography.

This phenomenon is perhaps most conspicuous and complicated in Frost's numerous recordings of "The Witch of Coös," where he acts the characters of mother and son to the hilt. Katherine Kearns has argued that "Coös" allegorizes voice in poetry, particularly "the potential of sound to circumvent or supersede stated meaning" through the figures of mother, son, and speaker/stranger, each "standing for" subtext, articulation, and imposition of meaning, respectively (123). The audiographic variant compounds a fourth figure, the reader himself—that is, Robert Frost—tempering and manipulating the poem's speakers much more like a stage manager than a rhapsode. He reads line 27 ("We'll never let them, will we, son? We'll never!") thin and pinched, the dropped /r/'s disappearing in craggy, throaty aitches and the final two syllables forming a hard, wailing spondee—"NE-VAH!" So, for instance, the speaker of "The Witch of Coös" appears in the context of the "two old-believers" of line 3 as a less rural, worldlier New Englander. His accent is far less attenuated, implying that the mother and son are worthy of aural reproduction, as well as the speaker's own (and his readers') difference from them. A print reader might suspect the speaker's implied difference by virtue of the poem's mere existence, yet all we know of him from the text derives from the poem's first three lines, which foreground "talking" itself as the poem's subject: "I stayed the night for shelter at a farm / Behind the mountain, with a mother and son, / Two old-believers. They did all the talking" (Frost, *Poetry* 202). There is nothing suggesting that his difference carries great significance except, perhaps, that he defines them as "old-believers," the implication being that he is not one of them. Yet in the voiced poem, this reminder of their virtually anthropological significance, evidenced by their "talking," is now a dramatized fact apparent in every line and maintained as the subject of the poem. Read aloud, the characters serve as emblems of cracked New England spiritualism, and the distance of the speaker from them rings out in every line. To underscore this differential gap, Frost often "directs" his audience by stepping outside the poem's narrative frame to offer stage directions: he uses the paratextual phrases "and then he says" and "and then she says" throughout. In this way, each line insists upon the marginal difference of speaker, mother, and son. This suggests a reader quite removed from the original creation of the poem, troping the voiced "The Witch of Coös" into a poem about the framing of voices.

Frost also controls audiographic effects and plays heightened expression off ironic distance by producing an expertly modulated vocal chiaroscuro, or deep contrast. I'm not the only one to have heard this auditory effect. In her liner notes for the 1976 Caedmon record of Frost reading at the 92nd Street Y in the early 1950s, the poet Grace Schulman suggests that Frost's vocal intonation plays contrapuntally against the bleak moral evacuation of a poem like "Fire and Ice." As she puts it, "[A]bsolute destruction [is] intensified by the speaker's calm manner." Essentially, Frost's voice in this reading could be described as "slow tumbledown"; it's monochromatic and dour, suggesting something either in denial of or perhaps abjectly complicit with the eschatological terror the poem projects. The tonal flatness also renders inoperative and virtually inaudible the hard end rhymes that might be interpreted as a reassuring familiarity and containment of this blighted millenarianism present in an unvoiced (printed) version of the poem. To be sure, Frost himself was aware of this possibility of vocal tone, as he writes in a letter to John Bartlett in 1914 about sentence sound, not literally meant to be, but figuratively standing for, spoken language: "Remember that the sentence sound often says more than the words. It may even as in irony convey a meaning opposite to the words" (Frost, *Letters* 113). In this most fundamental way, then, voicings of poems offer a literal tone that Frost can lay dialectically as an "oversound" against the poems' textual logic.

So far, I've been arguing that Frost's poetry performances deploy vocal tone as a way to look Orphically away from, and then back toward, the humanist lyric. Yet as the reading at Kennedy's inaugural ceremonies suggests, the fixed notion of a Frost poem can also be framed by the way his readings readily accede to contextual interpretive demands; readings risk embodiment, animating the poem from its essential completeness, putting the spoken voice before a world of onlookers—an audience. Mark Richardson's *The Ordeal of Robert Frost* (1997) draws on this observation by arguing that Frost engages a dialectical struggle between "internal" and "external" motivations. Richardson interprets as emblematic Frost's claim that "[e]very poem is an epitome of the great predicament; a figure of the will braving alien entanglements" (qtd. in Richardson 2). His supple reading of Frost's lifelong negotiation between "will" and "entanglements" that are social, cultural, linguistic, and historical reveals how slippery notions of agency can be. When Frost claims in "The Figure a Poem Makes" that a poem "can never lose its sense of a meaning that once unfolded by surprise as it went," Richardson points out that such a "transcendent" gesture as this will eventually lead Frost to "a fall out of agency and authority" (224). While such experiences feel productive, they lead to recognitions of various forms of "constriction" (224). According to Richardson, a mythic possessive individualism imagines some kind of shelter for a humanism of poetic expression, where the "surprise" of composition remains intact and can be reliably articulated: "Frost shows us how true 'authorial' agency lies much deeper, beneath the awareness even of the poet. And the partly mysterious encounter of authority and contingency on the stage of writing promises, in poetics, to place the poet in touch with these deeper possibilities of agency" (224). While Richardson's humanistic focus is on Frost's various struggles against "culture" and audience, I locate such trials in the metaphor of performance itself, literalizing what Richardson refers to as the "stage" of writing. Listening to Frost on real stages, we can glimpse this struggle between will and the contingencies of alien entanglement—the audience. This is what Judith Oster means when she claims that "Frost's possessiveness of self and text was in conflict with the need to share them, to be read right by the right readers of both" (17).

Indeed, Frost is canny about negotiating such a dialectic. For example, after reading "Mending Wall" at a 1955 event, Frost runs in a joke so quickly, it sounds like a new ending:

> He will not go behind his father's saying,
> And he likes having thought of it so well
> He says again, "Good fences make good neighbors."
> Somebody else told me that good fences make good burglars.

While this typography deliberately fails to distinguish between poem and commentary—the poem's actual last word is "neighbors"—I cite it as an example of the qualities of a Frost reading, which is always choked with asides, additions, emendations, and subtractions that impinge in direct ways upon the poems that fall hacked and cajoled in their midst (we've already seen some of this in the Kennedy reading). If these additions and embellishments were recorded in print, a textualist like McGann would surely consider them variants, but as recorded on tape in their audiographic variants, they don't seem to warrant that status. Yet certainly they help Frost manage and guide the reception of his poems by speaking diacritically before, during, and after performing. They also trouble a poem's sense of authentic reenactment.

Often, this process speaks as loudly as any tonal phrasing against the authenticity of humanistic reading. On March 28, 1954, Frost appeared in an interview with Edward Stanley on an NBC broadcast produced "in cooperation with" the National Council of Churches. The show begins abruptly with Stanley introducing Frost as "America's distinguished and much beloved poet" and asking him to read his poem "The Pasture." Frost obliges in guttural craquelure:

I'm going out to clean the pasture spring;
I'll only stop to rake the leaves away
(And wait to watch the water clear, I may):
I shan't be gone long.—You come too.

I'm going out to fetch the little calf
That's standing by the mother. It's so young
It totters when she licks it with her tongue.
I shan't be gone long.—You come too.

When finished, Frost says: "Well, that's been taken as an introduction to several of my books; I suppose it's an invitation to read me." Stanley responds: "I suppose it's an invitation to reflect, too, that there might be some religious, uh, significance in such a simple act of clearing a spring." A quick study of Stanley's need to satisfy his religious sponsor, Frost obligingly rejoins: "I'm waiting for the water to clear itself, the spirit to come back." Frost's substitution of the word "spirit" for Stanley's more insistent "religious" signifies Frost's willingness to recognize NBC's underwriters while not entirely capitulating to their religious sponsorship. This particular "entanglement" with Stanley shades our understanding of a critical assessment of a poem like "The Pasture" such as Judith Oster's. Oster wonders about the "factual" nature of this poem and its ability to "stand alone and unassociated" from figurative weight. The poem is integral and can never be overcome by its implications: "In Frost we never fully lose the 'realness' of the literal term, or subsidiary subject, when it becomes a figure," as she puts it (56). This claim is surely rebuffed by Frost's appearance on NBC, where he capitulates to the "figure" suggested by Stanley.

Frost reads "A Soldier" next, a poem with a more immediately plausible "spiritual" interpretation. After he finishes, Stanley again tries to frame this poem as a religious meditation, carefully beginning with a comment on poetic form that leads him, via an unpersuasive free association, to a "religious" one: "I'm a little surprised, I don't know why I should be, to find you working in the sonnet form with so much discipline. It would be fair to say, wouldn't it, that, uh, there's some advantage to working in a, uh, formal style in poetry, as indeed there is some in religion too. The forms we observe." Again, Frost obliges Stanley and NBC by saying his three-line poem "Pertinax," an epigrammatic acknowledgment of formal necessity, though he stops short of ascribing a "religious significance": "'Let chaos storm, let cloud shapes form, uh, let cloud shapes *swarm*, I wait for form.' That's one of mine, too." The misquotation of his own line suggests his general unease with being asked to fit his poems into this narrow interpretive frame.

Yet in many of Frost's readings, he discusses in clear terms his thoughts on "religion," and in quite different terms. These are the very first words from the December 2, 1962, reading: "I want to start in by talking before I read the poems. I'm going to get to them as quickly as I can tonight. Uh, you know, you get warned, in anything you do, poetry, or, or art, that you better look out and not get too near the politicians, you better look out and not get too near the academicians, you better look out and not get too near the religious, I guess. They don't warn you about that as much as they should, maybe." Compared to the previous two excerpts with Stanley, this comment seems contradictory. Taken together, they reveal how well Frost was aware of audience expectations during his readings and how willing he was, at least to some degree, to shape (or be shaped by) their reception. While Stanley aggressively reads Frost's nonreligious poems as poems on religious subjects—an interpretive move Frost frequently criticizes and carefully manages, even at the studios of NBC—Frost appears to go along, if reluctantly. Yet without an interviewer to frame reception, Frost often takes on that role himself, and the results can be similarly forceful in their framing effects.

The final point I'll make concerns Frost's use of commentary and sequence in readings. The voice, live and improvisatory to a degree not possible in print, allows Frost to experiment with sequences of poems that rely on a governing logic to connect them in conceptual terms, as well as to frame these sequences with narrative connectives and asides, to make emendations on the fly, to test out new possibilities for lyrics and longer narrative works that don't have, and perhaps cannot have, access to these framing measures in their print incarnations. And new sequencing of poems gives Frost an opportunity to riff in the equivalent of jazz sets, stringing poems together in habitual but consistently revised patterns, and plays against the humanist impulse to locate speaker and poem in a simultaneity of authenticity. Live reading gives the lyric itself freedom to move and slide in new ways that challenge the very notion of lyric form; in this way, playing the role of Stanley to himself, Frost's readings present similar challenges to the closed, or "bounded," lyric form, one that textualist critic Sharon Cameron argues Emily Dickinson's fascicles do: the reading pluralizes the poems by giving them relevance to a surrounding context that supports new interpretive possibilities.[8] Live performance provides novel possibilities of presence; the read text shivers ontologically, caught between pure lyric expression and Frost's articulation of it. Significantly, the lack of this plural, cohesive effect entirely evaporates on a recording like the Caedmon album, which includes clips from different readings rather than an entire program, or the Random House *Voice of the Poet* series recording, which includes a mix of live and studio excerpts. These audio texts leave a flat, documentary impression, more like a newscaster's recitation of script than a poet voicing poems, and don't capture the drama of sequence and comment Frost often achieves through the extension, compression, and bridging between aural ellipses.

Indeed, Frost's commentary and directives before, during, and after a poem can be forceful in creating and restricting meaning. At a reading for the Chesapeake chapter of the American Studies Association given March 31, 1959, Frost opens his talk by positioning himself between "science" and "witchcraft," calling himself (by this point I hope unsurprisingly) a "humanist" who mediates between the two. "I often talk about witches, I've known so many," he says. "Some scientist wants to come down and give me a scientific explanation of witches," he goes on but explains via a line from *Hamlet* that one doesn't have to be a partisan of either "science" or "witchcraft" to entertain either: "[S]o I have heard, and do in part believe it." In short, Frost prepares his audience to think of him, during this reading, as a moderator between two worldviews, and so when he makes reference to this substratum of shared meaning throughout the reading, poems that might appear surrounded only by white space on the page are reframed.

Frost often underscores these framing devices quite deliberately, playing them off against the lyrics. This occurs during two readings of "Never Again Would Birds' Song Be the Same," a poem that inscribes voice and sound as its subject. In the Chesapeake reading, Frost reads the poem and then says, "You see, that's modern science, that's crossing things." In the context of this comment, the poem might be read as a critique of scientific rationalism, personified as Eve/woman, insinuating herself as an "oversound" and an "eloquence so soft" into prelapsarian Eden. This directed reading offsets a variety of possible interpretations of the poem and shapes its reception quite willfully as "about science," a possibility hardly suggested in the poem's diction. So in the Chesapeake reading, "Birds' Song" functions as a lament over the encroachment of scientific rationalism on a pastoral, romanticized American landscape: Eve's "eloquence so soft" becomes an insinuating faculty of deception that masquerades as "laughter" but bears sinister implications. The line "she was in their song" loses its ambiguity in this new context to suggest a probability that the prediction of "never again" is really a lament. The Chesapeake reading thus suppresses a reading like Richard Poirier's, which explicitly inscribes the voice of Eve as the figure of a "sentence sound" in the text (*Knowing* 130). Such readings might seem particularly important to enforce in an actual performance of the poem since they regard the originary voice—Eve's and, by implication, Frost's—as enduringly productive. It is an odd association for Frost to abjure. Readings show how these poems sound Orphically, at once embodied presentations that cite the poem's identity and cautiously swerve from it.[9]

Encore

Frost's performances capture the way his poems' willed essences clash with embodied presences. Sighing repatriates a lyric to its land of creation, only for it to be exiled moments later through tumbledown; a poem gets framed and reframed. Sometimes Frost sequences his shorter lyrics to produce this jarring pattern, as in a reading marked in the Woodberry archive simply as "1955," where he explains: "Now I'm going to read to you, chiefly, and I'd like to say that in the middle of the afternoon like this I suppose that one emotion ought to be enough for the, for the, for the hour. I'm going to just show you three, four or five emotions in rapid succession, three or four different kinds of poems. And they're, you'll see if I can mix them right out of my head for you, mix them. First, two or three little ones that make a group of one, just one emotion." He introduces the first poem by saying merely, "One is called 'Stopping by Woods on a Snowy Evening.'" He moves so quickly into "The Road Not Taken" that the break is hardly perceptible, though at points he sighs various words in his typical manner, with phrases like "I shall be telling this" heavily retarded and almost treacly in implied significance. He launches into "Come In" with tumbledown speed but then calmly intones it, as if comfortable at last in the portion of his "emotional" sequence that allows for new possibilities and unfamiliar phrases. The poems come all in a rush, tripping over each other's heels. There is an urgency to the pacing, and often the flipping of pages and mumbles can be heard in between, adding to the note of spontaneity and improvisation. Lyrics once separate and distinct cross-pollinate and bind, each transforming the others into something momentary, of an altogether different ontological type.

This tension between Frost's self-presentation as a stalwart performer of his own voice and the way he undermines that voice at the lectern makes his readings a particularly fruitful site for beginning an examination of the 1960s poetry reading; they suggest why his self-immolating podium style is so significant for a range of younger sixties readers to come—poets who found themselves struggling against the same anxieties over poetry's shifting status in the public sphere. Frost's readings dramatize the tension between freshness of poetic sound and the sounds of re-sounding. Surprisingly, it's a very different kind of reader, Charles Olson, who draws upon a similar dialectic during the same decade.

3

Charles Olson's Textual Voice

Charles Olson: Allen, I'm just proving that
oral poetry exists, O.K.? Ain't I or not?
Allen Ginsberg: It's very good, it's beautiful.
Charles Olson: Isn't this oral poetry? Isn't this
improvisatory, spontaneous poetry?
—Charles Olson, *Muthologos*

The above exchange between Charles Olson and Allen Ginsberg was caught by an untended microphone during intermission in Olson's notorious appearance at the University of California Poetry Conference on July 23, 1965. His performance that Friday night is now the stuff of legend. Olson's biographer Tom Clark describes the poet arriving in Berkeley "[o]verstressed, jet-lagged, battling fatigue and competitive tension, wired on artificial energy provided by amphetamines and increasingly muddled by heavy counterdoses of brandy, Cutty Sark, and pot," and by any account Olson's antics onstage suggest the manic velocity of drug-inflected exhilaration (323). Certainly Olson was in rare form as he spoke in rambling fashion for four hours at the microphone in what Clark calls a "wandering, confused monologue" (324), George Butterick describes as a "tour de force" (Introduction ix), and a protective Ralph Maud assures us imparted "an entirely positive feeling" (*Harbor* 190).

Whatever judgments we make of Olson's juggernaut, it seems to have escaped no one's notice that this was a key event in the poet's literary career—perhaps least of all Olson himself, who claims at one point that he is "running for power" up at the microphone (*Muthologos* 115). Libbie Rifkin aligns herself with Olson's self-conscious careerism, arguing that the Berkeley reading reveals Olson jockeying among the postwar avant-garde: "However institutionally savvy, self-aware, and canonically secure Olson may have been, he was still compelled to put on a performance that was originary in its ambitions and embarrassing in its excesses. This suggests both that he felt his authority to be transient, and that revolutionary impulses can coexist with the more 'conservative' project of shoring up one's position via the creation of new institutions, new relations of production and reception" (27). Rifkin's emphasis on what she calls "the multilateral space of avant-gardist identity" (23) leads her beyond Olson's biographers' debate over the psychological dimensions or aesthetic and intellectual merits of his spectacle and toward the claim that Olson's "performance" should be understood as a negotiation of institutional legacy in a room containing not only Ginsberg but Robert Duncan, John Wieners, Robin Blaser, and Robert Creeley. As such, it may have worked. As an unidentified voice from the Berkeley tape calls out, to Olson's likely satisfaction, "You're the boss poet here, daddy!" (*Muthologos* 117).[1]

And yet the epigraph to this chapter suggests that Olson displays concern not only about institutional identity but also for the act of reading poetry aloud. In fact, for Charles Olson, readings weren't mere displays of spontaneous and improvisatory "oral poetry" but rather *battles royal* between the forces of page and stage, voice and text. Surprisingly, Olson's readings made a case not simply for "oral poetry" but also for speech understood as text. For competing with Olson's emphasis on the breath, graphic text itself was to him of equal value, and the tension between the two leads to this chapter's double claim. First, by drawing together orality and print text in awkward, often surprising ways, Olson's readings perform skeptical swerves away from the kinds of humanist presence he strived to engender. By listening to Olson's 1965 show at Berkeley alongside an earlier, sedate reading at Goddard College in Vermont, we can hear how Olson's readings articulate, quite literally, the problem of breath and its relationship to the printed page. Heard serially, Goddard and Berkeley display an Olson who discovers himself farther away than he might have hoped from—or, more simply, someone resistant to—the immediacy and presence of breath. As a poet endlessly inoculating speech with writing and writing with speech, the phenomenology of Olson's speaking voice deconstructs both gambits: live performances grant breath and authenticity to graphic text while simultaneously textualizing the voice, the whole act suggesting the enormity and elasticity of lyric boundary, which, by his reading, is extended beyond the page, beyond the voice, into some relationship between the two. Listening to Olson this way further helps resolve a critical dichotomy regarding Olson's status as an oral or graphic poet; what counts as "real" and present in a poem is found somewhere between voice and text. It also points to Olson's subterranean, Frostian ambivalence about sacrificing poetry to the gods of pure speech.

The second claim advanced here is that because Olson's recordings explode the boundary separating script and voice, they help resituate Olson in the canon of postmodern poetry itself, which has typically claimed Olson as a precursor or major founding figure while ignoring his relationship to actual performance. Olson was the first poet to appear in two widely read anthologies, Donald Allen's *The New American Poetry: 1945–1960* (1960) and Paul Hoover's *Postmodern American Poetry: A Norton Anthology* (1994). This fact, along with his enormously influential status, makes him something like the Walt Whitman of postmodernism, a grandfather figure standing astride the floodgates of a new era. And yet despite this eminence, despite his celebration of breath, Olson's identity as a reader or performer has been largely overlooked, even though performance is itself a fundamental aspect of postmodern lyric. A standard early work like Joseph M. Conte's *Unending Design: The Forms of Postmodern Poetry* (1991) names a variety of conditions that suggest the relevance of postmodern poetics to a performative ethos, one that stresses the uncontainable and contingent: "Poets such as Creeley, Oppen, and Spicer have discerned a serial order that is 'protean' and provisional. It incorporates random occurrences without succumbing to formlessness. Poets such as Ashbery, Mathews, and Cage have entertained a procedural order that is 'proteinic' and predetermined. It employs arbitrary constraints to generate the content of the poem" (11). While these aleatory, "provisional" and improvisational, experimental and "procedural" methods of composition have led to an emphasis on performance for writers including John Cage, Jackson

Mac Low, David Antin, and numerous others, Olson has oddly been left out of this lineage. (Conte cites him as "among the harbingers" [6] of later postmodernists though not quite of them.) Another early and important essay, on the poetics of postmodern performance by Marjorie Perloff, argues that Cage and Antin decenter and destabilize the "margins" of poetry via performance and suggests that both poets (she treats Cage's linguistic rather than musical work) rely upon performative utterance to break from the page's printed and conceptual edge. Perloff's main claim is that a poetry of performance like Antin's draws from formal traditions similar to what Northrop Frye calls "associative rhythm" (*Poetics* 317), a syntactic register falling midway between poetry and prose, and should be understood not as formless, digressive storytelling but as patterned, crosshatched narrative threads (319). Significantly, Perloff stresses Antin's formal qualities by citing Olson's "Projective Verse" as background, particularly the improvisatory, all-caps maxim that "ONE PERCEPTION MUST IMMEDIATELY AND DIRECTLY LEAD TO A FURTHER PERCEPTION" (qtd. in Perloff 318). Present but muted in this attribution is recognition that the legacy of postmodern performance draws from Olson's dicta concerning in this case spontaneity—each moment giving birth to the next—but also presence and a formal coherence that derive from the moment of poetic genesis. Listening to Olson at the microphone not only draws him more fully into the company of such performance-based poets but achieves something more precise: it suggests that Olson's writing and recordings should be read and heard together as part of an *assemblage* of texts, each media mode implicating the other. Just as later poets like David Antin challenged the page's margin, so did Olson, only with less deliberate fanfare. So it's not just what Olson said *about* the voice that's important; it's his actual speaking we should be listening to.[2]

If there's a lot to surprise us about Olson's reading, then perhaps it won't be too startling to underscore how much Olson's performances echo Robert Frost's. Both register a shared ambivalence in the early 1960s toward reading aloud, wondering (implicitly) if public reading is eroding poetry's authority and self-sufficiency. There are even clues, for what it's worth, that Frost may not have been entirely anathema to Olson. Ralph Maud describes an evening in which Wilbert Snow, Olson's early mentor at Wesleyan, and a friend sought to "convert" Olson to Frost, claiming, "We softened him up a great deal" (*Reading* 4). Maud assumes, perhaps anachronistically, that Olson would have had an attitude of "cajoling skepticism" during this conversation, though he also acknowledges how Olson's "knowledge was at all times available for play" and flexibility (4). In fact, Maud transcribes Olson's flyleaf notes from his undergraduate copy of William Trufant Foster's *Argumentation and Debating* (1908), Olson's textbook for preparing and delivering persuasive arguments, which extol Wesleyan as a "prelapsarian world" where "you can meet Vachel Lindsay, Carl Sandburg, W. B. Yeats, and Robert Frost in your professor's living room" (28). Olson's library, now housed at the Thomas J. Dodd Research Center at the University of Connecticut, also preserves his copy of Louis Untermeyer's *Pocket Anthology* of Frost's poems published in 1946, the very year Olson began publishing poems. Such examples don't demonstrate a deep affinity between the two poets, though they suggest that perhaps we should allow our own received ideas to be as "available to play" as Olson's own. In what follows, Frost's own brand of skeptical humanism is audible and replayed.

Print, Orality, and Technology

It should come as no surprise that out of the poets assembled at Berkeley in 1965, Olson would be the one to interrogate reading practices most thoroughly. His manifesto "Projective Verse" is one of the most cited postwar statements of American poetics, and indeed it does seem to make a forceful, if counterpoised, case for the primacy of "the breath" and "breathing." At the risk of making superfluous comments on this much-examined text, I want to clarify the importance of Olson's major statement on the way presence is generated by the body, by the voice, and by the breath itself. Drafted in February 1950, the document runs thick with claims about reviving breath for poetry:

> Verse now, 1950, if it is to go ahead, if it is to be of *essential* use, must, I take it, catch up and put into itself certain laws and possibilities of the breath, of the breathing of the man who writes as well as of his listenings. (51)

> What we have suffered from, is manuscript, press, the removal of verse from its producer and its reproducer, the voice, a removal by one, by two removes from its place of origin *and* its destination. For the breath has a double meaning which Latin had not yet lost. (57)

> But breath is man's special qualification as animal. Sound is a dimension he has extended. Language is one of his proudest acts. And when a poet rests in these as they are in himself (in his physiology, if you like, but the life in him, for all that) then he, if he chooses to speak from these roots, works in that area where nature has given him size, projective size. (60)

For Olson, breath is a trope for physical presence; it is prized as primary, originary, and unquestionably authentic. Without breath's primacy, both spoken and heard, language represented in print stands at a series of Platonic "removes" from speech, atrophying poetry's potential to be almost ontologically essential. This assumption is audible in the opening *Maximus* poem, "I, Maximus of Gloucester, to You"—the first draft written just months after "Projective Verse" (Maud, *Harbor* 139)—which inscribes a projective aesthetic by pleading for sound's liberation from print:

> By ear, he sd.
> But that which matters, that which insists, that which will last,
> that! o my people, where shall you find it, how, where, where shall
>   you listen
> when all is become billboards, when, all, even silence, is spray-
>   gunned? (6)

In *Maximus*, writing strives to approximate the articulated syllable ("mu-sick, mu-sick, mu-sick" [7]), and print equates to commerce and the deadening effects of capitalism: "the trick / of corporations, newspapers, slick magazines, movie houses, / the ships, even the wharves, absentee-owned // they whine to my people, these entertainers, sellers" (14). "Letter 5" continues this screed against print, structured around a response to the "Editor of a Gloucester quarterly" (22) who negatively reviewed Vincent Ferrini's magazine *Four Winds*, in which the poem appeared (Butterick, *Guide* 23.). This editor is a figure who seems less deserving of Olson's derision for attacking the poems as for committing the attack to print. In these opening poems, print erodes an imagined human community, the "absentee-owned" businesses of shipping and printing also referring to a more local absence where "measure" or verse stands for affect itself: "You see I can't get away from the old measure of care: how your magazine don't raise me" (26).

Some have taken this renegade orality at face value, and Olson's own formulations about language often get passed down intact, without a critical gaze. For instance, here is a reminiscence by Olson's student at Black Mountain College, Francine du Plessix Gray: "Olson was obsessed by the loss of energy between the rich immediacy of our emotions and the relative poverty of our scripted words: 'The dodges of discourse,' as he called it, 'the distinction between language as the act of the instant and language as the act of thought about the instant.' His infatuation with Mayan culture came from the directness of its hieroglyphic writing" (302). Scholarly writing buttresses this perspective. The critic Stephen Fredman claims that "the body in a particular setting" (47)—and breath in particular—"grounds" Olson's self spatially and temporally, serving as a response to an absence of "cultural tradition" (3). In an early and influential argument, Robert Von Hallberg calls Olson's writing "guerrilla theatre," claiming that "the conventional separation between audience and actor disappears," leaving pure "experience" itself to replace the dead letter of written text (qtd. in Szalay 269). While noting the "cowboy," masculine ethos of "Projective Verse" and how that ethos saturated the alternative poetry scene of New York City's Lower East Side, Daniel Kane credits the essay's "increasing emphasis on the human voice as shaper of poetic form" (29).

An unusual version of this critical echoing comes from Michael Szalay, who draws on tenets of modernist performance art that surrounded Olson at Black Mountain College (John Cage, Joseph Alpers) and later New York avant-gardes (Allan Kaprow, the Fluxus movement). Szalay imagines that Olson's texts and reading performances enacted a "fantasy market" that recalled New Deal institutions like the WPA, where artists were plucked free of the capitalist grind of production and consumption (269). For Szalay, "virtually all of Olson's most characteristic formal innovations worked to accentuate the performative dimension of poetry. His 'open form' technique, for example, also called 'composition by field,' used non-traditional typography to accentuate the spoken, communal nature of poetic expression," which would "indicate how to read his poems" (259). Szalay's error here, one that I think is common to writing about Olson and orality, is to uncritically adopt Olson's own claims about the breath's immediacy. Made in the absence of actual reference to Olson's performances, such an assertion leads Szalay to argue that as a performer Olson eroded the divide between poet and audience: "Collapsing the difference between consumers and producers, Olson produces an interactive community in which all can imagine themselves at work, laboring at the business of poetry" (269). For Szalay, this models the procedures of an imaginative community of writers, less political per se than an actual alternative to a capitalist economy, one in which Olson could have agency and control. While this is an inventive idea, Szalay relies upon the kind of "collapse" of speech and writing into an oral present that is the dream of Olson's manifesto. Yet such a collapse is not nearly as tidy as Olson, Von Hallberg, Szalay, or any number of the pie-eyed "consumers" who attended that perfervid night in Berkeley might have imagined. In fact, Olson's readings show him striving, in ways unremarked by even himself, to maintain a critical distance between orality and print.

More recently, it has become common to articulate a competing skepticism regarding Olson's claims to pure orality, usually by acknowledging what Nathaniel Mackey calls Olson's "graphicity," the visual qualities of text on the space of the page (123). Certainly, this has some bearing on Olson's writing in "Projective Verse," which is as rhetorically invested in metaphors of space as it is to breath. "FIELD COMPOSITION" conceives of a spatial poetry of the page propelled by voice but tectonically orthographic ("Projective Verse" 52). Even language, according to Olson, is conceived in terms of spatial scale, as when Olson says that successful poets attain "projective size," a phrase that itself transforms the nonspatiality of voice into terms of measurement and dimension (60). This is not really a new idea. In a persuasive and resourceful case for Olson's graphic aesthetics, Eleanor Berry has argued that projective verse is indeed accomplished "in large part through visual form" ("Emergence" 51), and Paul Lake more polemically urges us to accept that Olson "conceives of his poetry strictly in terms of visual space. The metaphors he uses to describe his new method are all drawn from the language of spatial relations, of geometry"—in the word "field," in the phrase "go by no track," and in the premise that poems should create energy at all "points" (26). Yet perhaps no one has been so perceptive about this as Mackey himself, who contends that graphicity is not contrary to orality, the two being mutually sustaining registers. "There is often something purely sensuous, intuitive, or gratuitous about the way a poem is arranged on the page," Mackey argues, "having less to do with musical specifications than with that very quality of openness, spontaneity, and even whimsicality often associated with an 'oral' stance" (123). Yet notice: in these three arguments the assumption of authentic or immediate source of expression still remains intact. It may be assisted by nonoral constructions, as in Mackey's graphicity, which serves the "openness" and "spontaneity" we associate with orality, but the Emersonian notion of an original relation to the universe stands unshaken.

Yet an actual listening encounter with Olson giving a reading—that is, standing upon a dais or sitting at a table and before a microphone, speaking words aloud to an assembled group—radically shifts this critical terrain. Faced with the immediate context of a speaking situation, the fabled poems of liberating breath encounter a variety of entanglements, including the haunting specter of text and the technologies of breath's mediation, like microphones and tape recorders. This phenomenological approach to questions of orality is long overdue in Olson studies, which with a few exceptions—Rifkin's analysis, some notes in Butterick's editorial apparatuses—has not taken his recorded readings much into account. And yet these readings are crucial interventions into settled ideas about Olson's relationship to breath.

BEFORE MOVING ON to the readings themselves, it's worth pausing to more roundly describe Olson's own attitudes toward orality, which are audible far back into Olson's biography. For instance, the Berkeley reading shows Olson repeatedly dwelling on his oratorical past. As a high school student in 1928, Olson won a series of speaking prizes, including one for his "declamation team," as well as "public speaking" and "oratorical" contests (Maud, *Harbor* 26). The *Worcester Telegram-Gazette* describes "the magnificence of his oratory," calling Olson "master of the art of speaking" (qtd. in Maud, *Harbor* 28). When Olson cries out from the stage at Berkeley "I feel like a kid" (*Muthologos* 111), he may be recalling these events, an association that grows more convincing in light of his numerous references that night to his role as public speaker. He cites the "*rhetor* . . . I was at seventeen, by speech, the most powerful figure in the world" (153), and the tape's last moments record him casting his mind back to this oratorical seed-time, specifically to the figure of René Ponthieu, the French contestant who beat him in the "International" competition in Washington, D.C.: "I don't even like those elocutionary poets, that I can be, and I was, at seventeen. Hah, you don't think I was in the Constitution Hall in Washington, being judged by the Supreme Court as to whether I was the primary orator of America, to meet Ponthieu—I remember it so well—who was the Frenchman who was so inferior to me if I was in hell" (156).

Clearly, Olson's time onstage at Berkeley recalled for him his oratorical past, although it isn't clear whether that recollection was in terms of his performance or the competition. In fact, one of the surprising discoveries of Olson as a reader is his similarity to Frost. Again, Joan Shelley Rubin's *Songs of Ourselves* supplies a relevant context. Rubin describes the "structure, content, and ideology" of instructional reading in the early twentieth century as "strikingly stable" and uniform and describes such pedagogical practices in schools across the American Northeast (where Olson grew up) in ways resonant with Olson's reading style (119). This ideology called for the instillation of moral value and, in the case of immigrant populations, citizenry through the memorization and recitation of poetry, the "memory gems" (110) described in chapter 2. Poems, mostly, and some bits of literary prose were to be committed to memory and recited, often for a few minutes each school day, in hopes that they would instill both morality and eloquence. According to Rubin, this was all in the service of politicizing and nativizing immigrant communities: "Borrowing from the ideology surrounding elocution, and sustaining traditions of oratory by importing them into the classroom," Rubin says, "teachers associated vocal training with producing an eloquent citizenry possessed of high principle and judgment" (113). It's not surprising, then, that Olson draws on the vocabulary of elocution and oratory and his memories as a reader.

Of more contemporary concern to Olson were recent discussions of orality and print media, twin cultural energies that Marshall McLuhan and Bronisław Malinowski described as locked in a dialectical struggle in terms similar to Olson's. Both theorists laid bare the ways in which orality was prized, even fetishized in postwar America yet also complicated by a sense of how technological change was altering it. Perhaps most initially striking among these texts is the consistent position that oral cultures were "primitive" and that speech somehow relied upon retrograde cultural energies. Malinowski, for example, who published his essay "The Problem of Meaning in Primitive Languages" in C. K. Ogden and I. A. Richards's extraordinarily influential *The Meaning of Meaning* (1938), coined the phrase "*context of situation*" to name the rootedness of primitive language to place (306, italics in original). Olson had read Malinowski in the 1950s and made repeated comments on his work, eventually including a Malinowski text on a course syllabus.[3] Malinowski, a cultural anthropologist who did his fieldwork on the Trobriand Islands (now the Kiriwina Islands) in Papua New Guinea, argued that what might appear to be "extreme simplicity" in verbal exchange among Trobriand islanders actually "hides a good deal of expressiveness, often achieved by means of position and context" (300). Charting his own misprisions of speech acts due to a lack of sufficient situational literacy, Malinowski claimed that oral cultures depend upon presence and embodiment to construct meaning, a position that not only resonates with Olson's investigations into Mayan literacy a dozen years later but also provides a basis for "Projective Verse" itself.

McLuhan's argument in *The Gutenberg Galaxy,* originally published in 1962, offers significantly more sophistication and lays bare contemporary tensions between orality and print. In ways similar to Malinowski, McLuhan positions visuality and technologies of print and type against all kinds of primitive tropes, including "oriental" "tribal cultures" (29) and the "Africa within" (45). For McLuhan, modern technology started with movable type and has metastasized into all forms of digital and communication media, which require "homogeneity, uniformity, repeatability," and an intense focus on visuality, abetted by print itself, which associated the eye with reason and rationality (58). McLuhan calls modern readers—who conceive of rationality as linear, sequential, and available to regulation—"literacy victims" and in so doing suggests that literacy and print technology override and alienate organic, "primitive," Rousseauistic orality or presence, just the kind that Malinowski describes (71). And yet it would be a superficial reading of McLuhan's book to miss his counterclaim that orality is staging a comeback: "As our age translates itself back into the oral and auditory modes because of the electronic pressure of simultaneity, we become sharply aware of the uncritical acceptance of visual metaphors" (72). Citing Gertrude Stein, T. S. Eliot, and James Joyce (McLuhan does not shy away from plumbing *Finnegans Wake*), he shows how orality can be assisted by textual means, often through alienation effects; for example, Stein's various "visual aids" are "a carefully devised strategy to get the passive visual reader into participant, oral action" (83). Indeed, McLuhan's shift here signals a position similar to Olson's own as expressed by Mackey's graphicity. For McLuhan, typography and literacy produced extraordinary changes, and his book—organized "mosaically," as he describes it, in short chapters, like tesserae—doesn't sound a clear note. Yet without question, orality and visual text were crosshatched for McLuhan as he describes the interdependence of publication and recitation, or what he calls "publication as performance" (84).

The work of Malinowski and McLuhan bear some striking resemblances to Olson's own commitments to orality and display similar tension between primitive unity and modern disjuncture, as I'll demonstrate below. For example, Olson is as canny as McLuhan in rehinging speech and text, abstraction and materiality; Olson's "breath" itself attains a kind of density that belies its primitive lack of spatial heft:

> Because breath allows all the speech-force of language back in (speech is the "solid" of verse, is the secret of a poem's energy), because, now, a poem has, by speech, solidity, everything in it can now be treated as solids, objects, things; and, though insisting upon the absolute difference of the reality of verse from that other dispersed and distributed thing, yet each of these elements of a poem can be allowed to have the play of their separate energies and can be allowed, once the poem is well composed, to keep, as those other objects do, their proper confusions. ("Projective Verse" 56)

Here Olson inverts McLuhan's dichotomy: spoken language, not typefaces, creates "solidity." It's hard at times to determine to what extent Olson's prose is being metaphorical—is "solidity" merely a trope for authenticity?—though this is also the point: Olson's aesthetic focuses on the "proper confusions" among these twining energies. On the page itself, the poem relies upon breath in the act of composition; and the spoken poem would suffer without being able to "keep," in Olson's language of postwar refrigeration, frozen in the preservative of type.

This complicated relationship between speech and graphic text, in which the latter erodes the seeming authority of the former, plays out most clearly in Olson's early book *Mayan Letters* (1953). The book is a selection of letters between Olson and Robert Creeley, edited by Creeley at Olson's request. The letters were written mostly from Campeche, Mexico, a coastal hamlet in the Yucatán peninsula to which Olson had abruptly traveled (a "sudden 'fluke,'" as Creeley describes it [*Mayan Letters* 5]). There, he found himself suddenly immersed in the amateur study of Mayan language, specifically hieroglyphs. Much of *Mayan Letters* is focused on breathing life back into dead script through argument and, it seems, the sheer force of prose; it's an effort at what might be called prosthetic embodiment, as if Olson felt the text's dead letters required his propulsive will and generously proportioned body to reanimate them. In essence, Olson's idea was that, rather than serving in various astrological projects, as some scholars (like J. Eric S. Thompson, whom Olson excoriates throughout) had suggested, Mayan glyphs actually functioned as a spoken language (62). Furthermore, this language is, via the glyphs, somehow still available today. When Olson says glyphs are primarily alphabetic rather than ritualistic and puts "the whole thing back to the spoken language" (62), "spoken" implies a world of sense—signs lead straight to their embodied presences in the world of touches and sounds, where abstractions found concrete existence: "[Y]ou can see, that time, in their minds, was mass & weight!" (62). "What continues to hold me, is, the tremendous levy on all objects as they present themselves to human sense, in this glyph-world" (66). In this way, the "glyph-world" approximates speech in terms of its presentism, immediacy, and access to the body. In his major essay "Human Universe," Olson stakes out the linguistic value of the glyphs, arguing for their healing of a metaphysical split in Western culture: "Logos, or discourse, for example, has . . . so worked its abstractions into our concept and use of language that language's other function, speech, seems so in need of restoration that several of us got back to hieroglyphs or to ideograms to right the balance" (3–4). Much like Pound's eager but flawed traducing of Chinese ideograms, Olson's faith in the "restoration" promised by early American texts is predicated on a woeful, modern dissociation of sensibility. Today, such complaints ring with a naïveté familiar to scholars of high modernist nostalgia, from which Olson's theorizing stems. And to a contemporary reader, the field of linguistics has emerged since Olson's Yucatán sojourn, picking up on and transforming much of what he argues here.[4]

Olson's project in *Mayan Letters* is to match the descriptive agency of the glyphs with his own, thus creating in language his own version of that embodiment. It's an impulse audible in his drunken aside to Allen Ginsberg in this chapter's epigraph: doing this would show how Mayan text attains living, oral presence. I suspect that some of Olson's animus for this project was gleaned from his copious reading at the time, especially the work of Leo Frobenius, one of the scholars on rock painting and writing whom Olson recommends (in a brief, idiosyncratic bibliography at the end of *Mayan Letters*) as one who could "give the Maya the present they once were, and are" (89). This gesture of *textual presentism*—the agency granted to text to reveal how past experiences are manifest in the present—is richly at hand in Olson's own writing and worth keeping in mind in the discussion to come of Olson's readings, which operate from similar assumptions. Olson gleaned the idea from Frobenius, who first describes his work with African cave art, which revealed links between European and African peoples, and then comes to the italicized formulation, "*That which existed once in Europe lives on among its epigones in Africa today*" (22). Frobenius is not simply interested in drawing on images and textual marks to understand the past; rather, he uses them to see the past "existing" in the present. The value of cave art for Frobenius is its uncanny property: an anachronistic mark signals a living culture. Here he writes about his younger self in the third person, realizing this:

> [W]hy should not the culture of the period have flourished in Africa as well as Spain? Were that the case, then one could imagine that when the water evaporated and the plains turned into a desert, the African branch of this culture, if one wished to call it that, had moved ever southward towards the moist interior, that it had penetrated as far even as South Africa. Were this, too, the case, then—and at the thought of it the young man caught his breath—then this culture still could be alive *today*, still could be observed, grasped, studied and understood *today!* (16)

I quote directly from Frobenius's essay because his childlike, Romantic fascination with the way written signs might thread back to living bodies, living cultures, peoples, and words is so palpably similar to Olson's own and offers a prose-like gloss to Olson's looping, discursive, epistolary exploration.

Mayan Letters attempts to create a similar kind of textual presentism through the agency of its own written fiat; the text calls forth an embodied presence, constituting an inversion of orality. If glyphs hold "weight" and "mass" for Olson, they do so as routes of access to the past; the material density, tactile immediacy, texture, and heft of these images grants access to the bodies that once articulated them. To achieve this directness of print, Olson's prose floods itself, saturating print's textual confinement enough to overflow its own parameters, a signal of his reaching beyond language and straining sense for the embodiment he describes: "what you & i have been (all along) talking about—viz., man as object in field of force declaring self as force because is force in exactly such relation & can accomplish expression of self as force by conjecture, & displacement in a context best, now, seen as space more than time as such" (67). A gloss of this Gothic exegesis might point out that Olson is seeking to eliminate time and suggest the present or simultaneous Mayan culture. This isn't history, it's actuality: "What has to be battered down, completely, is that this has anything to do with stage of development. Au contraire. The capacity for (1) the observation & (2) the invention has no more to do with brick or wheels or metal or stone than you and i are different from, sd peoples: we are like. Therefore, there is no 'history'" (68–69). Ironically for Olson, text—not spoken, oral language—has become, in its materiality, a means toward erasing that very materiality, erasing difference, erasing history. When Olson describes the "fluency" of the glyphs he means their role in the actual speech of the Maya and their capacity to grant access to it. Glyphs show that text and speech are mutually self-productive, neither one canceling out the other. It's just this slippage between embodied speech and written text, fixity and dissolve, that Olson's live readings engage.

Drawing on what I'll name Olson's "vocal text" and "textual voice," readings throw into question in radical and surprising ways the status of voice and writing, pulling them together and pushing them apart. In doing so, they help resolve critical disagreements over Olson's aural and "graphic" emphases, showing that these were not simply inseparable but mutually dependent. They suggest how troubling this relation is, and in some cases (as with his reading of "Cashes" at Goddard College) they serve as important iterations of the poems themselves that should be considered alongside published versions. Listening to three of Olson's reading performances suggests that reading provided Olson a forum—truly, a public venue for communicative speech—for testing out orality and its relationship to breath and text. Readings show that Olson locked himself in dialectical struggle with these twinned forces just as he reeled between Malinowski's primitivism and technological instantiation. In his essay "From Work to Text," Roland Barthes distinguishes between two modes of literary production, a relevant distinction here. *Works* are known things, monographic, available for inspection, "*moderately* symbolic," as Barthes says—that is, singular and capable of being apprehended due to participation in established discourses and interpretive epistemologies (158). Barthes calls the work "a fragment of substance" (15) affiliated with "the civilization of the Sign," the knowable, that which is able to be represented, examined, investigated, and coherently deciphered (158). *Texts*, on the other hand, are radically plural affairs—disjunctive, inviting collaborative readerly construction, thornily unconsumable, discursively intransigent. "Text is that *social* space," Barthes says, "which leaves no language safe, outside, nor any subject of the enunciation in position as judge, master, analyst, confessor, decoder" (164). Olson's readings underscore a similar tension between work and text and reveal, in ways perhaps not fully available even to Olson himself, how this may indeed serve as one of the "proper confusions" of his poems.

Olson at the Mike

Olson's poetry readings are deeply contrary events in which Olson avidly pursues a humanist authenticity of oral presence while simultaneously textualizing it back from the brink of living breath. His readings court and then deny the authenticity of speech. One telling phenomenon regarding this process is that an audience is transformative and essential for these two registers to materialize—that is, Olson's textual voice is less singular, rich, or responsive outside a live forum. At a recording Olson made at Black Mountain College (BMC) sometime during the academic year of 1954, there's an unusually close fidelity to graphic poem and spoken word. It is as if Olson is following precisely his description in "Projective Verse," quoted below, of voice and the typewriter:

> It is the advantage of the typewriter that, due to its rigidity and its space precisions, it can, for a poet, indicate exactly the breath, the pauses, the suspensions even of the syllables, the juxtapositions even of parts of phrases, which he intends. For the first time the poet has the stave and the bar a

> musician has had. For the first time he can, without the convention of rime and meter, record the listening he has done to his own speech and by that one act indicate how he would want any reader, silently or otherwise, to voice his work. (57–58)

Similar to Frost's entanglement of living speech and written sentences, Olson imagines a kind of audio-to-text circuit: the poet first listens to his own speech and then locks it into text with mechanically graphic precision; that text is then reanimated by the poet himself in the act of speech. (Though this is also quite unlike Frost, who describes the poet as listening to folk voices and more culturally valent "sentence sounds" rather than "his own speech.") Olson is seemingly more concerned here with composition than performance. He points out that Pound and Williams are already "composing" this way, "as though verse was to have the reading its writing involved, as though not the eye but the ear was to be its measurer" (59). The phrase "as though" implies that the ultimate destination of printed text matters less than the story of its composition. Yet clearly, while Mackey's "graphicity" is operative here, its status is underwritten (and undermined) by the voice that shaped it in the first place.

This balance between text and voice, machine and mouth, is readily audible in the BMC reading. Cut in the campus's small recording studio and subsequently transferred to vinyl, the recording cracks and pops as the needle navigates the polymer grooves. These sounds, along with the close air of corrugated walls and Olson's measured vocal sobriety, are all quite different from the psycho-activated stentor at Berkeley. Olson opens the BMC reading with "The Songs of Maximus," his phrasing corresponding to the print text with the mechanistic precision described above. "Song 1," for example, is arranged in staggered lines, though the left-hand margin is respected:

                        colored pictures
of all things to eat: dirty
postcards
                And words, words, words
all over everything
                                No eyes or ears left
to do their own doings (all

invaded, appropriated, outraged, all senses

including the mind, that worker on what is (*Maximus* 17)

On record, Olson's voice is shackled to the typography, with respectful and deliberate pauses following "pictures," "dirty," "postcards," and the third use of "words." At the parenthetical "all," which Olson notably "sighs" in the Frostian manner, a longer caesura falls before the double-dropped line, and then another one occurs after "senses" for the second double-dropped line. As the *Songs* continue, it should be admitted that some of this robotic exactitude gets mildly eroded by the animus of speaking, though this entire reading, just under twelve minutes long, follows the general graphemic pattern closely. There is no sense here that Olson is engaged in anything like "oral poetry," and no "context of situation," as Malinowski would call it, seems required to consume this diminutive vocal commodity. If this canned, forgettable recitation were all that was preserved of Olson's voice, we might be inclined to dismiss any claims to force, effectiveness, or intrigue regarding Olson's reading of poetry.

And yet such a reading makes clear how much this equation between text and voice is aligned with composition rather than performance, which includes Olson's interplay with a live audience. Olson acknowledges this distinction, as he explains in the second section of "Projective Verse," which begins by noting the difference between "reality outside a poem" and "the reality of a poem itself" (59): the latter draws the speaker into an "animal" dimension (60). So if "breath" stands for a compositional ideal in Olson's work, it clearly also stands for something like material presence and immediacy. Take his language from "Projective Verse" above, which describes "the removal of verse from its producer and its reproducer, the voice, a removal by one, by two removes from its place of origin *and* its destination." This studio recording captures just half of Olson's interest in the breath's relationship to the machine—their mutual compatibility. Contrary to Olson's BMC recording, however, in Berkeley a decade later we can hear a bid for unmediated production and reception with an actual audience—constantly, distractingly, obsessively so.

Live readings are categorically different from Olson's studio recordings, especially in terms of how he courts a sense of readerly presence. Both at Berkeley and at Goddard College, presence is sought in a variety of ways, though perhaps most apparently through a rhetorical self-reflexivity. Olson's post-structuralist heirs have touched on Olson's rhetoric of presence when reading. Barrett Watten argues that "Olson's refusal of closure"—his sprawling, seemingly endless torrent of vocabulary spat from the stage at Berkeley—creates an "affect of presence" (qtd. in Rifkin 21), one similar in critical tone to how Perloff describes the postmodern poetry performer's challenge to "margins" cited earlier. Ron Silliman imagines that "[i]n the Olsonian world, the text substitutes for the body of the poet," a formulation that cleaves closely to Olson's own assurances that the poem is a "score" for breath (370). Yet what does this kind of presence actually look like—or *sound* like—onstage? Incoherence, logorrhea, anecdote, and digression are only a few of his strategies for staging embodiment. For instance, self-reflexivity plays an important role in this process: "Gee, I'm moved" (*Muthologos* 104), he cries early on in the Berkeley reading. And later: "And I, at the moment, in that wonderful fact that you're here, and I am making it, just that, think it's one of the most beautiful poems I ever wrote" (107). And again, comparing his performance to a 1963 reading in Vancouver: "Honestly, look, I could read forever, right now. I mean, Christ! Oh, hah hah! This is better than that phony strength I pumped up in Vancouver. It's very sober. It's nice. I feel very comfortable and strong and resonant, and all that shit" (156). Olson's reading is constantly refracted through the prism of his various self-characterizations—here coupled with comparison to a previously "phony" performance; aren't you glad you missed that one?

This strategy gets modulated in a variety of ways. A more particular version is Olson's repeated claim that reading is a "publishing" event. In this way, the act of speech becomes (rhetorically, at least) equivalent to, or in some kind of competition with, material publication. "Reading is publishing," Olson cries to Lew Welch, sitting nearby in the Berkeley audience. "Any one of us in this room will prove that to you. There is no publishing—I am not published for many years, because I was not writing. I am now publishing, tonight, because I'm talking writing" (*Muthologos* 109). Interrupting himself during a reading of "Letter 6" from *Maximus*, Olson stakes out a geography of presence with about as much clarity as one could hope for:

> No, I wanna talk. I mean, you want to listen to a poet? You know, a poet, when he's alive, whether he talks or reads you his poems is the same thing. Dig that! [Applause.] And when he is made of three parts—his life, his mouth, and his poems—then, by god, the earth belongs to us! And what I think has happened is that that's—wow, gee, one doesn't like to claim things, but, god, isn't it exciting? I mean, I feel like a kid. I'm in the presence of an event, which I don't believe, myself. (*Muthologos* 111)

The "event" here is the sense of oral presence Olson is so vigorously trying to whip into a froth of being; the lack of "belief" is his acknowledgment of orality's essential impossibility. In fact, reading this text from a transcript of the event highlights the problems I'm describing here and throughout: the performed moment becomes just more print when transcribed. The poet Bob Perelman makes a persuasive and relevant case for the alienating effects of transcription, pointing out how "the evanescent charms of talk are difficult to discern in printed speech" (201). Further, the "presence of an event" here is, as Olson intuits, not to be believed for readers of it, who are at one remove. Consistent with his oral manifesto, "talking" and "reading" are equals (though of course, the spoken is privileged), the attainment of the projective moment so palpable and immediate, he shrinks from its revelation. This is why George Butterick's introduction to *Muthologos* lavishes praise on Olson's heroics of extemporaneity: "He would throw out an argument or a tale like Babe Ruth pointing to the stands, challenging himself, to see if he could meet the pitch. It was a healthy and resourceful activism, a drama of risk, part of the spontaneously creative moment" (x). Furthermore, Olson's sense of reading's function as a "publication" is consistent with contemporary orality's own recuperation of such an idea. As McLuhan pointed out, "public recitation was a principal form of book publication" for Aristotle and Tacitus and, later on, medieval culture at large (84). Olson's poetics of presence here attempts to value the oral act in much this same manner as McLuhan describes—thus Olson's haranguing of Ginsberg from this essay's epigraph. And so the Berkeley reading is saturated with contradiction: on the one hand, Olson strives toward implicating himself and his audience in an immediate action, an oral presence; and on the other, such acts are rhetorically reinscribed as something "solid" and textual.

As suggested above, Olson's attitudes and gestures toward "technology" are a further development of these questions; print and sound recording often function as delimiters of presence. *Maximus* itself is invested in positioning the poem's speaker in relationship to technologies of print and recording, especially regarding the immediately audible and visible. The first clear reference to this occurs in the opening poem, "I, Maximus of Gloucester, to You," "when sound itself is neoned in." Print is roundly excoriated:

> Let those who use words cheap, who use us cheap
> take themselves out of the way
> Let them not talk of what is good for the city
> . . . .
> Let them cease putting out words in the public print (13)

The voice of Maximus represents a local, immediate citizenry ("Polis now / is a few" [15]) who can literally hear words spoken aloud without amplification or mediation ("who can say who are / citizens? // Only a man or a girl who hear a word" [15]). It's worth pointing out here that one of *Maximus*'s most consistently chosen modes of address is apostrophe, a figure I think is used for its nonmediated availability to the senses. In the line "Isolated person in Gloucester, Massachusetts, I, Maximus, address / you islands / of men and girls" (16), Maximus seems to maneuver around the arras of print, the blather of radio and television, and distance itself, taking it upon himself to speak face to face with his people. In this way, apostrophe functions as a conceit of immediate, unimpeded speech. The figure of apostrophe is in fact significant: originally derived from oral performance, its literal meaning is "to turn away," which refers to the ancient Greek stage practice of an actor turning from his lines to address a Muse, a god, or an abstract entity ("Apostrophe" 82). Jonathan Culler argues that apostrophe produces a "special temporality" (153) in which absence (like Keats's "this living hand") is transformed into an imaginatively authentic sense of presence (154). Culler speculates that what he calls the "repression" of apostrophe in literary criticism (modern readers are mildly abashed at apostrophe's emotive form of address) may be the result of writing itself harboring "some innate hostility to voice" (136), which apostrophe signifies to a greater degree than other rhetorical tropes. Maximus's apostrophes might then be seen as figures for actual breath and speech in the poem and as being at odds with any attempts to mediate them. They stand out as steps away from the representational space of the page and toward unmediated presence.

Certainly this isn't always a one-way screed, and Maximus displays some concessions to print ("you do meet someone // as I met you // on a printed page," he writes in an address to Vincent Ferrini [Olson, *Maximus* 28]). Still, the poem establishes a kind of unresolved relationship between the voice and the print that mediates it, especially in print's associations with technological forms. At the end of "Letter 9," a four-poem sequence about the publishing of his poems in Ferrini's journal *Four Winds* and his book *In Cold Hell, in Thicket,* Olson rhetorically pits the voice against its mechanistic regimentation into "measure":

> I measure my song,
> measure the sources of my song,
> measure me, measure
> my forces
>
> (And I buzz,
> as the bee does,
> who's missed
> the plum tree,
> and gone and got himself caught
> in my window
>
> And the whirring of whose wings
> blots out the rattle of
> my machine) (48)

While we've seen that the typewriter ("my machine") was sanctified by Olson as an abettor of breath, a positive association he shared with Williams's glorification of the typewriter's granting of individual agency, here the organic buzz of a bee seems powerful enough to check the mechanical "measure."[5] And it's hard not to hear a kind of self-indictment in the triple anaphora of "measure." The tape recorder, too, plays a role in the poem. "A Later Note on Letter #15" is a direct comment on tape recording itself, which positions the recorder as a "lie" in relationship to being there "on the spot." From the middle of the poem:

& *that* concept of history (not Herodotus's,
which was a verb, to find out for yourself:
'istorin, which makes any one's acts of finding out for him or her
self, in other words restores the traum: that we act somewhere

at least by seizure, that the objective (example Thucidides, or
the latest finest tape-recorder, or any form of record on the spot

—live television or what—is a lie

as against what we know went on, the dream (249)

Recording is here figured as a "seizure" of action; it gives the lie to history itself. Olson distinguishes between two modes of history here: history as an "objective" and history as a "verb." Like Herodotus's works, tape recorders serve in Olson's imagination as "lies" that can't possibly lead back to "what we know went on." And yet, of course, what went on is a "dream," an inaccessible point of time that relies upon these mechanistic tracing devices.

Such technologies aren't only figural. As in his poems, actual objects of technological reproduction—microphones, speakers, tape recorders, and printed matter—play a prop-like role in Olson's readings and are made reference to with surprising frequency. In one piquant version I'll name "the drama of the microphone," Olson draws upon the presence of recording technology itself—a visible presence at these two readings—to establish the quality of "live" described by Jonathan Sterne in his cultural history of sound recording technologies, *The Audible Past* (2003). For Sterne, "authenticity and presence become issues only when there is something to which we can compare them" (220). The very idea of "live" performance arises historically as the obverse of recording itself; without reproduction, production would lose its lose-ability. For this reason, Walter Benjamin's *aura* is possible only when it falls under threat, as "the object of nostalgia that accompanies reproduction" (220). Paradoxically, a live reading without a microphone lacks the dialectical presence established by that magic wand, its visibility on the tabletop opening a productive gulf between the present moment and its promise of nostalgic recapture. Crucial for an understanding of Olson, this equation of orality as presence and "mediatization" as absence is actually inverted by Michael Davidson, who reads Olson's emphasis on voice as representing "ideals of immediacy and acoustics" (*Ghostlier* 196) just as I have above. Yet Davidson notes only that Olson used the typewriter as a way to "score" a voice with newfound precision—precisely the effect audible in the BMC studio recording (197). His discussion of poets like Allen Ginsberg and, more recently, David Antin, Laurie Anderson, and Steve Benson suggests that they drew on taped voice less as a "passive receptacle" and more as "an active agent in its deconstruction" by, say, bringing recording devices into a particular performance or act of composition themselves, as did Antin for much of everything he "wrote" (100). Such employments of language technologies—the typewriter, the tape recorder—assisted in "adapting the means of reproduction to productive uses" (117). While Davidson's reading is astute, he leaves Olson out of this later development of voice and recordings, citing only Olson's interest in the typewriter; yet the ritual of noticing recording paraphernalia and drawing it into the discursive present was a stock part of Olson's readings that allowed him to underscore difference between speech and its mediated capture. Furthermore, Olson simply isn't able to commandeer recordings in the deft way his contemporaries could. Microphones and tape recorders do help him establish "liveness," though they render him incapable of maintaining it.

Just a few phrases into Olson's Berkeley reading, this drama of the microphone begins to awkwardly unfold: "[H]ow do you do this if there ain't . . . ? Just connect . . . ? You see, this is life [laughter]. I mean, I either am the Hanged Man, or . . . [laughter]. Where do you put that, like? Where does that go? There's no hole! Where do you put it? You'd better show me. Mr. Baker. Able Baker [laughter]! You see, security. Thank you" (98). One might read this overtly lavish recognition as an attempt not to associate but to dissociate his own voice with what is being recorded. Or later, after trouble with the microphone cord: "I almost lost it. I feel as though I'm chained to the Catholic Church [laughing]. And I am, and I have been. And, in fact, if it's become a mike, with the condition in which I am tonight, I'm lucky" (108). Or yet later, again in reference to the mike cord: "Hm, Jesus, that mother will get me yet!" (120). The tape recorder—its microphone cord's hard-to-find hole, it's Otherness as competitor for the voice—allows Olson not just to play the Luddite but also to side with the audience. It's us against It, he seems to say.

But just what is "It"? At Goddard College in Vermont, this question becomes more pointed. The reading opens with a recasting of the techno-drama of the microphone:

> Unidentified voice: You don't mind using a tape recorder do you?
>
> CO: No. As a matter of fact I'm going to just watch it, [laughter from audience] like a fire, let's sit here and watch that tape [laughter from Olson]. What happens if it just goes on and I don't say anything? See, that's the problem with reading, it gets to be kind of a bore, because it—it's become a performing art, you feel as though you have an audience, and as if you're supposed to do a concert or something, and uh, I don't think I believe in verse in this respect at all. As a matter of fact, I know I don't. (Olson, *Goddard College* 1)

Here again is the familiar triangulation of Olson and the audience against the technological intrusion, though in this case Olson also refers to the tape recorder as a guarantor that what the audience is experiencing is the real thing, distinctly not a "performing art." Tellingly, Olson's trope for the tape machine is the primitivist icon of fire; the room and all the people in it are now figured as a small village audience listening to a shaman. Contrary to Sterne's argument about liveness, Olson's pose is that the recording device forces him to "perform," the word in this context implying a concert-like formality. What Olson doesn't acknowledge (or realize) is how the tape recorder's presence underwrites this claim, allowing the business conducted onstage to be anything *but* a performance. Claiming a possessive individualistic sense of voice is abetted, not distracted, by the mike wand and allows Olson to persuade his audience that what he's offering them is nothing less than the real thing—or what's named in "A Later Note" above as "what we know went on." The threat of performance hovers about the stage, he implies, but it won't get the best of him. What if he just watches it? He's in control, after all; no concerts for him.

Here it's crucial to distinguish between Olson's stances at Goddard and Berkeley, for their difference helps sketch divergent contexts for Olson's reception. First, each campus environment signified radically different things. Beginning in the early 1960s, Berkeley became the seat of an increasingly felt cultural shift, sparked by the Free Speech Movement but soon flowering into a more general social transformation. Citing the "cultural consequences of the Free Speech Movement" (343), Lawrence Levine describes how shifting values in personal demeanor and social hierarchy emerged from the organized efforts of the student protest movement. Speaking freely—loudly, with anger, confrontationally, or with explosive gusto of any kind—may have begun as a political necessity, though soon it more broadly saturated cultural attitudes and personal relationships. More specifically for Olson's readings themselves, Libbie Rifkin suggests how much Berkeley was made up of an audience of knowing peers with and against whom Olson was engaging in combustive struggles for dominance. Olson combined a welter of textual sources with oral performance to develop "a structure of value in which orality and spontaneity meet textuality and history in order to form a more 'authentic,' because less objectifiable, literary object" (Rifkin 24). In Rifkin's analysis, Olson was consciously playing to a room of compeers "well versed in their stable of greats," to many of whom Olson made liberal reference (24). In any case, Berkeley in 1965 would expect no less, and Olson knew that.

Goddard College, on the other hand, was and is a small, woodsy, liberal arts college in Plainfield, Vermont, founded in 1863. Olson's biographer describes how Olson and his wife, Betty Kaiser, were reprimanded for drinking with students and asked to "abide by community laws while there" (Clark 198). In his introduction to the Goddard transcript, Kyle Schlesinger reports that a Goddard literature professor said about Olson, "We threw that louse out of here," and "referred to Creeley as a 'love' poet" (xv). Far from Berkeley's free-wheeling rhetorical calliope, Goddard signified something more like Black Mountain's community ethos, though with a New England Calvinist edge. Like Black Mountain, Goddard was a progressive, arts-centered experimental environment inspired by John Dewey's educational theory, and Royce Pitkin, the school's founder, articulated the college's ethos of "plain living and hard thinking" (Schlesinger xiv). Olson read in the Haybarn Theater in front of a small group of students, some of whom had, the previous year, been present in the same space for a reading by Robert Creeley. In fact, in his opening remarks at Goddard, Olson makes reference to a tape recording of Creeley's reading that he heard so soon after its creation that "it was like hotcakes" (*Goddard College* 1). According to Schlesinger, Berkeley's own king, Allen Ginsberg, referred to Goddard as the "center of the universe" (xiv), though undoubtedly with knowing hyperbole. Goddard was decidedly small, so much so that Olson is first introduced by one "Miss Glazier," who doesn't "really know much about him" at all (*Goddard College* 1).

While these differences are important to keep in mind, the distinctions between the two readings themselves more crucially sketch out a difference in Olson's approach to voicing print. At Berkeley, Olson establishes what I'll call the "vocal text." This is voice given full rein over its textual predecessor; typographic, machine-scored breath-text loses to a flattened, nonspatial logorrhea. Poetry itself, which lays claim to the breath of composition, gets waylaid as Olson's sallies at reading are either delayed by digression or abandoned entirely, breath itself renegade, spilling over the boundaries of print. (Only a few poems are actually read at Berkeley, often at the pleading of an audience member.) Olson's typical gesture when voicing text is to suggest the uniqueness of the reading act—that the voicing is itself an occasion. Here he is, after being prompted by Ginsberg to read the poem he's been talking abstractly about, making sure to make the reading itself an occasion, a "first":

> Olson: No, I'm going to . . . O.K. that's I guess why I'm reading it. It's called "An Ode on Nativity," and I don't believe it's ever been read. I've never even, prac—except for this morning, I thought I'd look at it and I liked it, you know how you do. I don't think anybody has ever . . . By the way, did you reject, did you even bother to consider it, Bob [laughter; trouble with the microphone cord]? How far can I come with this tether?
>
> Voice: Go ahead and read it, read it. (*Muthologos* 100)

Ten minutes later in the same recording, Olson attempts to establish his speaking voice as prior to the written text, rhetorically fusing voice and writing in the way McLuhan describes above. Responding to Lew Welch, he cries, "I am now publishing, tonight, because I'm talking writing" (*Muthologos* 109), and then an exchange moments later:

> Olson: Reading? This is a—? Are you kidding? You think this is anything but a—I mean, I think this is a political occasion. . . . From my point of view, I'm addressing a convention floor. The only convention I care of in the whole earth is occurring tonight.
>
> Voice: Read some poems! (*Muthologos* 110)

Disavowing the act of "reading," Olson carefully evades the function of text as a score to breath entirely. Olson's tone acknowledges that the audience in these two exchanges is expecting poems to be read, and Olson's strategy, if that is what it can be called, is to fail that expectation. We can only speculate about why this is, though empirically obvious is that Olson's Berkeley reading jettisons text in favor of voice. Rifkin is entirely correct, then, when she points out that the Berkeley reading was itself "a text to be read"; that is, Olson's excesses of literary reference, anecdote, aside, and digression had supplanted any authenticating text prior to them (24).[6] So truly, the Berkeley reading is Olson's most vociferous claim to the textual voice—the voice that stands prior to any antecedent, that is self-sufficiently productive in itself: "[I]f I was reading poems tonight, instead of running for power, I'd read you the poem I published in *The Psychedelic Review*, which I think is—and John Wieners is one of the persons that has had, like, you know that way he is to say it to you so that you say, 'gee, that's just what I intended.' I wrote a very impossible to read (and probably I couldn't read it tonight) poem" (*Muthologos* 115). Talking, reading—they're not quite the same; in fact, the written poem in this instance isn't even "possible" to articulate. The voice, not the text, gathers its authority from this occasion, and in this dual act of rejection and assumption the reading hall vibrates with a sense of the moment itself—or, in Olson's own language, "what we know went on."

Olson's Berkeley performance is also significant in the context of reading, or talking, in avant-garde circles during and after the 1960s. Set against other modes of "talking" onstage, Olson's reading can be seen to worry the line between talking and reading, speaking *extempore* and vocally modulating scripted language—otherwise known as speaking out loud. Certainly, the sixties and seventies poetry reading was "meant to be revolutionary" (*Voicing* 129), as Lesley Wheeler points out. This was the era of deliberately "anti-academic" (130) reading that challenged a more or less sclerotic form of podium recitation. In the previous chapter, we saw how Frost clearly worked within and around that podium style, simultaneously embodying and undermining its conventions, and clearly Olson was more frontally revolutionary in many ways. A more relevant context here might be what Bob Perelman calls simply "talk" (200). Perelman describes his work editing the San Francisco Talk series in the 1980s, in which poets talked—or "talked," as these talks often blurred into performances—and were recorded and, later, edited. Figures involved included major voices in the then-burgeoning Language movement, including Lyn Hejinian, Steve Benson, and Ron Silliman. About David Antin, Perelman wonders, "Where, and when, did the art occur? In the performance, on the page, or in the longer-term, diffuse space of the literary field?" (207). Like Olson's, Antin's performances were improvisatory and based in part upon prewritten or pre-thought-out models or ideas. Unlike Olson, Antin engaged in self-conscious and deliberate performance work. For Olson, reading prior to Antin's antic antics, the spoken moment claimed its authority with much less careful self-assurance. More generally, Olson's talking should be seen as a clear precursor—and not just in theory but in practice as well—to the kinds of talk-based performances Perelman catalogs.

Yet by listening across readings, we can hear how the vocal text can change. During Olson's reading on April 12, 1962, at Goddard College, the relationship between voice and text was inverted, and without recourse to such a recording we might mistake the Berkeley reading for Olson's primary mode of reading and performance. At Goddard the text was in charge. If Olson's Berkeley reading was a vocal text, I'll name this vocalization as a virtual chiasmus: Olson's "textual voice." At Berkeley, Olson assumes his audience can follow his breadth of literary reference, though at Goddard, he opens by feeling out his audience in just this regard: "And uh, I have no impression, yeah, of how much this book is known—could someone give me some idea of how much you know *The Maximus Poems*? I'm, I'm really fishing, because if I go to the fifth volume [laughter from Olson] instead of the first, because the first is unknown, that makes it awkward for you, I believe" (*Goddard College* 5–6). Olson's solicitude is remarkable. Lacking here is a sense of the voice itself, which struggles in similar ways as at Berkeley to announce itself without digression. Unlike at Berkeley, at Goddard long swaths of explanatory notes follow some poems. Olson explains who Maximus was and how Olson appropriates Maximus's voice and then explicates numerous references. Olson is overly sensitive to his audience's needs and desires, possibly a recognition that he was not on coterie footing but in Melville's woods, where the legacy of Frost, not Ginsberg, would be felt more keenly: "You want that again? I don't know. Call me if you'd like any one of these again" (13). "I didn't feel as though that one made it with you, I—at least I—it seemed too obscure or something" (18). After a brief intermission, Olson returns to announce to the room that he understands his reading is losing some listeners. "I guess a lot of you are, I heard some, I got some impression, that like, the sort of like the references were like, especially the imperative historical was a little interfering with the, well, there's hardly much I can do about that" (39). He goes on to suggest that there are few "poems that are like poems" here, though because someone asked for "poems, like, about those you love or live with," he'll try (he reads "The Librarian") (39).

The point here is not simply that Olson is being considerate in 1962 and will later be uncouth in 1965. Nor is it that he is generating Barthesian "work" rather than "text." In other words, this isn't significant as a mere inversion of the Berkeley reading. The Goddard reading complicates the question of breath by staging writing as antecedent to belated voice—that is, the voice has become a "textual" voice. Goddard offers a virtual nostalgia for writing, as when Olson narrates the visual text version of "GRAMMAR—a 'book'" (which in the Goddard transcript appears as "'A Grammar—A Book'" [*Goddard College* 19]), originally published in issue 7 (1961) of LeRoi Jones's mimeographed newsletter *Floating Bear.* The Goddard audience is tantalized with the possibility of a voicing of the poem—really, just various notes on dictionaries and lexicons, including *Webster's Collegiate Dictionary*, Charlton T. Lewis's *An Elementary Latin Dictionary*, Liddell and Scott's *A Greek-English Lexicon*, and John Williams White's *The First Greek Book* (Maud, *Reading* 163). Notable here is Olson's sense of the printed text's mastery, one that he essentially backs away from to leave sacrosanct. After describing what *Floating Bear* is, he explains that Diane di Prima was responsible for its visual appeal: "[S]he took my typed copy and put it in mimeograph so there wasn't a—and it's all tilted and squeezed and shoved" (*Goddard College* 19). A moment later, he calls this "the greatest publishing I ever had" (19). And then, something remarkable occurs: "Now this poem, for some reason, I'm really, like everybody thinks is awful square. But then I've had more response from it from those who I, I, I should go on now—to make a pitch, you know [laughter from the audience]. I've ruined it. You never should make a pitch you know" (19). At this point Olson drops the idea of reading "GRAMMAR—a 'book'" altogether, moving on to recite "In the Face of a Chinese View of the City" from *Maximus.* Faced with reproducing visual text, Olson's voice falters; it's as if he says "I give" to the exceptional typographical authority of *Floating Bear.* The implicit message rings clear: this reading, my appearance here, can only do so much. Literary history has had its fun, and we can't listen in.

"Cashes"

Ron Silliman has claimed that, "[a]vant le slam, projectivism was American poetry's most aggressive argument for the text understood as a form of speech" (371). Yet listening to Olson requires us to invert this formula: projectivist reading, or at least Olson's example of it, was an argument for speech understood as text. Robert Grenier's "I HATE SPEECH," which appeared in the first number of *This* magazine in 1971, captures this attitude best perhaps in its outright rejection of "voice" and subject-oriented, expressivist poetics. For Olson, the most complex and developed version of this inverted textual voice occurs in his reading of "Cashes," a seafaring narrative drawn originally from a textual source. Here, voice, print text, and tape recording implicate each other in the telling of this tale and the reading of the poem. This performance raises questions regarding the poem's identity itself, as its sounding in the hall at Goddard College duplicates its own history of production; what can we make of such a reading, and how can we evaluate it in terms of Olson's voice?

In *Ghostlier Demarcations*, Michael Davidson describes "palimtexts" as archival draft versions of poems that, by their material presence, echo and disrupt published versions, calling into question the boundaries of poetry's scope and reach (his examples include writing by George Oppen and Susan Howe). Palimtextual study reads poem against manuscript to detect "overwriting" and "displacement," opening up "a window onto forces of stabilization in the culture at large" (92). In a similar way, Olson's staging of "Cashes" draws upon the poem's genesis and frames it as a poem interrogating poetry and the presence of voice itself. If the Berkeley reading reveals Olson striving for "oral poetry" as the evasion of techno-textual authority in favor of presence and immediacy, "Cashes" underscores a suppler orientation to written text—its value and status, Olson seems to imply, must be understood within the context of oral history. The "textual voice" in this case isn't mere hierarchy; instead, it suggests how deeply implicated voice and text can be. "Cashes" itself offers a miniature history of impingements of text on voice and tells us how Olson's work is careful to overturn oral immediacy in favor not of text but of a poetry as a relation between voice and the page. In the end, the palimtextual "Cashes" captures this transit by unhinging the poem from its spokenness and its textual history—it survives as an emblem of Olson's understanding of the mutual implications of speech and the page, the necessity of their existence.

There are at least five iterations of the "Cashes" narrative, which tells the story of the *Rattler*, a ship that, despite pitchpoling—that is, wheeling in a somersault, stern over bow—on Cashe's Shoals off the coast of Gloucester, Massachusetts, sometime around 1874, arrived safe in port with no casualties. The narrative is (1) a fisherman's oral history, (2) a Boston newspaper's account of that oral history, (3) the quotation and framing of that newspaper account by George B. Goode, (4) Olson's revision of Goode's account as the poem "Cashes," and (5) Olson's reading of "Cashes" at Goddard College (of course, other readings would count as yet other iterations). The third iteration of the story was recorded in George B. Goode's *The Fisheries and Fishery Industries of the United States* (1887), a book that Ralph Maud verifies Olson bought in Cambridge on 28 April 1959 (*Reading* 148). In the chapter titled "The Fisherman of the United States," Goode quotes the second iteration, from an unidentified Boston newspaper, which claims to offer "a fair example of the fisherman's dialect" and serves as a transliterated narrative with the New England accent intact. The fourth iteration is Olson's poem itself, though, interestingly, that work actually *tames* the dialect, conforming it to standard English. From Goode: "Wall, the Rattler, as I was a speakin' of, wus comin' 'long down the coast from Newf'n'land loaded with frozen herrin'" (Butterick, *Guide* 268). From *Maximus*: "The Rattler was headed along down the coast from Newfoundland loaded with frozen herring" (189). In this way, Olson's intervention into the story surprisingly strips the colloquial markers of "voice" directly away, textualizing and, one might even say, bowdlerizing the narrative's oral origins. What Olson makes of this version of the poem in the fifth iteration is the subject of this analysis.

What is most significant about the reading of the poem is what Olson says about it. The reading itself is mundanely faithful to this prose narrative, yet his framing of it is not. In the end, Olson's reading of "Cashes" suggests that language can strip itself of its orality to attain a contemporary, unmediated authenticity, ultimately implying that the poem's "atavistic" source is text, not voice—even though the poem is most definitely based on speech. The logic of this analysis is tortuous: on the one hand, "Cashes" is a poem derived from voice: it originated as a fair example of fisherman's dialect, and, as Olson explains to his Goddard audience, it was composed orally and "picked off the tape" by the publisher Gael Turnbull to be published (*Goddard College* 45). Furthermore, it's a sea-yarn and bears the traces of a told tale ("I tell you it's cruel," it begins [189]). And yet, the poem is actually born from a textualization of voice—quite literally, as Turnbull translated the poem into writing, but also as the Boston reporter recorded the fisherman's original story. In this way, the poem's literary production mirrors its historical production: an oral testimony, written down. The essential part of this story is Olson's claim that the text version of "Cashes" is really the atavistic one.[7]

How does this inversion work? As Olson explains to his Goddard audience, the poem is valuable for its ability to evade "metaphor," evade "image" and achieve a kind of preliterary stability, the kind of bedrock structure that serves as the opposite to breath's living dynamism. After suggesting that "Cashes" is not "captive" and is "free," he explains: "I'm suggesting that just such a thing as metaphor has broken down and to some extent we're involved in succeeding in picking up things which will not then behave as metaphors again, but what will put us in touch with what metaphor didn't put us in touch with, and never would, because metaphor is caught in a discourse system" (*Goddard College* 45). Here, metaphor serves a "discourse" and is at a remove from things that put us "in touch." The poem is valuable for its nonliterary evasions of doubled, or marginal, meaning and is more authentic because of that: "I think that you get inventions—I guess sort of like that—of all sorts of rhythms and faces by letting this thing stay back where you find it, and then in going back there, that kind of a thing, almost like an atavism rather than an image" (48). "Cashes" strips away image, strips away metaphor, and, as Olson says a moment later, strips away "dialect" itself. In his emphasis on "newness," Olson is clearly echoing his master, Ezra Pound: "That is, that deadness of our cultural, of our universal speech is just so dull, it's like dialectical, dialect, uh? I hate it. I would clean every—I myself would wish that all who spoke and wrote, spoke always from a place that is new at that moment that they do speak and not hang up on any of the places from which they may have acquired their speech, whether it's putative, purposed, or personal" (48). Olson refers obliquely to the fact that his retelling of the "Cashes" narrative denudes its irregularities and fashions it into standard English. Yet this stripping the poem of what might be considered its oral authenticity is itself the greater act of authenticity—it's an authenticity of the present, "new at that moment." Paradoxically, "making it new" for Olson means inverting an original revision of the authentic oral narrative. This brings it both closer to, and removes it from, the primary, oral, spoken source. For a poem about history, and a poem so deeply invested in the past, a poem that arose in the salted mouths of sailors and witnesses, this is a wild claim (though one perfectly consistent, really, with Olson's textual presentism). "Cashes" serves in this forum as severe textual voice. Though he reads the poem aloud, its service is to suggest the ways in which print can make voice—in this case, the "deadness" of dialect—living and new.

SO WHAT SHOULD we do with a Charles Olson recording? I think we listen to it, closely, as part of the Olson canon when we are writing or talking about Charles Olson, and especially when we are working to understand his complicated, sometimes sprawling and confused attitudes toward voice. Students should listen to these recordings in conjunction with the printed poems and essays. As scholars, we should attend to the audiographic Olson, perhaps in a way that's different from how we should attend to readings by Robert Frost or (as we'll see in the next chapter) Gwendolyn Brooks. Why? Because listening to Olson is essential rather than tangential to his work. Reading reveals Olson's poetry in its desublimated condition—unresolved in terms of voice and text. Readings don't help us determine Olson—they unravel him. They show us not that Olson was able to establish "oral poetry" in front of assembled listeners, or that he was a ludic wild man, or a nostalgic Mayan primitivist, or a graphic "poet of the page" despite all his fulminations about breath. Rather, readings portray an Olson who animates these relationships, reveals them to be mutually dependent, progressively productive. They show a poet struggling to find a language suitable for explanation but not so rigid as to ossify. If Mayan text was "fluid," it is also of consequential "weight"; if Maximus speaks "by ear," the poet writes by machine. Olson's real problem is mediation, by voice, tape recorder, typesetting, or book. Readings sound for us the insufficiency of mediation and how we might allow that its lopsided presence on tape may be, in a final paradox, the best way to hear this.

4

The Public and Private Voices of Gwendolyn Brooks

Every Negro poet has "something to say." Simply because he is a Negro, he cannot escape having important things to say. His mere body, for that matter, is an eloquence. His quiet walk down the street is a speech to the people. —Gwendolyn Brooks, "Poets Who Are Negroes"

Think of your efforts to be convincing and entertaining when you are gossiping. You use gesture, touch, tone-variation, facial expression. Try persuading your wordage—SOMEHOW!—to do all the things your body does when forwarding a piece of gossip.—Gwendolyn Brooks, in Brooks et al., *A Capsule Course in Black Poetry Writing*

In her autobiography *Report from Part One* (1972), Gwendolyn Brooks repeatedly notes the tonal qualities of the human voice, ever attuned to its resonance and capacity to communicate essential qualities nonverbally. "No one ever had, no one ever will have, a chuckle exactly like my father's," Brooks writes. "It was gentle, it was warmly happy, it was heavyish but not hard. It was secure, and seemed to us an assistant to the Power that registered with his children" (39). Young African women she meets on a trip to Nairobi are "appealingly soft" in speech, talking "with that shy musical softness I am beginning to revere" (96). Elsewhere, the voice and the body's movement are tropes for black identity. When she recollects her transformative experience at Fisk University's Second Black Writers' Conference in 1967 by emphasizing the "electricity, in look, walk, speech, *gesture* of the young blackness I saw all about me" (84, Brooks's emphasis), or when in the epigraphs above she equates voice to sheer physical presence, Brooks is arguing that black poets should aspire to the immediacy of conversational gesture. At the outset of *A Capsule Course*, a volume she helped edit, Brooks quotes the Black Arts scholar and critic Larry Neal, who claims that black poets "can learn more about what poetry is by listening to the cadences in Malcolm's speeches than from most of Western poetics" (4–5). Brooks liked Neal's idea enough to include it at the outset of her own contribution to the volume, an essay steering aspiring black poets toward vocal presence rather than material poetic production, which was to be held with suspicion. Even the physical existence of writing itself affronted the kind of immediate presence voice offered. After quoting James T. Stewart, who in the anthology *Black Fire* (1968) challenged Western "perpetuation of the product—the picture, the statue, the temple," Brooks adds in parentheses: "And certainly the piece of 'literature'!" (5). *Jump Bad* (1971), the anthology of black writing Brooks edited, includes an essay by Don L. Lee in which he lays out a similar case for the immateriality of black writing: "Black art, like African art, is *perishable*. This too is why it is functional. For example, a black poem is written not to be read and put aside, but to actually become a part of the giver and receiver. It must perform some function: move the emotions, become a part of the dance, or simply make an act" (37–38). Real mouths, real tongues. Voice, rather than print in books—commodities to be bought and read, saved and revered, housed and claimed and institutionalized—was a rich and essential medium for black expression. For Brooks, real voices mattered.

In this chapter, I argue that Brooks's "real" voice in recordings and at readings—in which Brooks speaks out, literally, to assembled crowds—dramatizes the slow, often contradictory, and ultimately incomplete transformation Brooks made from private to public poet. Voicings of her poems reveal Brooks as a public poet straining for expression in early private poems and, later on, a private poet nostalgic for an interiority lost or surrendered in public, even declamatory poems. Poetry readings allowed Brooks to devise and then maintain necessary distinctions between these competing emphases in her lifetime of writing, and they demonstrate that performance was a means toward satisfying requirements of social commitment that may have been at odds with Brooks's essentially craft-based, contemplative lyric impulse. Ultimately, Brooks transforms her mature reading voice into a sui generis vocal style, its deep and resonant tones embodying blackness while also keeping Brooks separate from its more traditional sounds of expression. My reading of Brooks, which is based on a diverse set of materials—an episode of a radio show, recordings of poetry readings, a Caedmon album, and a short film—intervenes into a long-standing critical debate about Brooks's poetic career, which is sometimes seen as bifurcated by the Second Black Writers' Conference. The conference itself took place in April 1967 and displayed a "Black Power thrust" (Kent 196), including a boisterous, energized crowd that, according to Brooks's biographer George Kent, signaled a coming together of Black Power and Black Arts (202).[1] In an interview with Ida Lewis in *Essence* magazine (and reprinted in *Report from Part One*), Brooks herself describes the Fisk event as a "turning point" (167), though elsewhere she downplayed its significance. As Lesley Wheeler points out, "[T]o draw too dramatic a contrast between the early and later works is to misread them; as Brooks herself insists, although the world around her has changed, 'I just continue to write about what confronts me'" ("Heralding" 229).

Yet drawing dramatic contrasts regarding the Fisk conference is not uncommon. In fact, Fisk is the most scrutinized episode from Brooks's biography, and it splits allegiances along political and aesthetic lines. Many agree with Brooks's description of the event as a "turning point" or schism, as does Haki Madhubuti (previously Don L. Lee), who divides her work around "the pre-1967 period" and after (81), and Houston Baker, who suggests Brooks was one of many black poets to experience "significant shifts" regarding political commitments in the late 1960s (117). The break as Baker depicts it is definite and absolute: "Jolted from what she calls 'a sweet ignorance,' Brooks cast her lot with the new generation" (118). Kent says that Fisk "would initiate a fundamental change in the poet's consciousness, her commitment to art and audience, and her perception of the black situation in America" (196). And yet, while there is no doubt that the events of 1967 catalyzed Brooks, radically altering her personal and political identity, I see her work along with other critics—D. H. Melhem, Betsy Erkkila, Kathryne V. Lindberg—as more consistently honed around an ongoing, agonistic drama of public and private voice, one present from the start to the end.[2] Henry Taylor makes the case that Brooks's career is less radically schismatic than the above writers encourage us to believe: it begins with writing from "personal history (not necessarily her own)," then "merge[s] social and political history with that strain," and finally is "on the brink" of successfully realizing a "larger historical scope" that synthesizes personal and political writing (274). I side here with Taylor, though I extend his reach by listening in to Brooks's voice on magnetic tape, video, and vinyl—and now the no-place of digital media—to claim that readings show not only consistency but also ways in which Brooks learned to negotiate between her public and private registers with increasing sophistication. Ultimately, readings allowed Brooks to bifurcate these roles, giving her the chance to perform, and thus exorcise, her public role of poet from the podium, stage, and microphone.

The central evidence for this claim is derived from four readings Brooks gave between 1949 and 1983 and constitutes the second section of this chapter. The first section details voice as a *figure* in Brooks's early and late poems; establishes working definitions of "public" and "private" in terms of Brooks's poems, black poetry, and lyric in general; and finally, relates all this to the subject of authenticity, a term that assumes a particular resonance, as black sixties poetry equated authenticity with publicity and privacy with whiteness. Part of this work is also the work of recuperation: despite Brooks's life of reading and public appearances, little direct evidence of these events is represented in treatments of her work. By her own count in 1981, Brooks says she was visiting "around 50" college campuses a year, where she gave readings and took part in workshops (Robinson). That's almost one a week, and such a figure doesn't take into account her many other, noncollegiate public appearances and activities. This chapter tells the untold story of Brooks's life as a poetry reader.

In the following section, I'll describe the antinomies of Brooks's sixties readings and contexts, which reveal her struggle between public and private experience. The following is just one example, though it helps to crystallize the sharp contrasts that can arise between characterizations of Brooks's sense of privacy. First, a passage from liner notes on Brooks's 1969 Caedmon record, written by Brooks's young mentor at the time, Don L. Lee: "Gwendolyn Brooks is a writer/poet without the yearly migration to the farm. There are no six months a year in upstate New York to write or contemplate the nuances of her people. The reality of the crowding chimneys will not allow or condone such luxuries; as her smoke is conceived she will have to inhale it also." And here is Brooks herself, writing just a few years later in *Report from Part One*: "That's one of my problems—finding extended privacy. I'm thinking now of going away at the end of summer—*some* summer—to a hotel in which I would have just such a situation. I would stay in my room, and have my meals delivered; and I would write, write, write" (133). Privacy, personal expression, craft, and the luxuries of bourgeois recreation—all are contested by Lee and approved by Brooks. It's precisely this conflict between publicity and privacy that informs Brooks's readings, which help redraw the lines around her conflicted and lifelong understandings of identity and social commitment. For Lee, the bucolic image of a farm in upstate New York calls up a Frostian world of reflective "contemplation"—presumably something an authentic black urban poet has no business doing. Lee's primary objection is to a poet's removal from context, a critical distance in which Brooks would pause and reflect, on her own, away from others. The black poet can find no such privacy in Lee's metaphor of "smoke," which is produced and consumed in the same "crowding" public space. This tension—between what Brooks saw as her modest literary requirements, the need to "stay in my room" and "write, write, write," and a public poet's charge to remain in and of the people crowding round—was addressed and worked through in Brooks's reading life.

The Figure of Voice in Brooks

Because voices are figuratively inscribed into many of Brooks's poems, early and late, beginning with a look at Brooks's use of figurative voice serves as an introduction into Brooks's lifelong treatment of what I'll call her private and public modes of lyric. As old as African American writing itself, black poetry has long drawn upon the tension between speaking as an individual free from the restrictive category of race (if such a feat is possible) and speaking as an affiliate. Brooks's first three major books—*A Street in Bronzeville* (1945), *Annie Allen* (1949), and *The Bean Eaters* (1960)—employ a range of figural voices that address this double perspective: persona poems from the voice of a speaker (e.g., "Negro Hero," "A Sunset of the City"); second-person address and ballads that speak to a particular character or persona (e.g., "the mother," "Ballad of Pearl May Lee"); and poems that draw in conversations, including dialogue and "quotations" (e.g., "Men of careful turns, haters of forks in the road," "Mrs. Small"). In these lyrics, private experiences, figured as embodied speech, mash up against a social order conditioning them, and the situational pronouns like "I," "you," and "we" don't easily decouple from black experience. In the lines from *Annie Allen* "And shall I prime my children, pray, to pray?" (*Blacks* 117) and "We are lost, must / wizard a track through our own screaming weed" (140), pronouns issue from the consciousness of the character of Annie herself, though clearly they attest to and displace the more general social dimensions of experience that gave rise to the poem. Brooks indeed saw her reading performances as ways to communicate in tone something of the politicized condition of her poems' subjects. Regarding her reading of "The Pool Players: Seven at the Golden Shovel" (beginning, and often simply called, "We real cool") and her hushed vocal intonation of each line's final third-person-plural pronoun, Brooks told George Stavros in 1969, "[Y]ou're supposed to stop after the 'We' and think about their validity, and of course there's no way for you to tell whether it should be said softly or not, I suppose, but I say it rather softly because I want to represent their basic uncertainty" (*Conversations* 44). Black audiences seemed to understand that they were being addressed as a larger sociopolitical category. One listener wrote to Brooks in a letter: "Upon hearing WE REAL COOL for the third time it was a revelation, the way you recited it. The insight I arrived at was that this other poem was about me. I don't mean the possessive 'me,' myself, and I. But, the collective 'me' in the experience of many brother [*sic*] and sisters who read the light between your lines" (Queen). The shifter "we" hit this listener hard: he felt implicated by its collective address and heard the collective echo within him, the "collective 'me,'" as he calls it. Some were less sympathetic to Brooks's complex handling of self-expression and its emotional effects. One contemporary critic refers to *The Bean Eaters* in ways that reveal such "revelation" wasn't audible to all: "If she were trying to exemplify T. S. Eliot's philosophy that poetry is an escape from emotions, she has succeeded admirably" (Ford 18).[3]

A survey of how voices function across Brooks's work, from her early books to her post-1967 works, suggests a persistent figurative use of voice that reveals fault lines between private and public experience. Focusing on Brooks's figurative use of voice across her career clarifies a shift from a private to a public poet. One metric: early poems are full of figurative voice that is noticeably distant from later uses of it. In "the mother," from *Bronzeville*, voice draws on the pathetic fallacy to describe a voice that is itself a figure: "I have heard in the voices of the wind the voices of my dim killed children" (*Blacks* 21). In contrast to the aural absence the poem describes, in which the aborted fetuses "never giggled or planned or cried" (22), voice's disembodied, abstracted state is a representation of what never was—the actual bodies of the speaker's babies. Other poems from *Bronzeville*, like "Hattie Scott," "the date," and "when Mrs. Martin's Booker T.," represent voice in a folk dialect tradition reminiscent of Paul Laurence Dunbar (e.g., Mrs. Martin, who is quoted: "But tell me if'n he take that gal / And get her decent wed" [*Blacks* 24]). Dramatic monologues, like "Negro Hero" and "Ballad of Pearl May Lee" in *Bronzeville*, affirm early on Brooks's adoption of persona as a way to articulate the speaking voice. *Annie Allen* includes the striking "Men of careful turns, haters of forks in the road," which represents the voice of a white speaker articulating the ideology of white oppression, though in Brooks's poetic idiom: "My friend, no thing is without flaw. / If prejudice is native—and it is—you / Will find it ineradicable" (*Blacks* 140). *The Bean Eaters* also includes dialect poems (e.g., "My Little 'Bout-town Gal"), monologues (e.g., "Old Mary"), and a more sharply drawn racist white voice in "The Ballad of Rudolph Reed." This last poem includes Reed's own lyrical voice, which longs for the mythic fundamentals of middle-class American life:

> I am not hungry for berries.
> I am not hungry for bread.
> But hungry hungry for a house
> Where at night a man in bed
>
> "May never hear the plaster
> Stir as if in pain." (*Blacks* 376)

In the same poem, whites sound the stock phrases of Jim Crow segregation ("*Why, you black old, tough old hell of a man*" [*Blacks* 377, italics in original]) and the poem's quoted word, "Nigger" (378). There are numerous other examples of voiced voices in these books, including "Jessie Mitchell's Mother" and "Leftist Orator in Washington Park Pleasantly Punishes the Gropers," which D. H. Melhem refers to as Brooks's first glimmer of the "prophetic voice" (*Poetry* 118) from her later writing, though the poem itself presents two voices in contrast: the orator-speaker, who predicts doom ("I foretell the head and yawn of eye and the drop of the / mouth"), and the lost souls, whose lostness is metaphorically a "screech" that can "only beseech" (*Blacks* 380).

"Leftist Orator" aside, voice in these early poems is noticeably *private*: it issues from individuals who may have undergone intense experiences that are social—lynching, racist attacks, class aspirations—but who articulate their experiences in a reflective, highly crafted lyric enclosure. For Brooks herself, this means careful management of the poem's, and the public's, hard edges. As she describes it, the private/social schism for her resembles Russian dolls, one implicitly contained in the other: "The poet, first and foremost an individual with *a* personal vision, is also a member of society. What affects society affects a poet. So I, starting out, *usually* in the grip of a high and private suffusion, may find by the time I have arrived at a last line that there is quite some public clamor in my product" (*Part One* 138, emphasis in the original). Whatever Brooks's writing process, later poems mark a nominal shift *away* from this early private voice. "Riders to the Blood-Red Wrath," about the Freedom Riders, and the three versions of "The Sermon on the Warpland," "The Wall," and "A Primer for Blacks," among others, all speak in a voice often described as "prophetic." In her 1966 review of Robert Hayden's *Selected Poems* for *Negro Digest*, Brooks articulates a case for lyric privacy in ways that recall a Wordsworthian tranquility of recollection in which the poem stands apart from the mud of experience:

> We need the poet who "lives in life," mixes with the mud, rolls in rot, claws the scoundrels, bleeds and bloodies, and, grasping in the field, writes right there, his wounds like faucets above his page, at once besmutching and ennobling it. We need, also, the poet who finds life always interesting, sometimes appalling, sometimes appealing but consistently amenable to a clarifying enchantment via the powers of art. His reverence for the word Art is what chiefly distinguishes him from Poet I. Poet II, moreover, may postpone composition until he is off the field, rid of the fray's insignia, and has had a bath. (qtd. in Kent 194)

This captures Brooks's distinct lean toward craft and "composition" itself, an act of cleaned-up and ordered proportioning rather than gushing "faucets" of verbiage. The kind of retreat and reflective space derided above by Don L. Lee are here what Brooks so prizes, as they allow for the dedication to "Art," or the act of literary craft. In this way, privacy also indicates for Brooks compositional quiet, lyric craft, and form itself. To be private is a necessary requirement of literary production. "Brooks creates a powerful kind of mother, a public actor, fusing her speech with that of a preacher or prophet, articulating an unusually authoritative, distinctly female voice," argues Lesley Wheeler, who in an important recent essay describes Brooks's use of apostrophe—especially in the three Warpland sermons—as a gendered means of collapsing private and public distinctions endemic to lyric itself ("Heralding" 228). I'll add to Wheeler's argument by demonstrating how actual voiced readings complicate, by making increasingly separate, the relationship between the public and private lyric modes.

It's important to emphasize how Brooks's later poems enact voice not only with "prophetic" difference but also as a figure that addresses audience from a black perspective, in which spoken voice is a revolutionary force that produces social or political change. Personifying the Freedom Riders in "Riders to the Blood-Red Wrath," Brooks equates the voice to struggle itself:

> My scream! unedited, unfrivolous.
> My laboring unlatched braid of heat and frost.
> I hurt. I keep that scream in at what pain:
> At what repeal of salvage and eclipse.
> Army unhonored, meriting the gold, I
> Have sewn my guns inside my burning lips. (*Blacks* 390)

Here, voice transforms private pain into public action, the "burning lips" crying against racial apartheid. The poem "The Wall," which memorializes Brooks's actual reading performance at the Wall of Respect in Chicago, a vast mural on which was depicted various figures from black American history, narrates Brooks's appearance there, which includes a community raising their voices collectively: "Women in wool hair chant their poetry," "hundreds of faces, red-brown, brown, black, ivory, / yield me hot trust, their yea and their Announcement," "And we sing" (*Blacks* 444–45). "The Wall" demonstrates how crucial the spoken voice was to her sense of African American uplift and political agency and urgency. Other voices—loud, whooping, soulful, pleading, deflated, hortatory—sound and resound in the later poems, not simply lyric and expressive voices of personal striving, declarations of sensibility, or private contemplations. The voice itself is tantamount to action. "Your voice is the listened-for music. / **Your** act is the consolidation," Brooks writes to Don L. Lee in "To Don at Salaam" (*Blacks* 492, bold in original). In "To Keorapetse Kgositsile (Willie)," about the young South African poet and activist, Kgositsile's voice blares in all caps, a representation of a national voice that "speaks":

> "MY NAME IS AFRIKA!"
>   Well, every fella's a Foreign Country.
>
> This Foreign Country speaks to You. (*Blacks* 491)

In fact, it's common in Brooks's writing after *In the Mecca* (1968) for a speaking voice to "call," as she puts it, blacks to make themselves known, affirm their "magnitude," "bond" with each other. These voices speak to and from collective black identity and are often troped as voice itself. In these later poems, voice is black voice.

Brooks's poem "Paul Robeson," written about the great civil rights leader, is an example of such a voice of "call," one that also demonstrates how important contexts of performance can be. Here is "Paul Robeson" in its entirety:

> That time
> we all heard it,
> cool and clear,
> cutting across the hot grit of the day.
> The major Voice.
> The adult Voice
> forgoing Rolling River,
> forgoing tearful tale of bale and barge
> and other symptoms of an old despond.
> Warning, in music-words
> devout and large,
> that we are each other's
> harvest:

we are each other's
business:
we are each other's
magnitude and bond. (*Blacks* 496)

This "we" refers to black people, and the poem serves as an apostrophe to Robeson's voice, which, in its sheer size and force, will break free of conventional, fettered range of utterance—the spiritual language of "Rolling River," the "tearful tale of bale and barge" from emancipation literature and music—and call people to unity. The poem can be read in this way as a paean to Robeson's fashioning of originality from ossified narratives and iconographic typologies. The communal "we" is created by evading the music provided black singers by a history of minstrel writing, the "old despond" of certified black music. Brooks invokes Robeson's voice to urge black solidarity for the collective "we," a corporate voice of action and self-fashioning.

Yet is this voice of Robeson's just a figure, just a trope? As I demonstrate below, voice became a persistent figurative tic for Brooks due to her actual schedule of readings, lectures, and appearances in middle and high schools, colleges, prisons, and poetry workshops, a schedule that snowballed over the course of her life. This phenomenal life of reading and having her work read and performed is a lost contextual record, one that can help deepen our understanding of Brooks's poems in relationship to their actual social circumstance. For example, in the context of reading and performance, "Paul Robeson" may refer not only to Robeson's voice as emblematic of black identity or social struggles but to his effect as a stage performer. This is signaled in the poem by the opening words "that time," which may refer to an actual event: Robeson's speech at the Peace Arch on the U.S.-Canadian border in 1952 after he was denied permission to exit the United States to perform in Vancouver, Canada, due to the revocation of his international visa.[4] Robeson had been the target of a long-term invasive and harassing investigation by the FBI due to his supposed communist activities, and troubling Robeson about visa matters was not uncommon. At the rally, at which Robeson was forced to remain on the Washington State side of the border, Robeson sang "Old Man River," deeply emphasizing the combative line that Brooks echoes in her poem ("the hot grit of day"), "show a little grit and you land in jail" (Duberman 433). Thus

Robeson's "forgoing" of these famous songs may serve as a literal reference to Robeson's actual voice, his resistance "that time" located in a real act of public rebellion. This context is both cited and repressed, and its citation suggests how much public speaking mattered to Brooks and how she envisioned a poetry of public calling and performance as crucial to "music-words," a language made public at specific sites. Its repression, its oblique and quasi-universalized address to a generalized voice of Paul Robeson, suggests a hesitation to specify the activist, public role too pointedly. Yet the uncomfortable fact is that hearing Robeson sing locates him, and his struggle, in the world Brooks inhabits; he is not singing to the ages, he is singing to the poem's "we"—blacks. The relationship between such performed voices and represented voices—voice and voicings—is the subject of the rest of this chapter.

Private and Public Brooks

On September 11, 1938, the twenty-one-year-old Brooks printed a carefully arranged packet of three poems preceded by a brief statement of poetic purpose titled "How I Think Poetry Should Be Written." The poems that followed—"Alteration," "Old Laughter," and "To a Brown Madwoman"—never found their way into print, but the brief *ars poetica* serves as a prescient early statement of her poetics: "I think poetry should be written from the personal experience of the writer. Think how many fascinating human documents there would be now, if all the great poets had written of what happened to them personally—and of the thoughts that occurred to them, no matter how ugly, no matter how fantastic, no matter how seemingly ridiculous." This definition of "personal experience" doesn't exclude, of course, social encounters—of discrimination, of struggle for equal rights, of black identity politics—but it does suggest that the private, interior, and experiential basis for poetry Brooks held dear was intact at an early age. For her, privacy equals honesty and unvarnished truth—the retention and unapologetic representation of thoughts that might be unpleasing or "seemingly ridiculous." The poem is a record of private imagination that ignores possible public judgment. It may seem that Brooks disavowed such privacy as she grew, and her later works—*In the Mecca, In Montgomery, To Disembark*—portray a poet deeply committed to public struggles for black equality from the perspective of a social observer to whom most everything described has indeed occurred. Yet it's important to distinguish in this case between thematizing publicity in her poems and enacting it in her more public roles as speaker, reader, and public figure. Certainly there needs to be no defense of the public stance many poems take, particularly from *The Bean Eaters* on. And yet Brooks's role as a public poet is less clearly demarcated.

On the one hand, there is Brooks's sense of poetic identity as someone speaking directly to the people, as in this excerpt from *Report from Part One*, perhaps her most famous post-Fisk statement of poetic intent:

> My aim, in my next future, is to write poems that will somehow successfully "call" (see Imamu Baraka's "SOS") all black people: black people in taverns, black people in alleys, black people in gutters, schools, offices, factories, prisons, the consulate; I wish to reach black people in pulpits, black people in mines, on farms, on thrones; *not* always to "teach"—I shall wish often to entertain, to illumine. My newish voice will not be an imitation of the contemporary young black voice, which I so admire, but an extending adaptation of today's G.B. voice. (183)

This "newish" stance (the adjective suggests how much she perceived continuity with older stances) is one she repeated with striking consistency, especially the idea of reading in a tavern. This tavern ideal derives from an experience Brooks had at a reading of sorts, one that she describes in her interview with George Stavros:

> Let me tell you about an experience I had in Chicago. I went around with a few of these poets that I've just mentioned [James Cunningham, Etheridge Knight, Walter Bradford, Carolyn Rodgers, Jewel Latimore, Ebon Dooley]. They go to housing projects and out in the parks sometimes, and just start reading their poetry; and right around the corner—across the street from the Wall in Chicago, the Wall of Respect . . . is a tavern, and one Sunday afternoon, some of the poets decided to go in there and read poetry. I went with them. One of them went to the front of the tavern and said, "say, folks, we're going to lay some poetry on you." And there had been exciting things going on! I wondered how they were going to respond to poetry. The poets started reading, and before we knew it, people had turned around on their

> bar stools, with their drinks behind them, and were listening. Then they applauded. And I thought that was a wonderful thing, something new. I want to write poetry—and it won't be Ezra Pound poetry, as you can imagine—that will be exciting to such people. (*Conversations* 41)

In many ways, this figure of the public poet mainlining poetry to "such people" was a lived fact, as her litany of readings demonstrates, though she found herself in schools more often than bars. When Brooks spoke with Ida Lewis in 1971, the tavern again played the role of public forum ("My idea is that we have got to read the audience the poets are reaching by going to taverns" [*Conversations* 66]), as it did in a 1974 interview in the *Black Books Bulletin* ("I was fascinated about seven years ago, when we used to go out, Don and me and the others, to taverns and other places to read our poetry" [*Conversations* 77]). Poems in the late prophetic voice, especially the Warpland sermons, seem to imagine a vatic form of public address, a door-to-door poetic of activist, site-specific, interventionist public reading. During this period Brooks also received word of her works being performed in numerous public venues by others. The stage luminary Ruby Dee Davis wrote to Brooks in 1964 that she sang "Queen of the Blues" and "We Real Cool" at the Village Vanguard with "George Coleman's most sensitive jazz quartet." Brooks also had a poem sung in *A Hand Is on the Gate* (1966), a successful Broadway revue (and eventual LP record) by the Establishment Theatre Company that included music by Roscoe Lee Brown and performances by Cicely Tyson and James Earl Jones.

Yet Brooks repeatedly grinds against this public ideal. For one thing, she often reflects that "The Pool Players" is perhaps the only poem that achieves the kind of tavernesque immediacy she holds so dear (*Conversations* 130). When Stavros follows up her description of the tavern ideal by asking if poetry should be "a social voice, a voice that can be heard," Brooks is equivocal: "I am not writing poems with the *idea* that they are to become 'social forces.' I don't feel that I care to direct myself in that way" (41). Stavros asks her if she wants poetry to return to "one of its original forms, that of the voice of the prophet, speaker to the people," and Brooks replies gnomically, "I don't want to be a prophet" (42). For all Brooks's avowals of public activism, she retreats as well. (Even her statement on poetry's "call" ends with an assertion of something inimical and sui generis, not a public voice but an original "G.B." one.)

This is something at issue for Brooks during the very years in which she became more deeply politicized. Her archives contain a copy of *Poetry* magazine from January 1967 in which Brooks has underlined the final lines of a review by Eleanor Ross Taylor of Sylvia Plath's *Ariel*. The review is largely negative and recalls Brooks's own attitudes toward reflective composition, stated in her review of Hayden cited above ("you wish there had been time for distilling and perfecting" [260], Taylor writes). Near the end of the article, Brooks underscored and marked with large brackets (I've used underlining) Taylor's final judgment on Plath's self-exposures: "The confessional poem seems so amiable, it is easily available to the reader; it makes the poet feel better; yet it uses the poet shabbily; the poem that seemed to him his very individuality tends to fall into a clinical type, and its grasp of the reader deprives that reader of one chief pleasure of poetry, the feeling of having come upon a silence, a privacy, upon intellect existing unselfconsciously somewhere out of reach of camera" (261). Taylor's language echoes the "extended privacy" Brooks herself longs for in *Report from Part One*. On the cusp of her Fisk appearance, Brooks was conscious of her sense of poetry's necessary privacy, away from public gazes and camera lenses.

A different way of seeing this is to note that Brooks was not what was then called a "joiner," as the following letter helps to demonstrate. This letter, from her archived papers in Berkeley's Bancroft Library, has no date or any contextualizing marks besides what's recorded below, though it does refer to her "fifty-year old heart," dating it as post-Fisk by a matter of months (the Fisk conference was held in the spring of 1967, and Brooks's fiftieth birthday fell that June). Probably a fair copy made prior to sending the actual document, the letter is notable for its enraged tone and adamant stance against official affiliation with a protest group. Brooks had obviously been "accused" of membership in an antiwar committee at least twice, once by Mrs. Hirschfield and once by Mrs. Bitterman. It reads in full:

> Dear Mrs. Bitterman:
>
> There have been SUCH mistiness and misunderstanding connected with my "involvement" that in this letter to you I intend to be absolutely specific, absolutely clear, absolutely unfuzzy. I thought I had been in a letter to Mrs. Hirschfield, but apparently not.

ONE: Some months ago, Paul Carroll, whom I admire very much, and trust, invited me to read a poem at AN IMMENSE "RALLY" (or whatnot) which would include performances by writers, composers, performers, painters, sculptors, etc.; the theme was "ANTI-VIETNAM!"; the place was (probably) ORCHESTRA HALL; the number of appearances was—O N E. Mr. Carroll assured me that this endeavor had his support, approval, and endorsing enthusiasm. He suggested that I attend a meeting, so that I might "get the drift of things."

TWO: When I arrived, I saw by the "literature" being circulated that I had been drafted as one of the <u>committee</u>. I was not <u>asked</u> to consent to this inclusion—I was just "included." I saw no point in raising a clamor about this—why dramatically demand that my name be snipped off?? But I knew that I meant to read a poem, and read a poem only. I knew that I was NOT going to get mixed up in any organizing, or sign-carrying, etc. etc. etc.

THREE: At this point you will ask chidingly: "Well, just what ARE you going to involve yourself in, Miss <u>Brooks</u>, aside from 'writing po'try'?" And my answer is specific indeed: I am involved <u>actively</u> in aiding the young blacks on the south and west sides of Chicago; these include teen-age "gangsters", [*sic*] young college students, young teen-organizers. I am "involving" them with creative writing. It is a task that calls upon every one of my resources—<u>body</u>, <u>spirit</u>, and <u>money</u>. I don't carry any signs, I don't do any *gabbing*; I just get the work done that needs to be done. And I'm getting results.

FOUR: THIS IS ALL THE "INVOLVMENT" THIS FIFTY-YEAR OLD HEART CAN STAND, MRS. BITTERMAN. I shall leave Vietnam to the skilled hands of yourself and your staff. Paul Carroll is gone, Pearl Hirschfield is gone, William Hunt is gone. There is no one left with whom I have had any contact. I AM "RESIGNING" FORMALLY FROM A COMMITTEE I NEVER JOINED. AND <u>THAT</u> IS THE END OF IT, MRS. BITTERMAN.

Beyond the flaming tone, it's striking how infuriated Brooks is by the idea of official association with a protest movement. She prefers to see herself as a local activist, "getting results" from her work with the Blackstone Rangers, school contests, and readings and workshops. Being "mixed up" in "committee" work and "sign-carrying" are activities that clearly tread too heavily on one side of the public line. Such a line also clearly involves a racial dimension: while she will "leave Viet-nam" to other whites like Mrs. Bitterman and Paul Carroll, her work with blacks continues. (Brooks belonged to the NAACP and donated to the SNCC, though even those affiliations were of limited scope, as she tells Roy Newquist in a 1967 interview: "I'm not active in a speaking or marching sense" [*Conversations* 35].) Part of her anger in the letter seems directed at the misreading of her emotional commitments. While not willing to be a part of Carroll's largely white Vietnam protest, Brooks does want to clarify that her social outreach is directed more locally, at Chicago's black poor. This kind of public role is far more limited—one might say, far less "public" at all.

Sometimes, this sense of the poet's inherently compromised public identity reflects back on the poetry reading itself. In a late interview, Brooks is asked about the oral basis of her writing, "if you write your poetry to be read aloud" or not. Her answer is surprising for one committed to the tavern ideal: "I myself would rather read anybody's poetry than hear it read by even the best reader. That is because you can go back and forth in the lines, you know. And maybe at line eleven, you can say, 'Hey, now I understand what the poet meant in line three or four.' You can't do that or pick up the little gems of expression and savor them when someone else reads" (*Conversations* 142). Reading for Brooks is essentially a private activity, aesthetically speaking, a point that comes up, as will be shown, in her poetry readings themselves. Just as she eschews marching and sign carrying, her poems aren't bound for the forum; for Brooks, poems' real effects are earned in private, reflective reading rather than in taverns and auditoriums and from podium microphones. This is a crucially important tension in Brooks's work and part of the antinomies of sixties reading more generally: Brooks is urgently devoted to the struggle for race consciousness, though she is unwilling to enlist poetry's private, internal, aesthetic effects wholesale to that project.

Brooks's papers at Berkeley's Bancroft Library are full of responses to her reading performances that illuminate the dramatic effect her physical presence and voice had on audiences, who often found inspiration at her mere appearance before them. Brooks herself clearly understood the stakes of navigating a black body through a public space. Recalling in 1967 her first major literary award, from the Midwestern Writers' Conference in 1944, Brooks describes how "gasps went through the audience" as she strode to the podium to accept her prize (*Conversations* 31). In 1979 Brooks received a letter from a student named Rhonda Prettow about a campus reading at Indiana University that echoed her own experience. Prettow speaks to the transformational experience of being a black reader, onstage and in public, and how physical presence could affect her sense of identity in terms of both race and gender:

> As it is now I see too clearly the games which I, as a black woman, am expected to play in order to be accepted by the black community. You know yourself, looking around the room at the dinner [here there is a question mark with a slash through it, crossing it out] reading the dressed-up, doll-like image of black womanhood was nearly painfully evident. . . .
>
> Which brings me back to 'A Blackness So Deep.' After I had the opportunity to read in front of them, dressed as I usually am, speaking in my usual way, without the games, cloying or facades which I have come to think were required, I found that many black people have come to take an intrest [*sic*] in me.
>
> I walk down the street and am often stopped by someone who would never have dreamed of speaking to me before and am congratulated and asked about myself and my life. It is as though realative [*sic*] success makes up for what some black people might see as my eccentricity and my nonconformity.

Like the writer cited earlier who gleaned public and private dimensions of black identity in Brooks's reading of "The Pool Players," this correspondent draws from reading poetry aloud a source of personal authenticity that evades prescribed personal behavior and style. Her poem itself, however, is not at issue; only the performance is. Another letter to Brooks, written just days after this one, said: "To see you reading, teaching, being that which you know and understand filled me with hope for my own cowardice" (Laws). It's impossible to know what Brooks made of these letters, though they capture the divide between "poetry" and "reading": one can listen to a reader, even read oneself, and achieve a variety of personal benefits; and yet the "personal experiences of the writer" that interested Brooks are seemingly not at issue here. In these responses, reading appeared to be less about poetry than about blackness.

It would be a mistake to conflate Brooks's commitment to public appearances and readings and activism with an unambiguous embrace of public poetry. Despite the crucial transformative potential of a reader's "call," the poem itself still retained, for Brooks, hermetic privacy. Another way to see this is in terms of her willingness, even enthusiasm, for the mediation of her poems in a variety of forms, including musical performances, recordings, and films. Often these mediated forms blur the lyrical boundary of the poem to create a public documentary quality, performing a publicizing role while not being instances of actual poetry due to their status as adaptations and remediated versions. Brooks's archive contains a midlength screenplay adaptation by one Winston T. Henderson that was never made for "The Sundays of Satin-Legs Smith," though Brooks kept Henderson's letter from June 1975 in which he asks her to collaborate on the production. The screenplay itself features montages of slaves in chains being loaded on ships for the Middle Passage, African American soldiers, ghetto streets, "faces of the hopeless" urban black Americans, and Madison Avenue advertising and its harmful representations of material values. Though we can't possibly know what Brooks made of this proposal, in the following section I describe Brooks's own forays into media versions of her work, some of which were effective means to represent Brooks as a public figure while also decoupling the poems themselves from their status as private lyric.

Brooks in Performance

How was Gwendolyn Brooks's voice heard? Articles, remembrances, and letters record responses to the speaking poet and the effects produced by her presence. In the early years of the 1950s and 1960s, Brooks is perceived as shy and retiring. The *Book Bulletin* of the Chicago Public Library from January 1951 included on its back cover in its "Meet a Chicago Author" section a profile of Brooks in which the writer describes Brooks's "soft" voice: "To hear soft-spoken Miss Brooks read her poetry is to hear the persuasion of deep sincerity. She speaks very little of the poem's actual origins—just a word or two. Yet the listener needs no biographical drama to feel their lyric penetration." In a letter, a fan responds to an article Brooks wrote in *Ebony* magazine, recalling "the rather shy, retiring, unobtrusive poet who so ably read from her books of poetry" (Carina). This "shy," "soft-spoken" style is echoed in descriptions of Brooks's physical bearing. In 1965 the *Chicago Daily News* presented her in suburban/Rotary Club gendered terms, calling her a "shy, South Side housewife, wearing a stunning turquoise chiffon dress." (The "housewife" association was typical of the period: Brooks saved a scrap of newspaper headline that reads simply, "Housewife Wins Pulitzer Prize for Poetry Book.") The year previous, the *Kansas City Star* emphasized her modesty of dress, calling her "[a] plainly dressed woman—navy blue sweater and skirt, no jewelry except a wedding band." Yet Brooks is not all demure. Many sources register her deeply affecting presence, her sense of realness and authenticity. "Your poetry alone is wonderful, but you give it even more impact with your delivery," writes the chairman of Off Campus Writers, a Chicago writing group Brooks visited in 1964 (Spelius). In later years, especially post-1967, listeners noted something less traditionally feminine, more profound, and they strove, sometimes awkwardly, to name the complicated effect she produced. A 1972 article from a newspaper titled the *Daily Illini* says, "Gwendolyn Brooks . . . reads her poems in a lyrical, rhythmic voice that speaks of the distance between white and black people seen from both racial perspectives" and notes the complexities of her persona as well: "Despite her mouth's perpetual frown, Brooks writes and reads poetry that is incisively humorous." The *Dickinsonian*, the student newspaper for Dickinson College, where Brooks read in 1974, actually touches on her performance itself: "The little lady with the large voice. . . . Gwen Brooks rises, propping nothing on the podium. She speaks from her past voices, and from what they told her were their favorites. The audience realizes her presence, though she speaks only to the dark. I sank back into the words and learned the oral tradition" (Caleb). This shift from shy housewife to prophetic sage is captured in a letter from 1980 in which an audience member reflects on how Brooks's voice has changed over time: "Although I have heard you read before, your voice on this occasion was most rich and resonant" (Hill-Lubin). This combination of Brooks's "housewifely" appearance and the electricity generated by her poems and physical presence often evoked surprise. After one of her appearances in prison, coordinated by Chicago's Malcolm X College, Brooks received a letter of thanks from the school: "[Y]our earthiness and soulfulness shocked most of us. To find that the Great Lady lived on our street and talked our language was our most beautiful experience" (Dotson). And in one of the many letters from schoolchildren Brooks received, an eighth grader wrote the following paean to Brooks's powerfully real presence with moving force: "I like the way you read poetry. You read all your poems with feeling and you act like your words are all in your heart. I like how you were yourself, and didn't try to be nobody else" (King).

Despite these testimonials, Brooks is typically overlooked as a poet of performance. For one thing, as previously mentioned, she disavowed the association herself. In a 1967 interview with Paul Angle, she protested, "I am a writer perhaps *because* I am not a talker! It has always been hard for me to say exactly what I mean in speech" (*Conversations* 21). "I'm not active in a speaking or marching sense," she said that same year to Roy Newquist on the subject of civil rights. "I guess I'm too withdrawn" (35).[5] "Oh, Gwendolyn Brooks," exudes Studs Terkel in a 1961 interview, "you said, you think you are inarticulate . . . but you are truly articulate in what you write and even in the things you say with such economy" (6). Twenty years later, she drew on the same self-critical (and to a contemporary ear, offensive) diction, according to a reporter for the *Los Angeles Times* describing Brooks's 1987 visit to Chapman University: "'I have a hard time saying exactly what I'm feeling,' she confessed at the end of her visit to Orange, just before boarding a train to San Francisco while she was in California to give readings. 'I guess that's why I write, because I am an inarticulate person, who has a hard time spieling out' ideas" (Moffet). Critical pronouncements follow suit, ignoring Brooks's engagement with "spieling." Tyler Hoffman's chapter on Black Arts poetry and reading in *American Poetry in Performance* (2011) mentions Brooks only once, and in passing—though to be fair, she was an older, less integral member of this poetic community (168). Voice as figure or trope, however, as described above, has been widely and consistently emphasized. D. H. Melhem's *Gwendolyn Brooks: Poetry and the Heroic Voice* (1987), the first monograph treatment of Brooks's canon, draws on voice as metaphor to be read in purely formal terms—in "analysis of poetic structures: by sight (on the page), sound, and sense; by prosody, diction, language, imagery, themes, motifs" (1).

Yet Brooks's actual performances have never been closely examined, despite the fact that performance was crucial to Brooks's writing. She read her own work, had her work read by others, and was involved in nontraditional reading formats—workshops, competitions, staged performances—with an intensity unprecedented for an American poet of her generation. This started extremely early: Brooks writes in *Report from Part One* that her mother, Keziah, was "rehearsing me in the delivery of recitations" for the Carter Temple Church in preschool (49). At the age of twenty-three, Brooks joined a "poetry-writing group" conducted by Inez Cunningham Stark, an influential literary doyenne and reader for *Poetry* magazine, an experience to which Brooks referred frequently as the beginning of her education in poetry (*Conversations* 19). Brooks would go on to create her own poetry-writing workshops with the Chicago gang the Blackstone Rangers and other young writers throughout her life and sponsor poetry competitions, which took the form of readings, in elementary schools. Radio and television, too, were important formats for Brooks. Upon the release of her second book, *Annie Allen*, Brooks read "Men of careful turns, haters of forks in the road" after a dramatization of her biography, titled "Poet in Bronzeville," for the radio program *Destination Freedom*, which portrayed her childhood and adult life in Chicago. In 1961 she was also interviewed by Studs Terkel on Chicago's WFMT, where she sat for numerous broadcast interviews, most of which included the reading of poems, in the years to come. The following year, radio would reveal her limited linguistic reach when a musical version of "De Witt Williams on his way to Lincoln Cemetery"—which contains the seemingly unproblematic line "just a plain black boy"—was barred from the airwaves because the word "black" was deemed risqué (Kent 154).[6] The public television station KCET in Chicago produced a short profile of Brooks in 1966 that included B-roll, or supplemental footage, of poor Chicago neighborhoods and footage of Brooks reading poems into the camera. Brooks also had her work performed by others in recordings and onstage. Sidney Poitier and Doris Belack read "when you have forgotten Sunday" for a 1956 phonograph record, and Brooks produced a full Caedmon album, with an audio introduction by Don L. Lee, in 1967. In late December 1969 an extraordinary event called the "living anthology" was created, inspired by Brooks's example: poets, painters, dancers, and musicians gathered at Chicago's Affro-Arts Theater and performed and displayed works in her honor (*Part One* 197). Brooks also taught poetry workshops at the University of Wisconsin, Chicago's Elmhurst College, Northeastern Illinois State University, and, most frequently, Columbia College, where she played audio recordings for her students of *The Waste Land* and *Spoon River Anthology* and poems by Robert Frost, Dylan Thomas, and Marianne Moore (*Conversations* 33).

Live reading at conferences and campuses would also come to take a central place in Brooks's writing life, sometimes creating dramatic and lasting change. Most famously, the Second Black Writers' Conference at Fisk University in 1967 politicized Brooks, though other events vie for importance, especially her appearance at the dedication of Chicago's Wall of Respect, a giant mural celebrating black life in which Brooks's image appeared, and the impromptu reading in a tavern directly afterward. As consultant to the Library of Congress (1985–86), Brooks traveled and read in the Soviet Union; held workshops in prisons and at drug and alcohol treatment centers and public schools, sometimes three in one day; and started the "Lunchtime Reading Series," an informal workshop held at the library (Toi Derricote, contemporary poet and cofounder of the influential black poetry organization Cave Canem, was an attendee [*Part Two* 81]). Tabulating Brooks's frequent appearances at universities and other locations would be a formidable job, as she was so often "on tour." Like Robert Frost, her schedule was packed.

Before Brooks's fifty-campus-a-year schedule settled into its regular rhythm, she appeared with dizzying frequency at numerous venues to read and give talks. Notable here is the extraordinary range of institutions and organizations Brooks involved herself in, many of them seemingly incompatible. The impression is of an ecumenical poet before and after her schismatic 1967 year. I'll try to give a sense of the scope of her appearances by plucking out a few representative appearances from the vast list that portrays her ecumenical roster of hosting groups and institutions:

October 8, 1961: Brooks reads from *The Bean Eaters* at the First Annual Calumet Area Poetry Conference and Workshop at Indiana University.

April 25, 1964: Brooks speaks at the four-hundredth anniversary celebration at the Friends of Literature's Thirty-Third Annual Shakespeare Birthday Program and Award Dinner, held at Chicago's Bismarck Hotel.

November 7, 1965: Brooks gives a talk entitled "Poetry and/or Life" at the American Association of University Women at the public library in La Grange Park, a Chicago suburb.

January 1, 1968: Brooks reads a poem, uncollected, entitled "Richard Gordon Hatcher" in honor of the city of Gary, Indiana's new mayor at his inaugural ceremony.[7]

January 29, 1969: Brooks reads her poems at the Douglas School, an elementary school in Chicago.

May 7, 1971: Brooks reads at Alabama A&M University's First Annual Fine Arts Week, where she discusses "The New Black Poetry."

March 21, 1980: Brooks reads at a celebration for Afrika Express, a Chicago organization founded in 1972 that sends African Americans to Africa every year. This event also includes a call-and-response poem printed on the back of the program titled "Gwendolyn Brooks, an African Woman," in which a speaker and the audience trade lines about Brooks's Africanness.[8]

This list could go on indefinitely, up through the 1990s, and include appearances at New Hope Baptist Church, at Cuyahoga Community College, for the King Memorial Fund, at the Tampa-Hillsborough Public Library, as well as at scores of college campuses, grade schools, and high schools. One contrasting pair of readings, however, may help to reveal Brooks's scope in capsule form. On February 10, 1969, Brooks read with Ron Karenga and Arna Bontemps at Oklahoma State University at a conference on race titled "The Black Awakening: The Dawn of Pride and Involvement." This was a Black Arts event attended by major figures in the movement, including Karenga, whom Brooks actually quotes for her epigraph to "The Sermon on the Warpland." A few months later, on June 19, Brooks was the featured speaker at the Illinois Banquet for the American Association of University Women's Biennial Convention, held in the Hilton Hotel and with a menu that included "Colombet Vin Rose Wine," "Chilled Fruits en Supreme," and sirloin steak. Equally available to Black Arts rallies and bourgeois white feminist causes, Brooks never settled into a particular program; she was a reader for all.

Listening to the audio record of such appearances—or, rather, the sliver of it that remains—dramatizes Brooks's slow transformation from private to public poet, though it's a transformation that is never adequately made, even as late as 1983, in her astonishing performance at the Guggenheim Museum. Brooks eventually learned to use the reading to play a public role, thereby keeping the work of poetry appropriately marginalized, in reserve for different forms of readerly consumption. I don't want to suggest a neat or linear narrative, however. In what follows, I'll emphasize how we can hear struggle in Brooks's readings, the struggle that characterizes her poetry's own balancing of private experience and social identity, as well as the larger context of poetry's shifting relationship to privacy in the years during and after the civil rights and Black Arts upheavals.

WMAQ (1949)

The first significant voicing of Brooks's work was a 1949 radio show written by the radio producer and former *Chicago Defender* editor Richard Durham and broadcast on September 18, 1949, on WMAQ's *Destination Freedom* program about black life in America. Durham's show was entirely unique in early postwar radio, which was a "white actor's playground," as the radio historian John Dunning puts it, with virtually no black voices to be heard (197). In fact, Judith Waller, WMAQ's program director at the time and supporter of Durham's program, had produced *Amos 'n' Andy* twenty years earlier (197). *Destination Freedom*, which aired from June 1948 to August 1950, narrated episodes from African American history and culture, including Harriet Tubman's Underground Railroad, a narrative of the Middle Passage, and life in the Jim Crow South. It also presented biographies of major black Americans in sports, politics, and the arts: Joe Louis, Richard Wright, Louis Armstrong, Satchel Paige, Ralph Bunche (196). In this context, Brooks is framed as a key figure in the story of successful black struggles against American racism, in which blacks drew strength from their communities and themselves to counter oppression. The episode itself is valuable for how it portrays Brooks as both someone conditioned by a restrictive social environment yet also an agent in her own life story—an individualist in the mold of a Horatio Alger protagonist. The private and public poet are locked in a mutually constructive relationship. This episode also includes autobiographical snippets—about the two white socialite women who visited her apartment and inspired "The Lovers of the Poor," about her experiences delivering quack remedies in the

Mecca building, about meeting her husband, Henry Blakely—that Brooks herself would invoke repeatedly at readings throughout her life. In this way, the program serves as a discursive template for her autobiographical descriptions to come.

The script is a dramatic rendering of the young poet's life, charting her rise from girlhood to adulthood and success as a writer. The narrative is framed by two society women, Mrs. Winters and Mrs. Pritchard, who visit Brooks's apartment, which is full of allegorical noises: a clacking typewriter, signifying the poet's persistent work; an El train rattling so loudly that it blots dialogue, signifying Brooks's supposedly oppressive living conditions; and an interruptive neighbor who drops her child off so she can run an errand, signifying a sustaining Bronzeville community. The visitors explain that they're scouting for "new talent," though they are dismayed to find Brooks in this noisy flat. "Where do you write this poetry?" they ask, and "Brooks" (played by the black actress Wezlyn Tilden) answers, "Right here," as an El roars by. The women say they seek poetry of "the more cultured variety," but they can hardly have a conversation, as Brooks keeps getting interrupted by noises and knocks at the door. "Brooks" then reads "kitchenette building" in a small, high-pitched voice reminiscent of Alice, played by the white Audrey Meadows from *The Honeymooners*. The narrative then flashes back to episodes from Brooks's girlhood, including a reprimand from her teacher for writing poetry in class ("I'm all for you learning literature, but you're learning the backyard kind. I want you to learn the front-yard kind") and being instructed by James Weldon Johnson (in the show he's called simply "Dr. Johnson") to "forget about poetry and do something useful. To be a poet, one has to have experience. Where have you been?" Yet Brooks perseveres through adversities, all drawn from the poet's actual biography: her drab office job as a typist; her application for a job as a salesgirl, where she encounters racism ("You see any colored sales girls?" asks the incredulous manager); domestic work; and assistance to a spiritualist charlatan. Her poems are rejected from literary journals, too, but the typewriter's persistent clacks in the background tell us she's not giving up. Soon, she meets her husband, who affirms that Bronzeville provides all she needs to know about the world, and she begins attending workshops with Inez Cunningham Stark. Tilden reads "People protest in sprawling lightless ways / Against their deceivers," and we're back in the room with the society madams, who say they "don't understand" her work, upon which she receives news of various prizes, including a Guggenheim, that say otherwise. Finally, Brooks herself—not an actress portraying her—reads "Men of careful turns, haters of forks in the road" in a high-toned, girlish tremble. It is bad, nervous reading, perhaps her first in a live medium, and hard to square with the deep, savoring basso profundo of her 1983 recording discussed below. The last line in particular is read in singsong fashion, with the final words elongated in a playful lilt—"screeeeming weed." Years later, listening to this performance, Brooks would cringe at its "high, sweet tones" (Kent 87).

This early radio play captures the duality of Brooks's poetic identity, at least as others were constructing it. On the one hand, Brooks is cast as a public figure and social poet representative of the larger counters of black American experience. The story suggests that Brooks has, like other heroic black Americans before her (literally, in the weeks before on *Destination Freedom*), overcome obstacles—of being a woman, an African American, and a poet without recourse to the kinds of "poetic" experience that a literary establishment values and, more importantly, funds. In this way, the show recognizes an emerging black aesthetic illegible to "cultured" whites. Brooks's neighbors and Bronzeville itself are not distractions or detriments, as the white interlopers imagine, but sources of strength and meaning. In this way, Brooks isn't a poet of subjectivity but one of social documentary, reading from three poems that reflect social conditions familiar to other stories of black success. And yet, the profile simultaneously serves in a second way as an audiographic bildungsroman testifying to Emersonian self-reliance: the poet is figured as earnestly hardworking and dedicated, an exemplum of bootstrapping self-improvement that will "make it"; as the show reveals at its end, major awards were indeed forthcoming. She will also transform the social conditions she experiences into something of her own, inverting what some see as limitation toward personal advantage. In fact, the script strives beyond fact to suggest how forces conspired against her, thus amplifying her individual strength in confronting obstacles: in actual life, her mother and James Weldon Johnson were very encouraging (Kent 87). The narrative establishes an uneasy relationship in Brooks's work between socially embedded themes and private life, which stand distinct and separate.

Asilomar (1964)

In August 1964 Brooks read onstage with Amiri Baraka, then LeRoi Jones, at the "Negro Writer in the United States" conference, held at Monterey Peninsula's Asilomar Conference Center.[9] The performance portrays Brooks's more careful and self-conscious tending of the line between privacy and the larger social issues her work describes. Unlike a radio show, now Brooks was in front of live spectators, with fellow poets and an inquisitive audience. The conference format itself is significant, something Harold Cruse, in *The Crisis of the Negro Intellectual* (1967), called a failure. "Negro Writers' Conferences settle nothing, solve nothing, pose nothing, analyze nothing, plan nothing, create nothing," he wrote, going on to describe a conference organized at the New School in New York City by John O. Killens, who also organized the second Fisk conference, which would so radically affect Brooks (498). Cruse is dismissive of "Negro conferences" not for how they had been ridiculed in the press (a *New York Times* article reported that the audience "hissed and hollered and debated one another for about seven years" [501]) but for two contradictory problems. First, they couldn't "separate literary art as content, theme, and form, from the material basis of cultural expression" (505); because they were held at Asilomar, the New School, or other mainstream white institutions, full-scale resistance to the "prevailing cultural superstructure" underwriting their oppression was impossible, according to Cruse (505). Second, Cruse excoriates the crude cultural politics exhibited by Killens and his associate John Henrik Clarke, whom Cruse accuses of petty attacks on writers like Ralph Ellison and James Baldwin for not parroting orthodoxies of black separatism (507–8). So on the one hand, conferences are hobbled by complicity with white institutions, and on the other, they're ruined by loyalist squabbling. One can hear in a letter Hoyt Fuller wrote to Brooks the weariness such events provoked in attendees when he refers to the "endless series of conferences I seem to be locked into."

James C. Hall's depiction in his book *Mercy, Mercy Me* (2001) of Robert Hayden's public skewering at the first Fisk conference offers a lens through which to observe how poetry fared in this political environment and suggests the nature of public scrutiny being cast upon poets and writers—something that may have indeed pushed Brooks toward her dramatic transformation.

Hall's book is an account of what he calls African American antimodernism, a cultural resistance to the inauthenticity of modernity by sixties artists, including John Coltrane, Romare Bearden, and Paule Marshal, among others. In Hall's view, sixties black art "claimed for itself an expansive social capacity" (5) in which black writers sought "to provide or capture in the aesthetic realm what students and ministers had delivered in the political or social" (47). From this perspective, experiences like Brooks's at Fisk in 1967 were part of a cultural style: "ideological conversion" itself became a trope for anger at the status quo as black artists and intellectuals made clear, definitive movements toward a black identity that could express the full measure of African American desire for cultural change (16).

Hall's account of the public quarrel between Hayden and Melvin Tolson at the *first* Fisk writers' conference in 1966 portrays a standoff between universalism and race consciousness. Hayden's position was, in fact, very close to Brooks's own, though hers was more nuanced. Tolson, with the crowd behind him, tore into Hayden for his assertion that a black poet might be one "who happens to be Negro" (qtd. in J. Hall 49). "Hap, hap . . . let me see," Tolson replied in his oratorical fusillade, "hap means accident. Is someone going to make M. B. Tolson an accident? You'll never make me an accident. . . . I'm a black poet, and African-American poet, a Negro poet. I'm no accident—and I don't give a tinker's damn what you think" (qtd. in J. Hall 50). This exchange is notable not only for the explosive emotion on display (at Fisk, a black university, the obeisance to white liberal propriety feared by Cruse was absent, even though the audience contained plenty of whites) but for how the humanist universalism Hayden proposed had become publicly dismissible, bringing Hayden close to the designation "Uncle Tom" (51). Drawing on an article by Kimberly Benston, Hall argues that the choice between universalism and community, "general" unraced experience and "blackness," is outmoded, though its roots are in the late sixties and early seventies Black Arts period (39–40). It's this very line between universal and raced expression that Brooks treads so carefully at Asilomar. But the fact was that conferences and public readings were beginning to play a new role, serving as a metric for authenticity in black writing. On this shifting ground, Hayden's desire for universalism was perceived as a desire for his poems to be treated as private expression—"the beauty of perception given form," Hayden calls it (qtd. in

J. Hall 50)—and that just wouldn't stand. A black poet needed to speak to blacks, and the time had come for this to be asserted in public fashion. As has been amply suggested in earlier sections of this essay, public visibility was the mark of black authenticity in the sixties.

The question of black universalism shades the events at Asilomar. Herbert Hill, the conference's white organizer, later wrote in an essay collection based on the conference's proceedings what amounts to a universalist's credo:

> The hope that James Weldon Johnson expressed many years ago is being fulfilled at last. "Standing on his racial foundation," the Negro author can create that which rises above race and reaches "out to the universal in truth and beauty."
>
> Thus Margaret Walker, writing for the two audiences now becoming one, can carry away an important poetry prize. Gwendolyn Brooks, in poetry such as her *Bronzeville*, can do things with the language of imagery that appeal to all humanity. (19)

This was written after the conference itself and perhaps inspired by Brooks's own performance there, which concerned this "appeal." Unlike her appearance in the scripted radio autobiography, Brooks was careful at Asilomar to separate poem and racial consciousness; in her reading, she repeatedly grounds her poems in private experience, which she distances from her public persona. She begins by reading the opening three paragraphs of her own foreword to Langston Hughes's recently published anthology of black writing, *New Negro Poets U.S.A.*, a collection of thirty-seven black poets of the next generation, including major figures to come: Jay Wright, Audre Lorde, Mari Evans, Dudley Randall, Julian Bond, and Jones himself—all of whom are dedicated to an ideal of public writing. Brooks's citing of an anthology edited by Hughes and her status as the author of its foreword position her as generationally removed from the poets therein—especially the deified Jones, who shares the stage with her. She also quotes her own writing from 1950, which includes the epigraph to this chapter—even "[h]is quiet walk down the street is a speech to the people"—thereby collapsing the distance between body and voice, linking the black body to authentic speech. Her main point in the foreword is to repeat this idea, what she calls the black poet's "double dedication" and "two-headed responsibility" (13) to write as a black and a poet. Striking here is Brooks's layered self-citation: she reads her own words from the foreword to Hughes's anthology, which, in turn, quote her own words from fourteen years before, as if to say, "I'm sticking to my guns." The guns, in this case, are booming the same DuBoisean duality: while black writers must acknowledge collective, racial identity—one half of their "double dedication"—they must also apprentice themselves to craft and form—to being, after all, poets. "But no real artist is going to be content offering raw materials," she goes on to say to the assembled crowd, not finishing the thought as she does in the original article: "The Negro poet's most urgent duty, at present, is to polish his technique" (15). Here, Brooks separates form and content; private experience, the "race-fed testimony," as her foreword names it, is detachable from the forms in which it survives. "Two-headed," "double dedication," "twice-tried": Brooks's language clearly establishes her perspective for the audience in northern California: private and public spheres may be kept—*should* be kept—separate.

This separation structures her reading. Onstage with Jones, Brooks—speaking first, despite by some measures her greater status—carefully grooms the divide between what happened "to her" and treatments of more general, social concerns. Sometimes a poem functions as a transcription of life, as when, after reading "kitchenette building," she assures the audience, laughing a little, "That's straight from my own experience." In her introductory comments to "A Song in the Front Yard," Brooks admits to some tweaking, though her changes keep intact the associations between experience and expression: "Many of these poems are out of my own experience, twisted and molded here and there so that they won't be too recognizable. And even so, my mother shakes and shudders each time I publish a book, wondering which of the neighbors I'm going to put in [laughs]." At other points, poems represent diverse social experiences about which Brooks has no personal knowledge and which she keeps wholly separate from "herself." She prefaces "The Mother," about a woman who received numerous abortions, by establishing her distance from the speaker through a persona poem, telling the crowd (with uncharacteristic grammatical awkwardness), "I am not the heroine. I sympathize with the heroine, but I'm not she." Before reading "The Preacher Ruminates behind the Sermon," Brooks describes the poem (as she often does) as a speculation about a public preacher's "private thoughts of his own behind the sermon." By saying this, Brooks establishes the preacher's life as neatly divisible between an inner, private life and a public persona that masks it, and the poem itself echoes this schism: the preacher implicitly compares himself to God, who "tires of being great / In solitude" (*Blacks* 30). All of these prefatory comments share the task of snapping chalk-lines between Brooks's subjectivity and her poems' social revelations. Her tone of voice when reading is apologetic. It's as if she's embarrassed to be nettling listeners with political poetry. Brooks reads "A Sunset of the City," a poem about an aging woman that includes an opening laugh line, directly following her much more politically charged "The Chicago Defender Sends a Man to Little Rock." Jones had publicly criticized this poem, in fact, something Brooks actually addresses onstage before reading: "I'll be brave nevertheless, and you can tear it to pieces later on." Afterward, she says in a mumble, "Race away from that!" The pose here is of a poet who doesn't wish to upset propriety with messy questions of racism—Cruse's very concern about the whiteness of such events. Yet such propriety and respectability are on clear display. When reading "The White Troops Had Their Orders but the Negroes Looked Like Men," which includes the rhetorical question "Who really gave two figs?" Brooks says, "Of course, the soldiers wouldn't've said 'two figs,' but I did." She prefaces "Sunset" by saying that middle-aged women can identify with this poem, giggling along with some in the audience after reading the poem's first line: "Already I am no longer looked at with lechery or love" (*Blacks* 353). The difficulties of "Little Rock" are defanged by whimsy.

In Brooks's introductory comments, she refers to the "twice-tried" black poet, one who is both poet and black. The effect of her performance at Asilomar in 1964 is to police the line that separates these roles, an act accomplished by colliding her self-presentation with the poems themselves, which don't always separate with such oil-and-water ease. The end of Brooks's reading moves into her more recent poetry, including poems concerning events surrounding civil rights struggles: "Little Rock," "The Ballad of Rudolph Reed," "Riders to the Blood-red Wrath," and "The Life of Lincoln West." Yet these poems are tempered by an accommodating persona somewhat at odds with the poems' subjects. She intersperses them with easier fare, like "Nora," written for her daughter, and "Marian Anderson," both of which she calls "children's" poems. But most significant, again, is Brooks's vocal tone itself, which helps unpeel the poet—writing descriptions of a social order drenched in omnipresent racist ideology—from the public nature of her poems, something that marks the reading of "The Life of Lincoln West," Brooks's long poem about a little boy so ugly that people shudder with revulsion and sometimes pity when they see him. The poem's climax occurs when, as young Lincoln sits watching a film in a theater, a white adult calls him the "real thing":

> One of the best
> examples of the specie. Not like
> those diluted Negroes you see so much of on
> the streets these days, but the
> real thing. (*Blacks* 487)

In printed text, these lines indict a white ideology of race that essentializes black primitivism, using the public space of a movie theater to do so. Yet in the lines that follow, when the man calls Lincoln "Black, ugly, and odd—the real thing," Brooks chuckles a little. In the next stanza, when Lincoln's mother "jumped up, / shrieked 'Go to ——'" at the white man, Brooks chuckles again, and this time the audience, now authorized, echoes her by guffawing lightly. Her voice itself is flat and without the kind of gravity or weight she'll give it even just a few years later. It's essential not to overdetermine such moments; it's impossible to ascribe clear intention to such voicings. Still, the Asilomar reading repeatedly represents the poet as positioned outside her own work, a reader of it rather than its embodiment. Her physical presence was in no way "a speech to the people."[10]

Voices of Our People (1966)

In 1966 Brooks participated in another media representation of her life, this time on television. *Voices of Our People: In Celebration of Black Poetry* aired in 1966. It was a black-and-white documentary on Brooks produced by KCET, a Los Angeles–based educational television station founded just two years earlier. In some striking ways, this program—which features Brooks reading directly into the camera and talking about her beliefs about writing—shares much with the Asilomar event and echoes the WMAQ radio show in 1949 by emphasizing, this time with generous footage of anonymous poor blacks in the Chicago area, Brooks's association with her environment. The format, however, is totally unique. Brooks talks about her poems and reads some of them, with the camera either on her or showing scenes of Chicago life. It's also a program clearly pitched at white audiences and features the poet addressing the viewer somewhat awkwardly, as if the poet is accounting for and explaining herself to a critical gaze.

Like both previous examples, the documentary stresses the distinction between private writer and social subject. Near the very beginning, Brooks looks into the camera and frames her poetry as about those who, in the fateful words Robert Hayden would use the very same year at Fisk, just "happen" to be black:

> My poems are about people. They are often about people who happen to have brown, black, or ivory faces, but aside from that they are people like any other. They have dreams, desires, hates, loves, fears. Circumstances are involved. Situations that are familiar to anyone. . . . My poetry has often been called Negro poetry, and I am considered a Negro poet. It's true I am a Negro, and I hope I am a poet. But when I begin a poem I don't have special social categorizations in mind. I am impelled by an emotion or thought and try to do the best I can by my emotion or thought. . . . That is my governing desire. Of course, being a Negro and seeing more of Negroes than others, there will be poems that refer to Negroes. ("In Celebration")

Perhaps more forcefully here than anywhere yet, Brooks slices through the tissue connecting race and identity. She begins by universalizing her poems' subjects as "people" (though this word does carry with it, of course, shades of "*the* people," "*my* people"). Her subjects "happen to have" black faces, though she says "social categorizations" such as race don't apply to her thinking. Brooks is arguing that her private self is only grazed by "seeing more of" blacks, as she is black herself. Beyond that, she implies but then occludes the various forces oppressing blacks by her use of passive voice ("Circumstances are involved," "I am considered a Negro poet"). Later in the documentary, she describes her process of composition as a distinctly *private* act of Romantic imaginative composition: "It's chiefly a matter of sitting with my chin in my hand and gazing out the window . . . and communing with myself and what I'm remembering or imagining. I feel that each one of us is alone in the specific sense of the word. There are times when we come to grips with other people, happily or unhappily, are able to mesh with them and qualify the aloneness to a certain extent. . . . I have always enjoyed aloneness, as distinguished from loneliness. I recognize myself chiefly when alone" ("In Celebration"). Brooks's acknowledgment of her address to black America is barely hinted at in oblique phrasings like "other people," which simultaneously represent and deflect her writing's real subject.

This repeated disavowal of race as a category (or even a term that can appear amid these euphemisms) that defines or limits her subjectivity is quickly belied. One of the striking silences in this production is Brooks's failure to acknowledge a treatment of race. The first poem she reads, as at Asilomar, is "kitchenette building," though in this instance before reading Brooks is suddenly cast in the role of cultural docent, helping nonblack viewers acclimate to the raced diction. It's a striking maneuver—denying any race-based qualities to her poems, Brooks immediately reveals the knowledge of black Chicago that one needs to adequately receive her work. Brooks explains what a kitchenette building is and describes its genesis: after certain Chicago neighborhoods shifted from white to black and poor, apartment buildings were segmented into tiny units into which large families crammed themselves. As she speaks, the film shows building facades from which sad-looking faces of an old African American woman and young boy peer out. Then Brooks reads the poem in a deeper, more confident voice than in previous recordings, and as she reads the film cuts to more images of the building. The poem ends:

> We wonder. But not well! not for a minute!
> Since Number Five is out of the bathroom now,
> We think of lukewarm water, hope to get in it.

Leading up to and through this passage, the film offers an encapsulated drama: a woman in a bathrobe waits impatiently for the door of the bathroom to open. When it finally does, a man saunters out and she slips in, though as the man moves down the hall, he wolfishly takes her in with his eyes.

One might argue that the film offers an adjunct, documentarian echo to the poem's articulation of a social condition, much in the way the "Satin-Legs Smith" screenplay did. And yet Brooks implicates herself in the drama, even by the choice of the poem, the first word of which—"we"—immediately draws a listener up: Whom does the "we" imply? Is Brooks one of these kitchenette dwellers herself, a persona "playing" one, or just one who imaginatively associates with them, as anyone might? And if so, to what extent does this complicate her insistence that her poems concerning black subjects are due merely to "being a Negro and seeing more of Negroes than others"? Furthermore, along with the B-roll crosscutting, Brooks's distinct, intentional manner of standing and reading, looking from time to time directly into the camera's lens, positions her not just as a reader of the poem but as a part of the world she describes—its chief spokesperson.

The film is just such a continuous balancing act of identity. Is Brooks speaking as an incorporated individual from whom race consciousness can't be limned cleanly away, or is she simply a poet-who-happens-to-be-black standing to the side of her blackness, a creature of pure privacy and "aloneness"? When Brooks reads "The Ballad of Rudolph Reed," she looks directly—one might even say accusingly—into the camera's lens at the word "Nigger." Yet when she tells the story of getting the call to tell her that she won the Pulitzer Prize, she says that "the winning of that prize was a tremendous thing to happen to me," clearly emphasizing the word "me." Pronouns are likewise important in the documentary's title, *Voices of Our People.* Is this one such voice, speaking its singular truths? Or is this a voice representing all blacks in Chicago, America, or the world? Or even just all Americans? To whom does "our" refer? As the credits roll, Brooks sits in the background, alone at a small table, writing, gazing out the window, and writing more—a solitary poet reflecting on the world around her. This trembling balance between privacy and publicity will undergo dramatic transformations in the next reading, her Caedmon recording of 1969.

Caedmon (1969)

"I interpret Sister Brooks as a popular poet, a public poet." So says Don L. Lee in his liner notes to Brooks's 1969 Caedmon album, her only commercial audio product. The album's cover takes a radical departure from the image of Brooks at work in her study: a deeply shadowed photograph shows a young boy, his shirt off to reveal a thin, vulnerable body, one hand covering his mouth in shock or surprise. He stands in a brick alley with wet and shining walls leading to an open door in which a man sits in profile in a chair. Is this the boy's father? Has the boy just seen something shocking occur inside his home? The image relies on a disjunction between an indoor privacy, in which the man reclines in domestic silence, and the outdoor publicity of an alley, where violence or trauma is possible. While the image's content is ambiguous, the "public" nature of the scene is unmistakable. This image promises that the content to be heard within will be urban, black, raw, and shocking.

The recording itself also offers a study in contrast. On the one hand, there is Lee's framing of the poems, which acts in some ways, ironically, like what Henry Louis Gates, Jr., describes in a well-known example as white authentications—or what he calls "attestations" (83)—of black writers like Phillis Wheatley. Whereas established literary and cultural arbiters would sanctify Wheatley's poems, in this case another black writer would attest to Brooks's antiestablishment credibility. Because Brooks still carries with her the whiff of literary institution, Lee's energy is pitched toward making her safe for Black Arts listeners. To this end, Lee stresses the ethics of the "call" to blacks, how it will "perform some function," as he puts it in his entry in *Jump Bad* quoted above: "This collection of poems/songs will sing a surprise to many: it will motivate listening crowds to a position of action and will help blackpeople [*sic*] toward their own measurements of existence" (Brooks, *Reading*). This "motivational" quality, in which the poems serve primarily as a spur to action, is coupled with a bid at authenticity and its linguistic seme, the "real": "The accent is on realness; this woman is outrageously real in a land that subtly moves to suffocate that which is human." No longer latent, the manifest framing of Brooks's poems is now totally performative. Lee makes no mention of the poems themselves, their aesthetic or formal qualities (in fact, they're now not just poems but "poems/songs"). Instead, Lee decouples the poem as a formal work of private expression or lyric craft from its social urgency and empirical effect.

Listeners who place the needle at the beginning of Side A will hear Brooks's poems introduced again by Lee, this time by his actual voice. The first track is Lee's poem, simply titled "Gwendolyn Brooks," which Lee reads in hipster cadences that date to Black Arts patois. This means heavy emphasis on certain syllables and a kind of drawling elongation and thinning of others. The crucial word "real" gets particular emphasis: the line "Her makeup is total-real" loudly pops the first syllable of "TO-tal" and swallows the second, almost entirely; the word "real" itself is strung out like a twist of gum—"reeeeel"—the /r/ read quite sharply, the rest of the word stretching languidly behind as if all Lee's energy is expended on the /re/, leaving the rest to dribble away in fatigue. These lines from Lee's poem cast Brooks as a public speaker who incites others to write and develop. There is little room between being authentic and "real" and being public when Lee reads aloud:

> and everywhere the
> lady "negro poet"
> appeared the poets were there.
> they listened & questioned
> & went home feeling uncomfortable/unsound & so-
>   untogether
> they read/re-read/wrote & rewrote
> & came back the next time to tell the
> lady "negro poet"
> how beautiful she was/is & how she had helped them
> & she came back with:
>   how necessary they were and how they've helped her.

Lee's poem describes Brooks as a reader—appropriate for the opening to her album. This particular kind of reader is "real" because she's in some communication with her audience, initiating a recursive process of reflection and writing. In this scenario, poetry functions as self-scrutiny and "help," a word reiterated; poetry is a public act of communal self-definition, and Brooks is a leader of that process. Lee's framing of Brooks draws on her role as workshop leader, teacher, and speaker, a role that was so prominent during this period, and helps articulate her public identity.

However, Brooks's actual voice and the album's organization tell a different story. For one thing, the album is ordered chronologically, beginning with selections from *Bronzeville*, then *Annie Allen*, *The Bean Eaters*, *Selected Poems*, *Black Expression*, and *In the Mecca*, which suggests a cataloging of literary output rather than a program built around a progressive social agenda; the table of contents is organized around and reflects the history of books, not Brooks's reading activities. But the most striking contrast is Brooks's voice, which sounds radically different from Lee's trendy intonations of progressive, revolutionary black politics. Her vocal tone is measured, even, and tame and in truth not noticeably distinct from her Asilomar reading in 1964. There are distinct midwestern tones that Brooks has retained from even her 1949 radio voice, like the word "time" in "kitchenette building," which has a distinctly nasal ridge and rhymes with "tine," and very hard /r/ sounds gulped down the back of her throat. Brooks's rhythm and cadence, too, are conventional, an effect most noticeable when Brooks reads "Queen of the Blues," a poem with stock refrains ("I loved my daddy / But what did my daddy / do? I loved my daddy. / But what did my daddy / do?") that sound as stilted and unembodied as blues refrains often do when plainly spoken. Brooks also dramatically retards the final line to signal the end, a common blues reading practice. Reading "Sadie and Maud," the bouncing cadences of the ballad are recited in the tones of a dutiful schoolchild, with elongations in expected places, typically trisyllabic phrases that call for a kind of lilting emphasis ("fine toothed comb," "this old house"). "The Mother" in the poem takes this dramatic pause to its heights as Brooks lingers exceptionally long before the final word in the final line, "I / loved you / All." On a first listen, the provocative quality of this recording isn't its Black Arts sounds but the striking difference produced by its framing as such and Brooks's regimented—almost in this case oppositional—voice and style. In terms of vocal sound, Lee's framing of Brooks as a public poet, declaiming for the masses, seems a woeful misprision of standardized articulation.

One might object here that, while far removed from the public semiotics initiated by Lee, Brooks's performance isn't necessarily "private" by default. Yet a closer listen reveals Brooks "doing" other voices in a way that suggests her lyrics' removal from public discourse more decisively. By embodying characters and "playing" the roles of voices in the poems, or employing what might be called vocal irony, the lyrics themselves become dialogic and in that way private. Though for Mikhail Bakhtin the "dialogic" describes a mixture of social discourses, he argues that lyric has a way of maintaining a privacy amidst otherness: "Even when speaking of alien things, the poet speaks in his own language," he writes. "To shed light on an alien world, he never resorts to an alien language. . . . Whereas the writer of prose, by contrast—as we shall see—attempts to talk about even his own world in an alien language" (287). Of course, Bakhtin had no recourse to later poetries that would draw on public language in new ways, but the point is that for Brooks the poet's private lyric voice is maintained in and by drawing on other social registers—here, its *difference* from other voices, which frames and implicitly judges them. At first in the recording, this polyphonic quality is introduced through subtle but audible dialect. When reading "Matthew Cole" from *Bronzeville*, the moving portrait of a lonely elderly man living in relative squalor, Brooks adds the first tint of tonal dialect in the final three words, which refer to Cole's childhood family and friends, "the old crowd"—the word "old" drops its /d/ and pops out as black English, appropriate for Cole's inner voice being represented. In "The Sundays of Satin-Legs Smith," Brooks reads in the jaunty, traditional style that contrasts Lee's introductory devices, except that certain places, like the line "and the L / That comes on like a slightly horrible thought" and the word "service" (which is actually in scare quotes in the poem itself), are intoned with drawling irony. "Service," referring to church, resounds with an /e/ so elongated it's comical. In "The Parents," from *Annie Allen*, Brooks laces the ending lines with ironic humor:

> But one by one
> They got things done:
> Watch for porches as you pass
> And prim low fencing pinching in the grass.
>
> Pleasant custards sit behind
> The white Venetian blind.

Reading these stanzas, Brooks bifurcates the poem: while the first two stanzas are read in a traditional, unmarked fashion, these last two are biting, her voice's labile pitch indicating irony. These are the stanzas that offer some "justification" for the parents—the "white" approval of their status as upwardly mobile gentry; thus, "getting things done" is pushed a little into question by Brooks's voice. There is, too, a distinct devilish quality to her tone in these stanzas, one that creates winking complicity in her reader; it might be called "conspiratorial." These are dialogic voicings in which Brooks's physical voice ironizes one set of positions, passing judgment on them, and in this way maintains a singular, private, focused gaze. It's the sound of a person, not a movement.

It should be emphasized here as well that this voice is utterly distinct from the kind of vatic, hortatory, and oratorical style of "The Sermon on the Warpland," which Brooks reads at the end of the record, in which the tone of voice is a constant, nondialogic line addressing a stable and knowing mass. This later voice is far closer to the kind of public persona Lee had in mind. Besides her reading of "Warpland" and "The Wall," as the recording progresses on side B this polyphony gets more developed. In part, this is because some of the poems themselves display more dialogic voices within them, though her reading loosens, and she injects a playfulness not heard earlier. Her voice itself becomes more labile, as when in "The Bean Eaters" she reads the capitalized (and thus "othered") words "Mostly Good" in an extremely lilting pitch, the /ly/ rising high in an almost song-like flight before her voice plummets to thud the word "good." Here, Brooks uses her voice to underscore irony and suggest, along with the capitalized letters in this case, the way the goodness of the humble bean eaters is of a sort thrust upon them, a social judgment the poem is leery of. Two poems in particular, however—"The Lovers of the Poor" and "Riot"—receive a dialogic treatment like no others on the record, pointing toward how much Brooks's poems rely upon a private reflective voice. In "Lovers," about the visit of "The Ladies from the Ladies' Betterment League" to a tenement, the voices of the women actually break in distinctly near the end. In the early lines referring to the poor being funded by the Ladies—"The very very worthy / And beautiful poor. Perhaps just not too swarthy?"—Brooks unctuously drawls "swarthy," as in "not too *swaaaaarthy*"; later, referring to the "nice Art Institute" the Ladies attend "when suitable," Brooks gouges the word "nice" with a sharp nasal twang signifying peeved mockery. The aghast exclamation "Oh, squalor!" is soaked in sarcastic derision. As Bakhtin argues, however, the voice used to ironize the Ladies' exclamations of pity, pride, and surprise isn't an excursion into other social discourses; rather, it's the speaker of the poem controlling how these other voices will sound. It's the capture and quartering of others, not their citation. To be sure, the scripted poem already includes these voices; Brooks's performance simply deepens, enlarges, and gives priority to them. On a record in which Brooks is introduced as a public poet, these readings—which reveal private contemplations of social type—suggest a conspicuous difference.

Brooks's late, great poem "Riot" participates in this same polyphony. The poem's epigraph from Martin Luther King, Jr.—*"A riot is the language of the unheard"*—again links bodies and voice, or "language" in this case. The poem tells the story of John Cabot, a white southern blueblood confronted and ultimately assaulted by a mass of rioting blacks. In the middle of the poem, Cabot's own voice is introduced both by quotation marks and by free indirect discourse, and Brooks again plays the role of Cabot for the listener: "Gross. Gross. '*Que tu es grossier!*'" and "Don't let It touch me! The blackness! Lord!" The poem's final words, spoken by Cabot, are an ironic, racist version of Christ's language—"Lord! / Forgive these nigguhs that know not what they do."—and Brooks suffuses them with simmering bile, using her voice to inform the listener that the wrongness of her words can't possibly be misunderstood. In doing so, Brooks employs a private lyrical stance, buffeted by vocal inflection, in the perspectival judgments these poems make in dialogue form. It's a voice in judgment on others—not a public voice "calling"—and in this perhaps more nuanced fashion, Brooks continues to preserve lyric privacy in the midst of her role as an increasingly public poet. Also, in a fascinating omission from the Caedmon album, the one poem Brooks repeatedly cited as an example of a newish, tavern-ready call to all blacks, her great "public" poem by many measures, isn't here. "The Pool Players" didn't make the cut.

The Guggenheim (1983)

When Brooks says in *Report from Part One* that her "newish voice will not be an imitation of the contemporary young black voice," she's referring to voices like Lee's, which on the Caedmon album actually sound themselves out (183). As a reading at the Guggenheim Museum for the Academy of American Poets on May 3, 1983, attests, Brooks's diversion from the sounds of Lee's voice and other male Black Arts voices is not merely figurative. The most striking aspect of this reading is the way that Brooks has fashioned what might be called her private voice of resistance—a wild idiolect that manages to span her public and private voices. In her extraordinary reading of the "Ballad of Pearl May Lee," for example, Brooks modulates her tone with deep gulfs and gulleys of rich sound, wails or oozes words, and produces what amounts to a sui generis vocal style that's hers alone. In "Pearl May Lee"—a ballad from the perspective of a black woman addressing her dead lover, who was lynched for having sex with a white woman—Brooks's voice is booming and loopy with peaks and valleys of inflection, full of liquids (the word "blacks" gets a particularly embellished treatment, the /l/ sound stretched out luxuriously) and musical phrasing. She virtually screams some lines ("cut my lungs with laughter!"), croons others ("lorner, lorner"), and loads others with such unctuous, sensual repulsion that it's hard not to hear a situated, particularized animus buzzing behind them: "Honey, honey, your taste of pink and white honey," Brooks drawls in the voice of Pearl, mocking and also revealing jealousy over her lover's fatal desire. There are citations of other vocal styles here, too—gospel, a preacher's call-and-response—but her voice is truly uncategorizable and unique, especially in the terms her previous readings have established. The performance itself suggests how much Brooks's voice of protest was spoken by her in a way totally her own, unassimilated into the register echoed by Lee or other black poets, not to mention more long-standing styles of white recitation—all of which she drew upon in previous years. When Brooks prefaces this reading by saying that the poem is "the testimony of a Black woman's heart," the ambiguity of reference in the phrase "Black woman" is crucial—is it a generalized black woman or Brooks herself? In her afterword to *Report from Part Two*, D. H. Melhem describes a reading Brooks gave at City College in 1971: "With meticulous aptness it combined the energy of African drums, the rhythms of Black music, its blues and jazz, the Black sermon, the Anglo-Saxon alliterative poetic, the ballad, and the sonnet, and forged something new" (155). This is precisely what Brooks means by her "newish voice" and "today's G.B. voice." The audience's polite and stunned smattering of applause after this atomic delivery suggests their inability to assimilate and categorize exactly what it was they just heard.

The Guggenheim reading reveals Brooks in her late reading voice, a development and crystallization of her earlier public and private modes, one in which she has reasonably settled the conflict of public and private. The solution seems to be a deepening of division between her poems and her role as a public reader or figure. This reading shows her comfortably assenting to the schism between privacy of lyric expression and publicity of the cause of blackness. This is why Brooks sets up her reading of "The Lovers of the Poor" with the following lengthy preface (in fact, even the increasing length of Brooks's prefatory comments suggests her newfound belief in what poetry readings could do):

> I know how hard it is to sit and listen to a long poem when there's a lot going on around you, or you're wondering if you have on, um, a black sock to go with your navy blue sock. Wondering what you're going to have for dinner if they'll ever let you out so you can get back to your, OK. So I usually leave long poems on the page. Then, when you're at home, privately, you can read, and when you get to line 20, say, you can say to yourself, "That's what she or he meant in line 3!" and bounce back to line 3 and just have a good time all by yourself taking your time. But you can't do that in a beautiful auditorium like this. But I do want to offer you "The Lovers of the Poor." I'm not going to read a poem like "A Bronzeville Mother Loiters in Mississippi. Meanwhile, a Mississippi Mother Burns Bacon," and I'm not going to read you "In the Mecca," which is a half-book poem, so I hope you'll go find those in your library yourselves. (Clifton and Brooks)

Poems are to be consumed in private; performance and publicity, the mark of the new black poetry, limits literary effect. Poetry—here, the experience of receiving poetry—Brooks announces, is still a private affair. This sense of privacy is burnished by Brooks's opening comments as well: "In my *Young Poet's Primer* I have a paragraph: In writing your poem, tell the truth as you know it. Tell your truth. Don't try to sugar it up. Don't force your poem to be nice or proper or normal or happy if it does not want to be. Remember that poetry is life distilled. And that life is not always nice or proper or normal or happy or smooth or even-edged" (Clifton and Brooks). Speaking to an audience of presumed young poets (or, at least, that's the audience assumed by "Primer"), Brooks is sure to locate the animus for poetry in private idiosyncrasy. Being "normal" in this case is ambiguous—is normality cleaving to traditional forms and diction or to the more contemporary sounds of black writing?—but it stands for a kind of acquiescence to a public style. In terms of how poems are read (and written), Brooks's sense of the poem is a moment of private expression—"life distilled," in her oft-repeated formulation. In the seething of "Pearl May Lee," one can hear the mother lode of expressive force to which Brooks refers.

And yet, the Guggenheim reading also showcases Brooks's ease of movement between a private, expressive lyric and the role of public poet to which she had grown accustomed. Like on the Caedmon album, tone and dialogism serve to ironize the hortatory singularity of voice. The first poem she reads is "Primer for Blacks," which is written in Brooks's late rhetorical style, which she prefaces this way:

> I'm going to begin with a poem called "Primer for Blacks." I see a number of blacks before me, and when I see a number of blacks or even one black I like to offer this poem and I like to [laughter, clapping] and I like to introduce it with a paragraph from the work of another poet, a very influential poet named Haki Madhubuti, known to some of you as Don L. Lee. Haki said, "We have bloods who are so heavy that they are now in their postblack period. Will tell you they've been through that black thang. That they were black last year. Or year before that. Can you imagine a white saying he's been through that white thing, that now he's in his postwhite period?" You notice that it's *thang* for blacks and *thing* for whites. (Clifton and Brooks)

By differentiating "*thang*" from "*thing*," Brooks emphasizes the accentual *sound* of blackness in speech, relying on the spoken word to demarcate public identity. Moreover, this preface embodies her idea of the "call" to blacks, as she's literally addressing "a number" of them directly before her—not, it should be said, in a tavern but in this "beautiful auditorium" at the lily-white Guggenheim Museum. In this way, she suggests that her reading is addressed to the work of cultural identity, not poetry. That's for private hours.

The reading of "Primer" is an embodiment of this double-headed style of public and private speech. Here, form and content are at odds—her radical, sui generis idiolect forges privacy from a poem of cultural address. The poem opens with a definition of "blackness" to an audience of black listeners:

> Blackness
> is a title,
> is a preoccupation,
> is a commitment Blacks
> are to comprehend—
> and in which you are
> to perceive your Glory.

These opening lines establish the poem's stance to its audience: it's an address to blacks themselves and a promise for cultural uplift. In this way, the poem is representative of Brooks's late, prophetic style of cultural address. As the poem moves forward, this theme continues. The "you" of the poem is of manifest preoccupation, as in these lines near the end:

> Self-shriveled Blacks.
> Begin with gaunt and marvelous concession:
> YOU are our costume and our fundamental bone.

As a "primer," the poem purports to be a pedagogical précis, teaching a "self-shriveled" public how to claim a fuller identity through racial pride.

And yet Brooks's voice is a contretemps. In the phrase "Blacks / are to comprehend," the tone of voice is disquietingly scolding—the word "comprehend" is read in three distinct syllabic bites, the middle one pitched high. The tone suggests that blacks have *not yet* comprehended their glory. Tonal distantiation continues in the way she mocks a voice of white authority, as in earlier readings. Brooks reads the lines "Blacks here— / Blacks there— / Blacks wherever they may be" with such breathy intensity, it's as if she's both registering excitement about black omnipresence as well as mocking a quivering, racist concern like that of a John Cabot. Yet it's the penultimate line, "Niggeroes and Niggerenes," its double neologism side by side with Brooks's full-blooded, singsong capture of the terms' clever originality, that elicits a big guffaw from the audience and that sits in dialogic contrast to the poem's final word and line: "you." If Brooks is writing a poem of vatic address to the people, her vocal gambit is to extract herself from the very group to which she's speaking. Privacy demands its privacy after all.

BROOKS'S POETRY READINGS capture this tension between private and public expression again and again. While they changed dramatically over the years, Brooks's live or spoken voice dramatized and facilitated her negotiation of public and private identity. This final version of the public poet has shown a kind of mastery over this bifurcated stance. Public figure, along with the ideal of a black subject, has been carefully but comfortably kept distinct from a meditative private poet and poem. Yet the narrative we've come to accept, in a way, about Brooks's shift over her long career from pre- to post-Fisk political consciousness is far less tidy than one would imagine. In fact, we hear in these readings and performances a poet surprisingly consistent in maintaining the line between herself and the movements that surrounded her and gave her so much life and riotous energy.

5

The Disability Poetics of William Carlos Williams and Larry Eigner

Get up and
speak

something   whatever it is

—Larry Eigner, *Collected Poems*

As much as or maybe more than Robert Frost, Charles Olson, or Gwendolyn Brooks, William Carlos Williams sounds the call to ground American poetics in living speech. "Where else," he asks in his manifesto "The Poem as a Field of Action," "can what we are seeking arise from but speech?" (*Essays* 289). Like his modernist compeers—including those addressed earlier in this study, all poets who genuflect in various ways to the spoken voice as source and symbol of lyric genesis—Williams saw in American speech grounds for progressive art. The "movement" of poems, he argues in his introduction to *The Wedge* (1944), is made known "by the character of the speech from which it arises" (*Essays* 256). At times, this entails speech that draws upon ethnic, polyglot, and socially stratified sources, as implied by his famous comment that his poems are derived from "the mouths of Polish mothers" (*Autobiography* 311), and is audible in his many dialect poems. Here is "At the Bar" in its entirety:

> Hi, open up a dozen.
>
> Wha'cha tryin' ta do—
> charge ya batteries?
>
> Make it two.
>
> Easy girl!
> You'll blow a fuse if
> ya keep that up. (*Collected Poems* 1:457)

After reading this poem in rapid-fire staccato at Harvard on December 4, 1951, Williams hits home the obvious point, salted with an awkward conflation of low socioeconomic class and authenticity: "I think that poetry comes out of the language that is spoken on the street." Originality, freshness, and "rare presence" gleaned from "listening to the minutest variations of speech" (*Autobiography* 362)—all were figured as organic, spoken language, and all were embodied by Williams's voice itself: pitched high, reedy, fluid and lithe, clipped and rapid, electric and lean. Williams onstage often sounds like Williams on the page.

What happens, however, when the speaker himself *can't* speak? How does vocal authenticity matter differently to one for whom motor speech has become a challenge? In April 1962 the poet Stanley Koehler trekked to Williams's house in Rutherford, New Jersey, to interview for the *Paris Review* the seventy-nine-year-old master, who by then had suffered three significant strokes and spoke with noticeable difficulty.

> The effort it took the poet to find and pronounce words can hardly be indicated here. Many of the sentences ended in no more than a wave of the hand when Mrs. Williams was not present to finish them. But whatever the topic, the poet's mind kept coming back to the technical matters that interested him in his later years. One of these was his concern with "idiom," the movements of speech that he felt to be especially American, as opposed to English. A rival interest was the "variable foot," a metrical device that was to resolve the conflict between form and freedom in verse.

Koehler captures here an essential linkage: for the older Williams, speech was not simply a figure, it was a problem. It's no coincidence that Koehler's opening remarks referring to the poet's difficulty in pronunciation lead directly to Williams's questions of idiom and metrical form. Far from a "rival interest," I think it was a complementary one: the impingement of physical speech upon the development of verse forms was this newly disabled writer's pressing concern. In the aura of such a struggle, we can see Williams's variable foot and other attention to matters of form as a disabled man's attempt to "correct" his speech impediment and make a bid at normal—that is, "normal"—writing.[1]

As I argue in this chapter, disability poetics from the 1950s—when Williams was first beginning to perform—through the 1970s—in the work of the more significantly and life-long disabled poet Larry Eigner—emerges within a cultural moment of dramatic change, as a politics of postwar normalcy was unraveling but before the full-fledged disability rights movement (DRM) had emerged. Listening in on Williams and Eigner reveals two poets deploying performances of voice to accommodate physical requirements and shape their reception in ways that describe the arc of this shift in sensibility. This act of transforming, or "cripping," poems (a term discussed below) portrays two poets at odds with 1960s readerly conventions of presence, though they achieve it, at times, in the gaps between scripted and performed poems. Williams struggles against his disability, an increasingly severe form of aphasia, transforming his live readings into contests between the poem as written and his own troubled mouth. For the late Williams, speech pathology is something to overcome, and normalcy—ironically, for this experimental modernist—something of an achievement. In this way, Williams's difficulty in speaking masks an authentically cracked-up voice, one that is "corrected" as best Williams can manage, through both his audible efforts at standard articulation and his formal organization of the poem itself. This all gets crystallized in his important late long poem "The Desert Music," which I read as a performance poem that accommodates a newly problematized voice. For the late Williams, the body is a site not of physical presence but of increasing simulation, and the "real" is audible in the vocal cracks and fissures, hidden and normalized to the reader's best ability.

For Larry Eigner, who lived with cerebral palsy and spoke with noticeable difficulty, disability actually shades into the performance of reading itself, smudging and smearing the careful work of his poems' graphic arrangement on the page and revealing a physical presence through the spoken voice. Beginning in the early 1970s, Eigner began his career as a reader and in 1974 produced a cassette recording of himself reading short poems. This tape, particularly in distinction from the public readings he gave prior to it, asks us to reevaluate Eigner's status as a typographical poet of the page and in so doing to see his performance of disability on tape as an allowance of nonstandard speech and a recognition of bodily presence. Eigner at the microphone performs a somatic immediacy that has been virtually scrubbed from his reception, even by those acolyte critics who champion his work and call for such embodiment. Eigner's lyric cripping also occurred at the outset of the early DRM, with which he eventually merged geographically in his relocation to Berkeley, crucible of the DRM itself. While neither poet fully engages in disability identity consciousness, to recognize Eigner's—and, to an extent, Williams's—performances is to push the timeline of crip poetics back a number of years and to focus it not on questions of identity but on lyric itself.

In the larger terms of this study, disabled reading torques the humanist-skeptical dialectic. Williams reading onstage performs as a (failed) simulation of a "normal" humanist reader. The naturalness and unmediated presence required of humanist reading is compromised by the struggles of a nonstandard, physically altered voice that now must strain to achieve what sounds like effortless or vital tone. For Eigner, reading aloud "untypes" his poems, which were generated by slowly, methodically punching the typewriter keys with his right index finger, creating humanist effects not by earnest speech but by ironic distance between speech and writing. Difficult to render back into the standard and recognizable sounds of American English, Eigner's voice translates into aural fumes the very thing the poems' written forms seemed to promise—the presence of a life lived as a disabled man. Both poets speak in relationship to a perceived standard of normalcy, and, reading aloud, both Williams and Eigner limn the poles of nonstandard, "normal" speech to reveal the ways the idiosyncratic voice can upset expectations of normalcy and produce as a result new forms of presence. Onto the stage of 1960s reading wanders Williams, performing a new poetics of disability consciousness without knowing it. And to a booming scene of poetry in performance, Eigner speaks back to unsettle its certainties.

Finally, by reading the disabled poetry reading, this chapter establishes new vistas in terms of poetry read aloud. The preceding arguments in this book have relied upon the assumption of a standard, unimpaired body onstage (though I've also shown how susceptible performance is to even the inevitable human debilitations, like age in Frost's recitation at Kennedy's inaugural). A disability perspective reveals new vantages from which to consider poetry reading and the body. For Eigner, performances often *killed* presence because of the ways in which his poetry was managed and contained by the reading apparatus, which included typed poems projected on screens or other such "aids." In this way, readings limited possibilities of immediacy other sixties readers courted and won. For Williams, vocal disability led to a struggle for the presence of adequate, or "normal," reading and was ultimately simulated rather than fully achieved. By examining Williams and Eigner as performers, we see how much sixties reading assumed ability and eschewed disability and how a culture of spontaneous transmission couldn't accommodate difference of this kind. How might we listen differently to poets of disability than we do poets of ability? What about poets of advanced age, with faltering voice and vision? What are the consequences of voice-restricting effects like aphasia on readings by Williams but also on figures like William Meredith, who read with the help of supportive friends and colleagues and in a shaky, moving bid at articulation?[2] How do we "listen" to Deaf performers differently, whether they speak aloud or sign or project images of their poems as they read, or all three? What of blind poets who recite from memory? Poets who roll to the lectern in a wheelchair or walk with the aid of crutches or braces? In short, how do these circumstances change the reception of the poems the readers perform? How do they affect the presence generated by the reading, and to what extent do they work in concert with the written, textualized, scripted poems being articulated? Such questions ground and hover above the following discussions.

Lyric Cripping

The term "cripping" (or "crippin'") has a complexity of meaning surprising for its young life. As it's typically used, to crip is to transform language, or signs of disability, in ways that reveal the ideology of able-bodiedness that underwrites them. In my own use, the term "lyric cripping" refers to ways in which poetic language is spoken in concert with text to unsettle received or expected possibilities of meaning. Cripped poetic language is a performance in breath that acknowledges and challenges unthinking normalcy by establishing a double voice, speech itself, to ironize print and reveal its distance from the body that produced it. This can occur in terms of form (e.g., cripping a line to accommodate vocal necessity) and also representation (e.g., cripping a trope or received image of disability). In either case, lyric cripping functions by attenuating the distance between print and performance to reveal the ways in which the body and the line are mutually constituted. As I demonstrate below, when Larry Eigner speaks his poems aloud, their textual, scripted precursors (which some argue are already cripped in formal and spatial terms) are refracted and doubled-up and ironized. The phenomenological voice itself is thus crucial to lyric cripping, which relies on the work of comparison to achieve its effects, which are to transform a poem's embodiment in print into a relationship between print and voice.

In disability studies more generally, cripping has come to refer to the establishment of an identity position in response to categories of "normalcy" that assume its inherent difference. While my focus is on language and lyric, in critical discourse at large, to crip is both to reveal the falsely naturalized distinctions between ability and disability and to articulate self-descriptions that avoid the typical limitations and sorrows ascribed to nonstandard bodies. For this reason, Michael Davidson describes cripping as "an oppositional critique of bodily normalcy" (*Concerto* 4), in which the typically marginalized disabled body is revealed not as a medically defined object but as a more or less arbitrarily demarcated *other*. Because the disabled body has been used so often to establish through opposition norms of physical (and moral) perfection, the cripper has lots of material to work with. Upending easy associations between disability and inability (or misery, or death, or moral turpitude—choose your negative) constitutes the bread-and-butter jobbing of the crip practitioner. Literary history is rife with representations of disability that construe legless, blind, hunchbacked, impotent, insane, and dwarfed bodies that help establish what the critic Rosemarie Garland-Thomson calls, recognizing the constructed nature of disability's literary representations, the "artificial category" of disability in literature (*Extraordinary* 13). When a poet or a poem gets cripped, he, she, or it is alienated in the Brechtian sense, the "disability" itself evading a prefigured category of reception like *tragic* or its sunny obverse, *uplifting*.

While my focus is on the cripping of language and lyric form, typically the emphasis in crip studies is on questions of identity. Even Jim Ferris, the former president of the Society for Disability Studies who wrote a seminal essay on crip poetry, refers to cripping in terms of identity, arguing that "[o]ne of the major impulses of crip poetry is to resist stereotyping and the limits of the socially imposed 'handicapped' identity through a process of self-definition." Ferris coined the term "crip poetry" in 2007 to crystallize such an alternative, one "centered in the experience of being out of the ordinary," and he argues that disabled poets need to produce self-representations, articulate their own alternative physical and cognitive experiences. For this reason the crip theorist prizes *transformation*, "the possibility, the edgy potential, the openness and even likelihood of transformation" gained from cripping (Ferris). Robert McRuer, who has written one of the central, recent crip treatises, describes the ways cripping is about "collectively transforming" (32) a culture of able-bodied hegemony. As I'll demonstrate later in more detail, crip studies of poetry has emphasized such questions of identity at the expense of what might be called more purely literary concerns.[3]

But why am I claiming that the poetry reading itself is so important to lyric cripping? Because disability is often (though certainly not always) visible on the body, performance itself is crucial to crip studies in general. If the crip experience is marginalized, silenced, or conceptualized into muffling categories, the body and the voice—which are the origins of crip experience—can ably break through such static in reliable fashion. Disabled artists and memoirists often describe the performances of disability not only onstage but in "everyday life," to cite Erving Goffman's phrase. Simply getting on a bus, for the disabled playwright John Belluso, resembles stepping before an audience.[4] This "theatricality of disability," as Carrie Sandahl and Philip Auslander term it, is a fundamental aspect of its experience, which is essentially and diurnally performative (5): performance produces occasions of rupture, with live bodies tripping up a priori categories. While the discipline of performance studies itself troubles the boundary separating authorized and everyday sites of performance (as described in chapter 1), this chapter focuses on intentional performances of disability, those in which poets with limitations on their speech deliberately put their voices front and center.

Voices, in fact, are important. Much has been made of visuality in disability studies just as voice has been silenced. Michael Davidson traces the way "scopic regimes" of power survey the body in Western culture in service of the "master narrative of normalcy" (*Concerto* 18). The medical gaze, as Foucault describes it, "naturalizes" bodies, and Goffman's definition of social stigma traces that phenomenon to a somatic origin (18). Garland-Thomson describes a process of "beholding," which she calls an alternative to "staring," itself the discomfiting and asymmetrical gaze directed toward and interpellating a disabled person's physical appearance ("Beholding" 204). For Garland-Thomson, beholding establishes a "visual activism" in which disabled performers (both aesthetic and everyday) might construct a "visual politics of deliberatively structured self-disclosure" (204) and assert the agency of the performer to be beheld, sidelining the stare and the gaze and foregrounding the subject's own agency in self-representation. This kind of performative judo, based on vision and sight, stands at the core of the disability and performance nexus: once subject to the stares of others, the body now "stares back," as the title of Kenny Fries's influential anthology of poetry—*Staring Back*—written by disabled poets (including Eigner) would have it. Thus visibility, typically freighted with judgments and preconceptions, is understandably the primary concern of writers on disability and performance.

Yet what about voice? What about speech? Visuality's runt cousin, aurality, receives less critical attention than the body and its consumption by visual means. For poetry in performance, however, the putative content is primarily audiographic, notwithstanding the obvious importance of a poet's appearance, dress, and physical bearing. In her essay "Delivering Disability, Willing Speech," Brenda Jo Brueggemann argues that performances in which disabled speakers—including Deaf performers and those with "speech idiosyncrasies" (17)—speak in concert with able-voiced speakers (or "interpreters"), as well as signers in ASL and graphic writing itself, show that "no man is a rhetorical island" (22).[5] By destabilizing the "myth of the great individual speaker," Brueggemann posits that such performances countermand the long history of rhetoric itself, which is founded on the fundamental paradigm of normalcy that writers like Davis are so careful to revise (23). In terms of rhetoric, "[m]ost important to the delivery of speech was the energy and propriety of the orator's performance," which must "perform 'normalcy' even as it incites and inspires some difference (otherwise, we would not be moved by, or remember, it)" (20). Disabled speech, on the other hand, "can critique—can revise and reinvigorate and rehabilitate—the system of 'normalcy'" by showing its essential constructedness (20). It's just this conflict and distance—between the posited normalcy of spoken language and the way disabled speech challenges its conventions—that tells us something important is happening when readers with speech idiosyncrasies (I hereby pilfer the term) stride, limp, or wheel to the podium microphone. This is what both Williams and Eigner in their own ways do.

Williams's Mouth and the Achievement of Normalcy

"On June 18," Williams wrote to Louis Martz in 1951, "I shall read a new 17-page poem at Harvard for the Phi Beta Kappa ceremonial at the Sanders Theatre. It is an important event for me. Since my illness I have been working on it. . . . I feel that many of my culminating ideas as to form have entered into this poem" (*Letters* 300). Williams not only read his new long poem "The Desert Music" onstage at Harvard that year; in fact, he wrote it for the occasion of the reading itself. "The Desert Music" was the first major work to address Williams's new conditions of physical impairment—and to do so with performance in mind. As would happen increasingly over the next decade, Williams's poems were inflected with the promise of performance to come, and in some important ways, they worked in concert with it. As his body suffered repeated strokes (he had three major strokes—in 1951, 1952, and 1958—and then a series of TIAs, or "mini-strokes," into his final years), he also slipped into periodic depressions, one so severe he required inpatient treatment at Hillside Hospital in Queens (Leibowitz 420). A heart attack preceded these strokes, and aphasia, developing from mild to acute, followed them. Walking up to a lectern and reading his poems, both new and very old, and often to a growing audience of acolytes and followers, Williams confronted a paradoxical situation: on the one hand, his newly disabled reading—with which he struggled more and more throughout the 1950s and early 1960s—created an extraordinary quality of presence and immediacy; as he stumbled through poems, sometimes straining with the effort, the effect superseded any kind of spoken authenticity (not to mention the effects the poems themselves might engender). His impairment, that is, accelerated presence. And yet on the other hand, unlike Ginsberg, who wished to initiate "transmission" and immediacy, Williams strove to represent the poem in its disembodied, pure state—to *normalize* it by cleansing it of vocalized and spoken abnormalities. This impulse stands at suggestive odds with his lifelong claims to the naturalness of "speech" as a source for poetry. Presence was now obstructing the poems' original sound. Garland-Thomson makes the point that if the disabled "pursue normalization too much," they "may edge into the self-betrayal associated with 'passing'" (*Extraordinary* 13). Never a poet of disability consciousness, and entirely unconcerned with the politics of disability, Williams might be seen as seeking (and failing) to pass as his normal old self.

This ideal of normalcy for the late Williams readings clashes with some received ideas about the poet's appearances later in life. Norman Finkelstein says that the Phi Beta Kappa reading produced in Williams "anxiety" and "revolutionary fervor": anxiety at "facing those who were synonymous for him with the academy and more especially with the camp of Eliot (one of Harvard's most famous sons)"; and fervor at performing "his own rebellious strip in church, singing about—of all things—a whore in a cheap Mexican joint," as "The Desert Music" does indeed refer to such a figure (274). By this account Williams is still in the 1950s thumbing his nose at Eliotic modernism, and the "whore in a cheap Mexican joint" is a defiant image of proprietary insurrection. Williams's biographer Paul Mariani similarly frames this important reading in terms of Harvard's institutional grandiosity, noting that Williams himself referred to the "semi-ecclesiastic" university setting in a letter to Louis Zukofsky (635). Certainly there is truth in such accounts, though I'll demonstrate that these analyses privilege questions about Williams's literary identity over his more recent health and speaking problems. In fact, the poem and its performance concern the establishment of Williams's own poetic agency, scapegoat his physical disarray by projecting it upon others, and articulate a formal means to accommodate his newly troubled lips, tongue, and mouth.

Though he is not typically seen as an important reader or performer, Williams is in fact a very useful figure for tracing the rise of poetry readings at American universities directly after the war. His reaction to them captures, in its surprise and excitement, their newness. Williams's *Autobiography*, first published in 1951, the year of his first stroke, describes his early invitations to read at universities, the sheer number of which he found cause to proudly list—"Dartmouth, Pennsylvania State College, Cooper Union, Vassar, Mt.

Holyoke, Buffalo, Middlebury, Harvard, N.Y.U., Bard, Brandeis, Salt Lake City, Puerto Rico all invited me" (309)—and his unschooled, amateurish perspective on them. His description of a reading at Penn State shows him learning on the spot that readings required preparation rather than simply winging it: "I remember that talk (it was one of my first): for the first fifteen minutes of it I heard myself discoursing pleasantly, but what I was talking about was not at all what I had intended to say. At that moment my wits returned. It was a valuable experience. I found that from then on I should never be at a loss for words" (310). As time goes on, he acclimates to what he calls the "strange experience" of giving readings and describes a particularly successful reading at UCLA:

> I hadn't prepared a damn thing. "The first thing to do in hearing poems is not to try to understand them at the start at least, but to listen. The arts are sensual in their intention to impress. Let the poem come to you. Put all you have into trying to hear the poem, hear it. Otherwise, how can you know it is a poem? Later, perhaps, if you are superlatively able and perspicacious you may discover what it means"—or something like that. They took it in complete silence. So I read, and talked and talked between what I read. You could have heard a feather fly. Once or twice they laughed, heartily. I surely felt no restraint. Then I quit. They almost took the roof off: there was no temple mood to that crowd. It brought the blood to my head. (*Autobiography* 386–87)

What's notable here is that Williams describes this event at all; it may sound rather conventional now, though we can hear the bravura inherent in his lack of preparation, the studied indifference ("or something like that"), and the stirring effects of what was clearly an entirely new experience for this book-bound writer. Perhaps most importantly, Williams can be heard celebrating a kind of unscripted, improvisatory style. It's this ease and faith in the ability of audiences simply to "listen" unimpeded by vocal stumblings that would undergo a shift in readings to come.

It is perhaps coincidental but in no ways incidental that Williams's "cascade" of readings, as a different biographer puts it, roughly coincided with Williams's physical decline (Leibowitz 405). It's hard not to hear behind his ambitions for the reading a sense of Williams's own need to reflect back on his poetic history, as well as develop his capacities as an able showman. In a letter to Wallace Stevens, he describes his disappointment when the first stroke keeps him from a new experiment in performance he was going to undertake at Bard College: "I had planned to do a daring thing, I was going to speak extempore, taking a chance on the result. I had never done that before for a whole hour. I was a little scared but that only whetted my appetite" (296). Reading had become for Williams a forum for articulating his literary principles, and his actual speaking voice—"speech" long being Williams's trope for what lay behind the line, and now wavering in its ability to simply speak itself out—served as proxy for the poem's vitality. A 1955 reading at Berkeley captures this phenomenon. Williams's voice in this recording is halting and awkward. He stumbles over longer words and phrases and sometimes simply slows down his pacing to accommodate a polysyllabic line. Here and there, difficulty simply articulating certain words is clearly apparent, as is his desire to achieve verbally what the text of the poem silently promises. "This should be read rapidly," he explains before reading "To a Mexican Pig-Bank," from his book *An Early Martyr and Other Poems* (1935). "And since I'm not able to read as rapidly as I like, uh, I'll read as I can." At first, he picks his way carefully through the tiny couplets of just three to five syllables, pausing and halting as the words come trickling slowly. It's not a confident reading, but he's managing. Soon, however, he stumbles over the phrase

at the
    top—

Hair-pin
    wires

hold up the
    sheep

and misreads the description of the pig's "green / ears" by calling them "pink." Stammering, emitting tiny puffs of frustration, Williams is clearly stymied by his inability to simply "read rapidly," as he had hoped, and at the end of the performance he gasps an audible "sheesh!" It's affecting, and the audience's dead silence is palpable. But then, without warning, he starts up again, saying, "I want to get"—and then just barrels into reading the poem a second time, more quickly now, and with more fluid success. His voice is still wooden, and he noticeably strains with effort and concentration, but he gets all the way through more quickly and with no mistakes.

Such displays of normal fluidity and verbal dexterity are also on exhibit during his reading of his poem "The Dance," a poem that he read often after his stroke. The poem itself—and dancing as a more general trope for the strength and vitality of poetic language—is a touchstone at readings for Williams. Again at Berkeley in 1955, he begins reading "The Dance" very slowly and carefully, though he soon mistakes the word "bugle" in line 4 for "tweedle," a word that appears earlier in the line, and laughs awkwardly at his mistake. Then he struggles over the somewhat tortuous lines "to bear up under such / rollicking measures, prance as they dance / in Brueghel's great picture, The Kermess," fumbling through the crowded line. The crowd laughs and lustily applauds, partly, it seems, at the poem's fantastic rhythms, though certainly a good portion of their applause derives from his adequately accomplishing the lingual acrobatics these rhythmic, thumping lines demand. "If you pardon me, I'll loosen my tie," Williams says before reading "The Dance" at UCLA on November 15, 1950, just prior to his first stroke. It's an indication, perhaps, that this poem required something like physical dexterity and looseness, and he reads the lines with a deliberative precision and finesse absent from the Berkeley reading. An even earlier recording of this poem, captured on an album titled *Pleasure Dome: An Audible Anthology of Modern Poetry Read by Its Creators* (Columbia Records, 1949), reveals a confident, robust Williams intoning the poem with almost stentorian force (unusual even for him and his lanky, nasal timbre). The poem's thudding iambics (rare for Williams, of course; he prefaces his Berkeley reading by referring to them as the "rhythms of the classroom") are emphasized in his performance, suggesting the poem's own rhythmic argument, which equates Brueghel's peasants with the lines that translate their movements into a mimetic syntax, the dancers' own "rollicking measures." Now struggling to enliven those vital lines with physical presence, his failure to do so is poignant.

These moments in reading show that Williams's career as a reader coincides with his nonstandardized mouth and that these two things bear upon each other. The poetry reading had become a stage upon which to prove his and his work's vitality, presence, and relevance. For this reason, many of these readings are built around a narrative of his poetry's historical development, as if he is making a case for his literary fame and legacy and seeking to educate his audience in the modernist aesthetics he helped develop. The Berkeley reading showcases this, referring repeatedly to the past in a retrospective and nostalgic gaze. After reading "The Pot of Flowers," he says: "There again, it is a, when it was written twenty-five years ago, it was very revolutionary for a poem. Because it said nothing but presented what it had to say. It was an imagistic poem. And the imagists were not too well thought of. All these poems written twenty-five years ago were received by the, the schools in absolute silence [laughter]. Uh, we had no reactions at all to what we were writing. Uh, they were not considered poems. Uh, and they were treated as if they were not." Onstage, Williams's reference to "absolute silence" at the imagism he clearly felt was in need of some kind of historical framing cannily provokes an audible response from the audience—laughter. This homily further implies a narrative of success: *they couldn't hear what you clearly can because you're sitting here, listening to me.* The reading transforms the moment of reading and listening into an act confirming both the poet's and the audience's perspicacious good judgment and cultural relevance. Williams's efforts here are to override any glimmer of physical eclipse—a glimmer that was audible, in fact, in the very voice arguing it down—that might signify a loss of lyric potency.

The key poem in this discussion is "The Desert Music" itself, which along with "Asphodel" was one of Williams's two major late poems. Williams typically referred to it as his "fifteen-minute poem" or his "seventeen-page poem," seizing upon Harvard's request in terms of length and time as a way to suggest the performative stamina the poem demanded. It was important to him as a return to his full force as a writer in terms of its function both as a late career *ars poetica* but also as a living example of his life and liveliness. Earlier in the letter to Louis Martz, in which he discusses "The Desert Music," he sums up his feelings about his need, in the wake of his stroke and disability—"most have put me down for a rough sort of blindman," he writes, figuring himself as physically compromised (*Letters* 299)—to make some kind of literary summation: "As a result of the enforced idleness and opportunity for thought, it may be, I have brought hard down on the facts of a situation which can no longer be delayed in the bringing of it to a final summary. I must now, in other words, make myself clear. I must gather together the stray ends of what I have been thinking and make my full statement as to their meaning or quit" (298). This "summary" concerns metrical and technical matters. In the same letter he writes, "Verse form, the actual shape of the line itself, must be as it is the first visible thing" (299).

This explicit link between physical disability and Williams's turn toward the three-step, or "triadic," line has been suggested before, though never within the actual context of performance.[6] Actually listening to Williams perform his late poems reveals the nexus between reading and performance, a link he makes quite explicit himself. Reading at Harvard in 1951, Williams urges his audience to experience the auditory poem rather than the textual one: "Don't attempt to understand the modern poem. *Listen* to it. And it should be *heard*. It's very difficult sometimes to get it off the page. But once you hear it, then you should be able to appraise it. In other words [very long pause], if it ain't a pleasure, it ain't a poem [laughter from the audience]." This is a surprising directive for a poet who only that year was describing his interest in live reading for the first time. Here, Williams suggests that the actual live reading of a poem precedes intellection, judgment, appraisal, analysis; an act of "pleasure," reading is suddenly an entrée to modernist poetics. On the one hand, it's not surprising, as Williams had long championed "speech"; yet on the other, this literal situation was entirely novel.

And though it's never been seen as such, *The Desert Music* itself is Williams's great book on disability. There are figures of disability in all but one of the book's poems, and, surprisingly, most are fortunate in their predicaments. The first poem, "The Descent" (originally a portion of *Paterson III*), chronicles the body's decline, as well as the unsuspected profits that might be wrung from it: "No defeat is made up entirely of defeat—since / the world it opens is always a place / formerly / unsuspected" (*Collected Poems* 2:245). The next poem, "To Daphne and Virginia," refers to Williams's family history of speech pathology (referenced in his *Autobiography*) but also to his recent difficulties with and overcoming of verbal articulation, albeit obliquely: "In our family we stammer unless, / half mad, / we come to speech at last // And I am not / a young man" (2:248). Typical for Williams, a lopsided but decidedly charming creature—here, "a heavy goose / who waddles, slipping / noisily in the mud of / his pool" (2:250)—stands in for the poet's own stroke-knocked body. "To a Dog Injured in the Street" is perhaps less sanguine and catalogs the poet's encounters with a number of wounded or dead animals, identifying with each—"It is myself, / not the poor beast lying there / yelping with pain / that brings me to myself with a start" (2:255)—and ending with a self-canceling refusal to grant legitimacy to the compromised voice: "The cries of a dying dog / are to be blotted out / as best I can" (2:257). Still, this list of the broken, mutilated, physically compromised, disabled, and diseased goes on and on, often with redemptive possibilities. The "crooked flower" (2:257) with the "deformed stem" (2:258) from the poem "The Yellow Flower" leaves the speaker "openmouthed," staring at the "twisted petals" (2:258) in a trance of identification. "Without the quirks / and oddnesses of invention / the paralytic is confirmed / in his paralysis," writes Williams in "Deep Religious Faith," a polemic poem urging a link between faith and a creative energy that can produce El Greco's "distorted saints" (2:262). "The Mental Hospital Garden" revisits Williams's old mise-en-scène of the hospital, with the young people "careless / under license of the disease" (2:265). In "The Artist," a man executes an agile entrechat for the poet's mother, providing another figure of a leaping dancer; in this poem, however, the mother sits "in her invalid's chair" and, unlike the poet himself, is rendered "speechless"—a word that references Williams's own struggles with speech in this late book (2:268). I say these figures are "surprisingly" fortunate in their disabilities because in Williams's writing, figures of disability had until this time typically been either pitiful or grotesque. From *The Doctor Stories* alone there is Jean Beicke, a physically deformed infant (2:72), the "peculiarly bowed" legs of the wife in "A Face of Stone" (2:85), and the preponderance of children with "psychoneurotic symptoms" in "The Insane" (2:105). *Spring and All* includes "To Elsie's" "deaf-mutes" (1:217) and the "old / jaundiced woman / rolling her / saffron eyeballs" (1:216), along with the ill legions implied by the "contagious hospital" cited in the volume's opening poem (1:183). *The Desert Music* seizes on the disabled figure for all but one of its poems, and with peculiarly redemptive force.[7]

"The Desert Music" itself is a performance poem that both acknowledges and attempts to normalize physical limitations literally inscribed on Williams's own body. As I demonstrate below, the poem's construction, which moves graphically and syntactically in short bursts of form, is particularly accommodating to the disabled mouth and, read in terms of performance, an example of Williams's lyric cripping. The poem describes a trip Williams and his wife, Floss, took from El Paso to Juárez in the company of friends when he was in the Southwest. It opens in medias res with Williams's figure for linguistic energy—dancing—before shifting to the body of a twisted, deformed human shape:

> —the dance begins: to end about a form
> propped motionless—on the bridge
> between Juárez and El Paso—unrecognizable
> in the semi-dark
>
> Wait!
>
> The others waited while you inspected it,
> on the very walk itself
>
> Is it alive?
>
> —neither a head,
> legs nor arms! (*Collected Poems* 2:273)

This decrepit figure recurs throughout the poem, an image of a body wrecked beyond sensible apprehension of form. Set dialectically against this figure is the "dance," a favored image of physical strength but also here, along with the motif of "music," an emblem of the poet's communication with a larger, Gnostic meaning. In this way the poem proposes a kind of struggle between disabled and fluid bodies: the "form" here, the body itself, is an "inhuman shapelessness" and "Egg-shaped" (*Collected Poems* 2:274); it is indeterminately gendered ("—it looks too small for a man. / A woman. Or a very shriveled old man."); and it serves as a grotesque reversion to a fetal blob—"a birth of awful promise" (2:284). Even the bodies of street children in "The Desert Music" are flawed, as in the begging boy with "obscene fingers" (2:276). These two figures—the warped, compromised body and the dance—merge and combine in the figure of the "worn-out trouper from / the States" (2:279), a stripper in a Juárez dive bar. Though she is "worn-out" she somehow locates for Williams the source of the music:

> What in the form of an old whore in
> a cheap Mexican joint in Juárez, her bare
> can waggling crazily can be

so refreshing to me, raise to my ear
so sweet a tune, built of such slime? (*Collected Poems* 2:281)

Here, the flailing, failing female body offers in its sleazy unction a second figure of physical decay. Both are sanctified by their brokenness, emblems of deformity. By the end of the poem, the original, contorted figure on the bridge reappears to bookend the narrative, further dehumanized by the wider range of figurative description:

shapeless or rather returned
to its original shape, armless, legless,
headless, packed like the pit of a fruit into
that obscure corner—or
a fish to swim against the stream—or
a child in the womb prepared to imitate life. (*Collected Poems* 2:284)

The achievement of the poet is to hear the "music of survival" (*Collected Poems* 2:275), as he puts it earlier, and speak it out as the poem. The poem ends:

Now it is all
about me. The dance! The verb detaches itself
seeking to become articulate

And I could not help thinking
of the wonders of the brain that
hears that music and of our
skill sometimes to record it. (*Collected Poems* 2:284).

The dance here becomes a linguistic one: to "articulate" actual words, of course, was the purpose of this poem, which marked his return to poetry and to speaking onstage; thus, we get the quasi-medical language of "the wonders of the brain," which had so recently bounced back from physical trauma. Written for an actual performance, too, the poem's penultimate word, "record," tacitly acknowledges the tape recorder that would be (and we now know was) onstage at the Phi Beta Kappa reading, recording Williams's lyric tuning of the music of survival.

Garland-Thomson argues that disabled figures that serve as representations in literary texts typically use "the monstrous body to demarcate the borders of the generic" and "the pathological to give form to the normal" (*Extraordinary* 20). Moreover, typically this body is female (20). As a "symbol of otherness," the disabled female figure can normalize the narrative perspective demarcating as such or figures within the representational text as well (29). "The Desert Music" deploys a similar tactic: Williams scapegoats the "shapeless" and possibly feminine form and the old stripper, thereby reserving for himself a standard, "normal" perspective. One of the poem's refrains is, in fact, that only the poem—the "counted poem" (*Collected Poems* 2:274) and the "made poem" (2:275)—can capture the music, and the poem's penultimate declaration is of Williams's own poetic identity: "I *am* a poet! I / am. I am. I am a poet, I reaffirmed, ashamed" (2:284). In this way, the poem is itself an effort at identity by the deployment of exclusionary categories; being a poet is necessarily not being a grotesque; to hear the "music" of reality, something must be "made," sturdy and well, not broken or deformed. This bid at normalcy is eventually treated literally: when a man approaches Williams and his wife and friends sitting at a table in the Mexican joint, he says, swaggeringly, "So this is William / Carlos Williams, the poet," while Williams depicts his little crew as engaged in the deliberately mundane activity of consuming lettuce salads. The man picks up on this, remarking—in the poem's most understated moment of overstatement—"You seem quite normal" (2:282). *Seeming* but not *being* normal is achieved by the distinction between the able-bodied Williams, as seen and judged by another, and the can-waggling strip-teaser and decrepit form on the bridge, both figurations of abnormality. Drawing on Goffman's notion of "stigma," Garland-Thomson argues that such stigmatization "legitimates the status quo, naturalizes attributions of inherent inferiority and superiority," and "obscures the socially constructed quality of both categories" (*Extraordinary* 31). By casting others as disabled and compromised, Williams normalizes himself, drawing upon the larger categories of social order implied by the broken bodies he describes. And by normalizing, he passes—or at least tries to.

It's not incidental that the word "form" appears in the first line of the poem and in conjunction with the crippled figure on the bridge. Yet Williams's engagement with the normalization of speech pathology goes deeper than simply representation, as Garland-Thomson would have it. In fact, one can view the entire project of the triadic line, and what Olson called the "composition by field" in which "The Desert Music" is written, much in the same way as a ramp assists a person in a wheelchair or a back brace "corrects" a twisted spine: by accommodating the breath in a new representational form, the poem's physical spread accommodates the poet, or "he whose brains / are scattered / aimlessly" (*Collected Poems* 2:282). In the 1962 Koehler interview in the *Paris Review* cited at the opening of this chapter, referring to "The Descent"—by Williams's own account, the first poem to employ the three-step line—Williams emphasizes the link between voice and "measure": "I wanted to say something in a certain tone of my voice which would be exactly how I wanted to say it, to measure it in a certain way." This may sound like a repetition of earlier associations between speech and poetic idiom, but in the context of this interview, the connotations are much more precise—the poem's formal measure is strictly tied to the body that produces it and that will reproduce it aloud. "The measure," he says in the same interview, "is what you encounter on the page. As it was with the Sappho. The measure must be transferred to the page from the lips of the, of the poem, of the poet." In "On Measure—Statement for Cid Corman," written in 1954—just as he was publishing "The Desert Music"—a vivid image of a disabled mouth characterizes a misguided return to old measures: "We must invent new modes to take the place of those which are worn out. For want of this we have gone back to worn-out modes with our tongues hanging out and our mouths drooling after 'beauty' which is not even in the same category under which we are seeking it" (*Essays* 339). Considering its timing, the metaphor is striking: "drooling" mouths with "tongues hanging out" are mouths that seek to articulate language in old forms; the implication is that measure itself springs from the requirements of literary speech. We've already heard Williams struggling through a reading of "To a Mexican Pig-Bank," striving to mouth the measures with his tongue literally hanging out, drooling after old beauties. To what extent does the triadic line, which is the measure for all the poems in *The Desert Music*, along with the scattershot composition by field of the title poem, reflect this new physical, *performative* requirement? To what extent is it an accommodating brace? A wheelchair for the voice?

In one way, this is an old question in the critical canon on Williams's poetry, well summarized by Eleanor Berry:

> The variable foot has been taken as (1) a temporal unit, each step of a triadic line being equal in duration to every other (Donoghue, Weatherhead, Breslin); (2) a stress-based unit, each step of a triadic line containing a single major stress (Duncan, Hedges); (3) a syntactical unit, each step of a triadic line being a single complete phrase or clause (Solt, Hofstadter); (4) a unit of meaning or attention (Goodman, Jofstadter); (5) a unit of phrasing in reading, the triadic lineation constituting a score for performance (Wagner); and (6) a visual unit (Shapiro, Perloff, Sayre, Cushman). Each of these interpretations had made its appearance by 1969. ("Triadic-Line" 364)

Each attempt to make sense of these lines has its value, though only one mentioned here considers the performative aspect of the form. More recently, Michael Davidson wonders to what extent Williams's stepped foot was "a typographical response to speech disorders resulting from a series of strokes," smartly making the crucial link between disability and form, though Davidson doesn't pursue this point (*Concerto* 119). Furthermore, I'm arguing that this is not a mere "typographical response" but an accommodative corrective to a problem with speech itself. Answering this question is crucial: if the poems in *The Desert Music* reflect Williams's newly "scattered brains," then they're merely mimetic—a "typographical response," as Davidson would have it. Yet if they serve as an accommodation to an aphasiatic voice, they function as structures of accessibility, those verbal wheelchairs. The disability rights activist Harriet McBryde Johnson describes removing her back brace and letting her spine deform into "its own natural shape." Since that time, she says, she's been "entirely comfortable" (574). In this way, formal mechanisms devised poststroke might show us Williams accommodating his new physical limitations with the prosodic equivalents, letting his lines turn and twist as they will for greater vocal and visual comfort.

Actually listening in on the Harvard Phi Beta Kappa reading of "The Desert Music" shows how much the performance was guided by the speaking voice. The lines themselves provide this accommodating formal measure, audible as Williams reads the opening slowly, closely tracing with his voice the phrases' graphic layout; this happens, generally speaking and with some exceptions, throughout the poem. His voice is clear though weak, struggling gingerly through words like "interjurisdictional," almost as if he had set himself a performative challenge and just barely passed. The three-step lines that appear create the necessary pace for breathing and visual shifting that his voice clearly tracks. Further, the poem is provided with what might be called resting places: declarative, summative refrains posted throughout the poem, such as "How shall we get said what must be said? // Only the poem. // Only the counted poem, to an exact measure" (*Collected Poems* 2:274). These lines, in various versions, are both grammatically plain statements and familiar landings for the beleaguered voice to steady itself on wide, flat ground. The resting places also provide pivots, or turning points, for his voice to move and dart in new directions. Speaking in short syntactic and cognitive bursts clearly provides Williams fewer challenges than do long, uninterrupted passages. The poem notably moves between voices, too, allowing for these pivots to find regular place in the poem. Describing the Old Market, the poem reads:

> the place deserted all but
> for a few Indians squatted in the
> booths, unnoticing (don't you think it)
> as though they slept there .
>
> There's a second tier. Do you
> want to go up?
>
> What makes Texans so tall? (*Collected Poems* 2:276)

In these few lines, there are three vocal shifts, if one includes the parenthesis. This pastiche form is by no means revolutionary, of course, though for this poem the quick breaks and shifts allow Williams's voice to bump amiably along rather than snag on the perils of long, attentive focus on a set narrative or form. This clarifies as the performance moves forward, when Williams can be heard to struggle more and more with the challenge of an extended reading. The rhetorical question "how can we get said what must be said?" takes on its more literal cast: he slurs the word "legs" (*Collected Poems* 2:273); he stumbles over the phrase "supporting girder" (2:274) near the beginning; and when he arrives at one of the poem's key phrases, he murkily flubs it: "a music of survival, sub— . . . a music of survival, sub*dued*" (2:275). But when he comes to the long passage on the aged stripper, indented and arranged in short quatrains, he reads with the stumbles and hiccups that have been happening throughout. This extended scene, the longest set piece in the poem itself, seems to require these lines of typically four words each, a useful crutch for the lengthy passage's technical requirements.

Writing to Richard Eberhart on May 23, 1954, Williams says of the variable foot, "It gives us resources to the ear which result in a language which we hear spoken about us every day" (*Letters* 327). The third-person plural here is misleading: in fact, the coincidence of formal and physical change led Williams into a poststroke disabled mode of cripping lyric, in which poetic structures served to accommodate and normalize his new physical requirements. Performing his poems before audiences allowed him not only to summarize a poetics but also to argue for the normal functioning of his body and mind. Seeing Williams in this manner is instructive: no longer is he bending his will against the problems of Anglicized or Continental modernism; instead, he's invested in demonstrating his own physical, and therefore lyrical, dancing vitality.

Eigner, Aloud and Allowed

Larry Eigner is typically associated with both the Black Mountain College and Language schools of American poetry. The first affiliation was made by Donald Allen in his influential anthology *The New American Poetry: 1945–1960* (1960), in which Eigner's poems were grouped with poems and statements on poetics by Charles Olson, Robert Duncan, Robert Creeley, and Denise Levertov. The association with Language poets was made concrete when Ron Silliman dedicated his equally influential anthology, *In the American Tree* (1986), to Eigner, though as Benjamin Friedlander points out, Eigner had been in close contact with key figures from the movement well before that time, including Barrett Watten, who wrote an early important essay on Eigner, and Robert Grenier, his eventual caregiver at Berkeley and most prominent editor (115). Silliman opens his anthology's introduction by squaring Eigner with the Language poets' concern with speech and writing by referring to Grenier's "On Speech" (which famously begins: "I HATE SPEECH"), the inaugural text for the inaugural issue of *This* magazine, in which Eigner appeared. Despite this disavowal, says Silliman, *This 1*, in which Eigner's poems appeared, was "obsessed with speech" and aligned itself with both Olson's projective verse as well as "the self-consciously anti-academic tradition of the 50s and 60s, a wide range of writings whose only points of agreement were an insistence on the centrality of the influence of William Carlos Williams and a preference for poetry that, read aloud, sounded spoken" (Introduction xv).

More recently, Eigner has become perhaps the key poet in disability studies. In particular, Michael Davidson's "Missing Larry: The Poetics of Disability in Larry Eigner" draws on Eigner not to interrogate figures of disability in his work (there are few of these, says Davidson) but to more broadly conceive a "poetics of disability" in which "poetry defamiliarizes not only language but the body normalized *within* language" (*Concerto* 118). Davidson argues that this is particularly germane to a 1960s "thematics of embodiment" (118) generated by the New Left and various social and aesthetic movements that metaphorically privilege the normalized body: "gesture, breath, orality, performance, 'leaping' poetry, 'action' painting, projective verse, deep image, happenings, spontaneous bop prosody" (118). Eigner's work raises broader questions about how postwar poetry is conceived in ableist terms—even as it foregrounds myriad forms of social injustice—and how we might begin to read against that grain by watching syntactic and graphic refiguration unsettle an assumed physical or psychic normalcy.[8] This framing of Eigner as a poet who deploys syntax and form from a disabled perspective also underwrites Barrett Watten's early essay on Eigner, "Missing 'X,'" which argues that Eigner's fragmented line and sentence structure imply but don't embody completed grammatical units, as well as George Hart's "Enough Defined: Disability, Ecopoetics, and Larry Eigner," which demonstrates how Eigner's disability perspective reframes Emersonian ideas of limitation. In all these cases, Eigner has been drawn into the orbit of larger movements, grafted to collective identities, and aligned with formulations about language and its presence and antireferential, performative functions.

I wish to develop and deepen Eigner's identity as a poet of disability by listening in to a tape of Eigner's reading voice—the cripped, cracked, coagulated morass of vowel tone and loopy cadence that takes its place, or sounds its yawp, in the landscape of Eigner's enormous body of work. Unlike Williams, Eigner's vocal struggles dated from birth. Because of a botched forceps delivery, Eigner was born with cerebral palsy. Though he could walk, he used a wheelchair, and though he could speak, he articulated words with noticeable effort. Robert Grenier, Eigner's close friend and editor of Eigner's recent and titanic four-volume *Collected Poems* (2010), says that when he first met Eigner, "I couldn't understand *At All* what he was saying" (*Collected Poems* 1:vii). Despite this—or perhaps because of it—the speaking voice itself was crucially important to Eigner. As Eigner describes himself in his first-person biographical note in Allen's anthology, Eigner's turn toward poetry itself dates from a 1949 broadcast of Cid Corman reading Yeats on a Boston radio show in a style of recitation Eigner questioned. "I disagreed with his non-declamatory way of reciting," Eigner explains, a surprising quibble for such a nondeclamatory poet (436). Allen's introduction points to the crucial role poetry readings played in circulating the "larger amount" of the avant-garde postwar poetry he'd collected, a fact not often remarked upon, and Eigner attended such readings in the early 1950s—one of his first was by a poststroke William Carlos Williams at Brandeis in 1952 (Eigner, *Collected Poems* 1:xxii). Eigner even felt bold enough to participate in a Q&A after a Charles Olson reading in Gloucester in 1954, asking Olson, in reference to "Letter 5" in *Maximus*, "Why did you attack Vincent Ferrini in your poem?" (Friedlander 118). By 1973, the year he recorded his audiotape, he had begun performing readings himself, and references to readings begin dotting his letters and poems, as when writing to his friends David and Maria Gitin in ways that suggest the everydayness of this activity, going "to rd at whatever poetryfest in Michigan or elsewhere" (1973). Some of his readings were modeled on the standard, stand-alone performances like Olson and Williams were doing, as in a 1978 reading at Berkeley in which Eigner reads uninterrupted for over twenty minutes. As I describe below, readings, Eigner's impaired voice and the face-to-face, spoken environment of poetry in performance were crucial parts of his poetic career.

And yet despite these facts, Eigner is typically read as a poet without a speaking voice. Olson's ubiquitous comment that Eigner's poems were "stone-cutting all the way" (qtd. in *Collected Poems*, dust jacket) sums up a received image of Eigner as a sculptural craftsman very much at odds with his physical constraints: a hypermasculinized, muscular chiseler who left hard facts in his wake. Olson's image is truly of the strong and silent type. In one way, this is part and parcel of Eigner's lineage as a fellow traveler of the Language poets, for whom, as Marjorie Perloff explains, voice is eschewed entirely: "One of the cardinal principles—perhaps *the* cardinal principle—of American Language poetics . . . has been the dismissal of 'voice' as the foundational principle of lyric poetry" ("Language"). Abetting this genealogy, Eigner has been read as a poet solidly print-bound, typographic, and of the page itself and wholly unconcerned with, and in no direct relation to, voice.

And yet that is precisely what I wish to challenge. Listening to Eigner unsettles this settled image, providing a seemingly unauthorized, strikingly discomposed figure of speech to have a say and to "untype" his typing. Eigner *aloud* is Eigner, finally, *allowed*: allowed to speak, allowed to sound "different," allowed to move beyond the page-bound and syntactically fractured aesthetic for which he was justly known. By making this case for Eigner's lyric cripping, I hope also to show that the repeated and uniform emphasis on Eigner's graphic aesthetic erases his physical self. Even Davidson's argument, which redresses Eigner's silenced body by working "not simply to find disability references but to see the ways Eigner's work unseats normalizing discourses of embodiment," obscures Eigner's physical self even as it makes it a grounding concern (*Concerto* 121). What would change if Eigner's voice itself was heard? How would the textual silences, or his poems' canny use of form to speak from a disabled subject position, transform if the disforming burl of his voice was heard twisting itself through sound? To what extent does Eigner's voice muddle the carefully wrought strategies so radiantly articulated by Davidson, Watten, Hart, and others? Allowing Eigner to actually talk suggests that his reading voice proposed a distinct alternative to his other various strategies of embodiment.

Listening to Eigner in this way also asks us to rethink some of the most fundamental suppositions about Eigner's use of language, which is often read more for syntax than semantics. Michael Davidson, for example, attends to Eigner's "silences" (*Concerto* 121), in which syntax reveals a disabled consciousness, how "the material limits of the poet's physical act of writing govern the creation of rhythm" (128), and physical limitations on movement project themselves, similarly to Williams's "pivoting" stanzas, into "irregular" lines, stanza shapes, and grammatical units (133). Crucially focused on the recovery of Eigner's body and physical bearing, Davidson still takes his lead, as he says himself, from Watten's "Missing 'X,'" written in 1985, when Eigner was still thriving as a poet. Watten set the stage for the critical history to come by showing how Eigner's syntax has the effect of evaporating embodied presence. Watten argues that Eigner breaks from a "metaphysics of referentiality" (179) by writing "predicates" for subjects that are absent and outside the poem (178). There are no complete sentences, rarely are there actual subjects (though they are implied), and so the poem becomes, drawing on the terms of J. L. Austin, an illocutionary act itself: "[F]orm and content are the same, and the time of the poem is one of constant attention. The poem does not defer a present but, rather, *is* a present, and for this reason the poem does not possess an outer boundary or box-like limit" (177). For contrast, Watten analyzes the syntax of Hart Crane's "Royal Palm," which is organized both by reference itself (to an actual palm tree that is then made symbolic) and a "self-contextualizing" (177) modernist poetic enclosure—a well-crafted poem. Crane's syntax refers to a temporal consistency established by the lines themselves and draws upon the stable subjects—the poem's "absolute object" (179)—it describes and, in so doing, authorizes them as to be reasonably articulated by an observing consciousness. Eigner's writing works differently: the poem's subjects lie outside the lyric boundary, and the poem is *predicated* on their invisible and implied existence. "Reference," says Watten, referring to John Searle, "involves the intention toward a unique object. Predication, on the other hand, does not" (170).

This is a fundamental argument for language-based poetics, familiar to anyone who follows this strand of American literary history, and it's one that Davidson works to update with crip consciousness. And yet we might pause over Watten's use of the term "unique object." What "unique object" might be relevant here and overlooked by this nonreferential turn toward the grail of syntax? Could it be Eigner's body itself? Watten never makes reference in this essay to disability of any kind, and his language emphasizes this disembodied quality in a number of places, perhaps most strikingly with a telling image describing Eigner's non-box-like, antireferential poetic: "The poem begins and ends. It might truly be likened to a hologram" (177). Commenting on Eigner's use of syllabic stresses and "metrical and grammatical isolation of the words," Watten says that the "architecture of Eigner's poem is kind to language, leading to a precise articulation" (184), referring to an imagined scene of verbal "articulation" that overlooks Eigner's own incapacity to actually articulate words himself. I'd like to suggest here that such critical writing writes Eigner himself out of the scene. "Holographic," immaterial, figured as a poet of "precise articulation" whose syntax eschews reference to "unique objects"—from a crip perspective, these things serve to silence what is so fundamental to Eigner's poetic work: his voice itself, which helps us lift off from the typewritten page.

Of course, it's undeniable that the page itself was crucial. Eigner's page clearly drew from Olson's doctrine of compositional "field," something that has become perhaps the most repeated judgment about his work. The most visible instance of this can be seen in *The Collected Poems of Larry Eigner*—published in 2010 in four oversized, barely luggable volumes, totaling over sixteen hundred pages—which preserves the poet's favored medium: typewriter-sized paper and Courier font. The editors, Curtis Faville and Robert Grenier, make a virtual fetish out of the typewriter's centrality to Eigner's work, including numerous references to his 1940 Royal typewriter in the preface, along with facsimile pages of edited typewritten pages. They also draw on a term Eigner himself devised, referring to Eigner's "typewriter calligraphy" (*Collected Poems* 1:xii) and, in a long essay at the end of volume 4 titled "The Text as an Image of Itself," situate Eigner's use of the typewriter in the long history of movable type as it emerged from its oral and spoken origins (4:xxvii) and gave rise to modernist precision and experimentalism (4:xxviii–xxx) and finally to Olson's "Projective Verse" itself (4:xxxi). "Larry Eigner's career as a poet could not have happened were it not for the invention of the manual typewriter," summarize Faville and Grenier (4:xxxii). Almost all of the collection's back-cover blurbs, too, composed by critical and poetic luminaries with seemingly conspiratorial uniformity, attest to the importance of Eigner's page. Charles Bernstein notes how the editors' work "rigorously adheres" to the manuscript originals; Ron Silliman explains that "Eigner took responsibility for every element that showed up on the page"; Benjamin Friedlander says Eigner was "the first poet to realize the syntactic potential of the page"; Albert Gelpi notes Eigner's "cuts and turns of lineation, the flow and pause of spatial arrangement"; and Stephen Ratcliffe refers to Eigner's "invention," as he calls it, "of space on the two-dimensional page." "Eigner's is decisively a poetry of the page" (124), Davidson agrees in "Missing Larry." "The page—specifically the 8 1/2 by 11 typewriter page—is the measure of the poem, determining its lineation, length, and typographic organization" (124).

There is no sense in refuting any of this. It's true that Eigner wrote, voluminously, by using his right index finger and thumb on a 1940 Royal manual typewriter and had trouble with handwriting (his archive at the Thomas J. Dodd Research Center in Storrs, Connecticut, holds examples of this, and it is difficult to decipher). His poems, arranged with all the orthographic essentialism described above, do indeed make extended use of white space, not only spacing lines at unpredictable distances from the left-hand margin but also adding space between words or even letters:

OR FEAR ITSELF

o l d   s i l v e r y   t o n e s

The gentle voice, whining
a people

joy in their moment

that it was

some vigor

crippled (*Collected Poems* 1:267)

Here, the word "crippled" ends this passage with powerful effect after the syntactic delays of the preceding spatial moments. As the eye tracks down from "that it was" to "some vigor," it's prepared for a punch of delivery, which "crippled" duly socks forth.

I include this last example not only to acknowledge Eigner's rhetorical use of the page but to again start chipping away at some of the received wisdom on this important midcentury poet. First, Eigner does in fact address the disabled body at times, and with some regularity, a fact that's rarely admitted.[9] The words "fear itself" allude, of course, to FDR's famous speech, and here Eigner treats Roosevelt as the disabled man he was. Roosevelt's voice—maligned by the terms "silvery," as in false, and "silver-tongued" and "whining"—emerges from "some vigor / crippled," his own healthy but wheelchair-ensconced body. The poem goes on to make clear reference to expectations of conventional masculine hardihood—referring to "the unconquerable men" who receive "a 'good education'" and get "a 'useful job'"—and implies, via Roosevelt's achievements, that this language of midcentury normalcy might not be appropriate for the speaker, who ends the poem saying, "you should pardon me when I sit down." The scare quotes around terms like "good education" and "useful job" also serve to throw these benchmarks of social conformity into question.

Elsewhere, Eigner is even more direct on this topic. "The amazement of these cripples around me," begins an early poem and then goes on to make associations between the "cripple" form and voice itself:

> The amazement of these cripples around me
> at a few words,   unable
> in my feet and so forth,   ah
> truly beautiful voice (*Collected Poems* 1:254)

Here, the speaker's stance ironizes the gaze of other "cripples" on him. He can, it seems, manage "a few words" despite his wracked body, or "my feet and so forth." We hear the encouraging words of others—"terrific, somebody says"—and the poem ends in what sounds like a defiant call to crip solidarity: "well, maybe we're caught   but we're movin, too / the slow sun is winning." Punning on the words sun/son, Eigner's final line—coming as it does from a man with two brothers and a close family structure—may indeed be a claim for personal pride, invoking that superannuated term for mentally disabled ("slow") only to deny its predictive force. He is "winning," after all. Other poems, many of them, have clear references to the disabled body, including the early poem "T h e C r i p p l e s" (*Collected Poems* 1:99) and the later one "a b l e m a n" (*Collected Poems* 3:862).

Yet more compelling than such representations is Eigner's voice itself, which page fetishism altogether occludes. First off, just as Eigner indeed referred to disability in his writing, he also frequently wrote about voice. He referred to his speaking voice more than once as his "sotto voce," emphasizing his vocal limitations and questioning, like a lyrical Derrida, the privileging of speech over text, or, scooping critics who often make this point, simply the clear link between physical limitation and style: "Sotto voce has resulted in the suppression of words," he claims in "Method from Happenstance" (*Areas* 6). In "Has Enough Seemed Nobody with a Pretty Strange Language or Just Accent Can Think Much at All," Eigner meditates on "voice in mind," the voice both internal and spoken, wondering about this binary: "All or almost all writing is based on speech, you'd think," he says, "though *a b c* or *&* and *o* could have been devised and then named, rather than the other way around" (*Areas* 15). In "Letter to Carroll F. Terrell," Eigner responds to Silliman's talk of speech in *In the American Tree*. Here, Eigner displays a more equivocal stance toward spoken language, one that I think is developed in his readings and performances: "I forgot, and Sunday overlooked, Silliman's words about *This* #1, it was 'obsessed with speech,'" he begins, going on to say that Silliman "might have agreed with Ted Greenwald (whose statement comes right after R.G.'s 'On Speech,' as Silliman has placed them) about speech, 'words in the head,' voiceless and breathless yet in some way audible speech, whisper of the whispered although speech can of course be like fireworks enough, in varying degrees too. No need to imitate talk too slavishly" (*Areas* 122). Here, "speech" straddles the unspoken, inward, unvocalized voice of a text, the actual speech or "talk" that we actually hear around us. How can speech be "breathless" and "yet in some way audible"? This is a paradox evident in the tautology "whisper of the whispered"—is it the first instance here or the second that's figurative? In any case, for Eigner, speech shouldn't be marginalized because it can be "like fireworks." This interrogation of the unspoken text is rife in poems as well, like this one dated September 17, 1973, which casts a skeptical eye on lineation:

in pages

what kind of poetry is
a horizontal line

in pages

pages

words (*Collected Poems* 3:1172)

Without claiming judgment about typed poems in "a horizontal line," the idiomatic use of "what kind of poetry is" rings with critique, as does the second use of "pages," which might function as a verb—pages "page" words, or dutifully, menially call them back to the page itself.

In "for Jonathan Greene," speech is associated with "possibility" and "encouragement":

<u>how</u> <u>to</u> <u>make</u> <u>it</u>

<u>possibilities</u> <u>of</u> <u>speech</u>

new

encouragements

in words sounds breath

wave on top of wave (*Collected Poems* 3:912)

Breath recurs in "wave on top of wave," emphasizing its recuperative nature. It is difficult to lean too hard on such nonassertions from the poetry—Eigner's syntactic hesitancy swerves away from direct claims. What is the subject in the poems above? What is the "it" to be made into "possibilities of speech"? Without reducing Eigner's poems to claims, I wish to emphasize patterns worth recognizing.

As mentioned above, readings themselves played a key role in Eigner's career as a poet, though they were far from the ecstatic experiences of authentic presence celebrated and undermined and toyed with by other poets in this book. Most of his performances (at least those that are preserved on tape) suggest that such reading was heavily mediated. In a reading at Berkeley from 1978, the emcee actually cuts Eigner off near the beginning of the poet's introductory comments, speaking over Eigner's voice to explain the format of the reading:

> Okay, before we start with the first poems, I would just comment that, um, the reading has been, sort of, the works in the reading have been chosen collaboratively. They're not all Larry's choices, they're partly Larry Eigner's choices, partly mine, and partly Ron Silliman's. And uh, so, then the order is pretty much mine and Ron Silliman's. And it runs basically that the first poem is a recent work that's come out in Jerome Rothenberg's *Big Jewish Book*, and there is, uh, a commentary that follows it in the projection, which you can read but Larry's not going to read.

While Eigner did indeed get his time onstage, this was not a typical reading format: the schedule was laid out beforehand, and the reading itself was organized and run by Eigner's fellow poets rather than Eigner. Further, the "projection" of the poems on a screen served as subtitles. This ensured that listeners could make out the words Eigner read, which could be very difficult to audibly decode, though it also had the effect of eroding authority in the spoken voice itself. (On the MP3 of the Berkeley reading from PennSound, I can't make out more than isolated phrases, though that may be a function of the recording's mediocre quality.) A few years prior to this reading, in a letter from May 9, 1973, to the Gitins, Eigner lays bare his feelings about a similar reading, this one at the "Cambridge St. Artists' Coop," in which other voices and graphic images worked in concert with Eigner's speaking voice:

> I'm forgetting what actually got to be read, mostly, but I did quite a few on tape, this having slide projections of tss to go with it (!), and Bob Teage a Marblehead actor and director rendered "Occasionally" et al before that and afterwards ##550,702 and I think some others. The slides, blow-ups as you may imagine (some of them of pretty faded crbons on yellow paper), an idea of Teague's. Frank Minelli . . . made them sl..s and the tape, were quite a sight for me, and likely I wd've done a sght better thn on audio just reading the poems of f the screen, in the homey atmosphere afer Ferrini's 40 minutes, during which his comments (I and others) turned to dialogue and the refreshment break.

The parenthetical exclamation point along with the crediting of Teague with the idea to project slides of poem carbons suggest this was the first time Eigner had experienced such a format. There is also audible bemusement and mild frustration at how video and tape and an actor's prosthetic voicing of his work silence him. "I wd've done a sght better thn on audio," he fumes, noting next that Vincent Ferrini got a full forty minutes. Such experiences suggest how much Eigner was concerned with poetry readings and how marginalized he felt within them.

Indeed, for Eigner the text itself is in need of some audio aid, rather than the other way around. In a letter to the Gitins from January 23, 1975, Eigner describes a night spent listening to Ezra Pound reading the *Cantos* in Italy in 1967: "Friday night six of us sat around listening to Pound reading from Cantos, the or one of the records made at Spoleto, on Bob's stereo phonograph, quite a treat, again an audio aid for me, the sense of going through however many pages without zigzags or won-whether to speed up, slow down, pause, etc.—bogg(l)ing." Notable here is how Eigner's experiences with Pound's *Cantos* repeats his audience's experiences with his own, though in reverse. Whereas his listeners relied on the text to navigate the "zigzags" of Eigner's voice, for Eigner the "audio aid" is to hear the text aloud, which reveals what the page can't. In fact, the voice alone reveals what even the body onstage can't, something Eigner will take to heart in the production of his own tape recording.

This relationship between the written and spoken was never settled for Eigner, and his negotiation of it is part of his attentiveness to those around him. Readings were paradoxical experiences: Eigner could finally speak in his own, authentic voice, and yet he was keenly aware of how much he had to navigate his speaking voice's abnormality. In an interview, Eigner talked about his spoken voice on tape and his sense of alienation from it: "Others have been able to understand me better on tape than I can myself, while of course while I'm saying something, thinking aloud, that is, it sounds like my speech is normal, though when I strain and try to say things loud or fast, I can tell it's not so clear. My monotone in playback is always a surprise" (*Areas* 154). This captures well Eigner's confounding orientation to voice: the tape recording shows him calibrating his voice to the world that receives it. As I'll describe below, such a concern for "normal" sounds ties Eigner to a period of shifting sensibilities about normalcy and disability.

THE MOST IMPORTANT source of Eigner's voice is Eigner's tape recording itself, where lyric cripping occurs most notably in his life as a reader. Recorded on July 1 and 11, 1974, in Swampscott, Massachusetts, by Michael Köhler, the tape is 13:05 minutes long and contains twenty-seven poems, all read by Eigner.[10] Titled *around new/sound daily/means: a selection of poems*, the cassette has a mustard-gold paper cover and a folded slip of liner notes, the central portion of which, in the section titled "author/speaker," reads: "LARRY EIGNER has lived almost all his life in Swampscott on Massachusetts Bay's North Shore a few miles from where he got muscle in-coordination at birth in 1927—mostly he's been on top of the world and in a wheelchair, while it's a puzzle for one thing, enough is elusive and a lot comes within sight and hearing through glass and radio and TV. From many pieces he's written over a dozen books and booklets have been compiled, including the representative collection of the 'Selected Poems' (Oyez, 1972)." Notable here is how Eigner is framed as both disabled and "on top of the world." Limited by "in-coordination," his wheelchair, and "glass and radio and TV," he nonetheless has gathered from these media sufficient observations to generate a large body of work. In a late interview, Eigner says that "radio and TV have been audio-visual prosthesis," educational like "a fast blackboard" (*Areas* 163). The liner notes suggest he is both disabled and not, confronted with the "puzzle" of life in a wheelchair but also managing just fine through the same media consumed by everyone else. Even the term "in-coordination" serves here as an elision of the medicalized and diagnostic term "cerebral palsy." Eigner is elsewhere referred to as a "spastic" (183), a term used by Samuel Charters in the biographical note at the end of Eigner's 1977 book *The World and Its Streets, Places*, though here such language is softened into a vaguer, nonmedical diction. Perhaps the most striking thing about these liner notes is what's *not* included—the poems themselves, in printed form. Unlike the readings Eigner had experienced, in which his voice was doubled or normed by text or other voices reading his poems, here it is naked and presented only by itself, with no mediating apparatus. Beyond the notes transcribed above, there is no introduction or introducer, no explanation given by others, no other version of the text to turn to, no further readers or information—just the tape and the tape alone, showcasing his voice with its cracks and crinkles unstraightened and unscrubbed.

And what's on the tape? The poems are mostly from the early 1970s, though three are from the 1960s and two are from the 1950s, though the order on the recording is not chronological. (For two of them—"At Death Olson's" and "Tribute to Cage"—I've not been able to find a textual basis.) Most importantly, Eigner's voice crips the voice that earlier readings were engineered to correct. Now we hear Eigner's voice unadorned, which is very difficult to follow at first and without repeated and careful listenings will not make its words clearly heard. Yet an individualized voice does come through. In some poems, particularly "How Much a Squirrel," one can clearly discern Eigner's Massachusetts accent in the flattened /a/ vowel sound in "after" and the dropped /r/ in "dark" ("dahk"). And there is a clear rhythmic and vocal style. In an interview, Eigner once described his vocal cadences in relationship to Allen

Ginsberg's. Ginsberg actually read some Eigner poems in a short film on Eigner titled *Getting It Together: A Film on Larry Eigner, Poet*, and Eigner immediately registered the vocal disparity by remarking that Ginsberg "has rising inflection, like questioning, where I have falling cadence at the ends of the lines, stanzas and phrases, emphasized words" (*Areas* 154). This is a fairly apt description of his voice, which dips and sometimes fades out at the end of a line or phrase. In all, the tape provides an audiographic signature, a sense of presence through obfuscation, muffling, tonal sludge, mauled and muted articulation.

In this sounded way, the reading makes implicit claims for Eigner's relationship to language. In many poems, the figurative use of language or voice is ironized by the spoken recording, which in its verbal presence stands for the voice itself and the body that projects it. Take the poem "Dying," from "c. 1952–52," as dated in the *Collected Poems*:

D y i n g

And yet they hunt the great whales
the beauties they see
finally dwarfing them

Around the world
What's more
they name them, and these are not tags
but inexpressibles

their function

and even the unwanted,

and time

to think lower than
spheres (*Collected Poems* 1:87)

It's significant that Eigner chose to begin the tape with this poem. By pitting the names for whales against their natural beauty, the whale-hunters ("they") have created "inexpressibles," a term at once metaphoric and literal. On the one hand, language itself misses its mark when it attempts to create adequate representation in sound for the signified creatures, who in their majestic beauty disable or "dwarf" the namers. And yet these words are also, for

Eigner's own mouth, quite literally "inexpressible," as any listener will quickly discern. The tape opens with a challenge to the adequacy of language, underscored by the errors *deliberately retained* in this version of the recording. As his voice wends through these lines, it makes two noticeable mistakes: repeating the word "finally" as if in a stutter, and then the entire phrase "their function / and even." No other poems make "mistakes" such as these. The poem's final word, "spheres"—a reference to the ideal music of heavenly perfection, absent in this human and nonideal performance—is almost altogether swallowed in what is surely an example of what Eigner calls above "falling cadence." For the recording's opening poem, this is a crucial performance of lyric cripping: it makes its way without a net, showing the awkward, lumbering, sometimes indecipherable, and error-prone voice sounding a language that it finds a challenge simply to express. Typed up, things look a bit tidier.

This thematics of expression is echoed in "Unyielding Rock," a poem written on May 31, 1971, and the recording's tenth poem. "Unyielding Rock" is mostly descriptive of the poet's perception of sound and noise sitting on his parents' porch in Swampscott. He notes that "cars pull off" the road, "and there's a fog horn" and "circulation / air and water," the sounds and subsounds of a recording consciousness (*Collected Poems* 3:1013). And then:

voices

    bear

on the wind

        shapes

          branches

              birds

       leaves run together

        the moon
        field in
                    the earth

           articulate
              beyond walls (*Collected Poems* 3:1013)

The voices speaking alongside the whoosh of cars and foghorns take real shape, presuming that we read the lines above as "voices bear on the wind shapes: branches, birds." Yet "voices" here are not the poet's but those of the townscape itself, and the poem's conclusion suggests the "articulate" nature of the world "beyond walls" confining the speaking subject, whose "leaves" of a book have "run together" in a blur of text that can't match the sounds he's hearing. In Eigner's poems, "walls" typically refer to his front porch's four walls and signify his stance toward what's "out there." The title of Eigner's collection *Windows/Walls/Yard/Ways* captures the poet's recurring anatomizing of domestic space, which delimits as much as it grants sensory experience. Here, articulation is given to that which stands outside the walls of his room. It is, as is written in line 5, "what you hear." This audio variant puts in tension the question of an "articulate" world outside, as the voice actually speaking these lines—despite its oozy aural delivery—is so effectively articulate of what it describes. In this way, Eigner's speaking voice is ironically played against the articulate nature of the world outside, something lost in a purely page-bound reading of the poem. The recording crips the text's seemingly simple description of the metaphorical language of a night's diverse sounds.

Perhaps the most striking poem to figure voice in this way is "You Gotta Have Steam," a poem originally dated July 30, 1965, and dedicated to Charles Olson (in the recording, Eigner begins by reading the dedication, which is typed in the left-hand margin). The poem describes a bicycle accident that the speaker witnesses and includes a series of cries and screams:

you gotta have steam but
there's no pipes it's
blow -out

A ccident! Accident! yelled
the kid riders my
* for Charles direction
Olson * with my goon face

their fellow sprawled

(far as he could) then
got up

the road hit him
quietly

What now, I
shouted next
so all could hear
he rode under
tree-climbing ??

(*Collected Poems* 2:658)

In his reading of the poem the syntax clarifies, just in the way Eigner once marveled at how Pound's own line breaks and phrase units clarified when heard on record. First, Eigner's reading of this poem is remarkably consistent with its scoring by the text: he gives rhythmic pauses after the first and second lines and adds a brief caesura between "blow" and "-out." In the poem's final stanza, the way Eigner modulates his voice makes it clear that he's asking, "What now, tree climbing?" while the lines in between serve as dependent clauses. This poem is remarkable, too, for its stable, "lyric I" perspective, not totally unknown to his earlier poems though crucial to this poem's performance (and antithetical to Watten's descriptions of Eigner's predicative "total syntax"). Most notable here is the way Eigner has chosen poems to accentuate and ironize the distinction between figurative and literal voices: the shouting speaker, admonishing the boys, has a "goon face" but is also capable of hurling words across some distance. This final act of yelling suggests, too, the speaker's psychological dimensions of regret—is there admonition or admiration that the kids can climb the trees? By introducing us to his goon face, the poem invites us to wonder.

In all of the above cases, Eigner's voice plays contrapuntally alongside the written text (a text invisible to listeners, unless they actually collect all the various books the poems have appeared in). Why? I've been arguing that Eigner's tape redresses his voice's normalization and silencing in readings by speaking without any scaffolding typically provided: a page of writing on a screen, an actor reading his poetry's lines. Yet more than that, I'm suggesting that these poems represent voices themselves, and Eigner's readings of them open and reveal a distance between the silent voice of the page and Eigner's actual, cracked-up warble. Eigner's taped voice demands something like Garland-Thomson's ideal of "beholding," though in this case it's not a gaze that asks for reconsideration but a cocked ear. I'd extend this, too, beyond figures of voice to images of sound and noise, which occur throughout this recording as well. This shows, I think, Eigner choosing to voice aloud representations of sound that the poems themselves often trouble, sometimes by simply pointing to differences between the written and spoken.

"Love Children," for instance, written June 13, 1966, contrasts a "noisy world" with a list of things that, in the very form of a greeting card–like list, serve as virtual tropes for sentimentality. The poem reads in full:

love children
  poems
 the unexpected

    in a noisy world (*Collected Poems* 2:725)

We might read this poem simply as a list followed by a claim about it: "Love, children, poems: the unexpected in a noisy world." In fact, that's the syntactic phrasing that Eigner gives this poem in the recording; commas, represented by abrupt pauses, seem to follow the poem's first three words, and the colon is signified by a double beat. Yet the page's own phrasing creates a different kind of "unexpectedness," of syntax this time, in the first line break, asking readers to perform some syntactical reordering as they go. The words "love children" in line 1, for example, might be an imperative ("love children!") or an adjectival phrase (the phrase "love child" was current enough at the time to serve as the title for the Supremes' Top 20 Billboard hit in 1968). On the tape, however, the voice clears this up, showing that what's "unexpected" here is his voice's own clarity and precision, not the phraseological ambiguities that a page reading seems to invite. "Love Children" is a poem meant for performing, and Eigner's voice in this case rectifies and organizes the page's syntactic play.

Other poems that cite sound in the recording often align it to the natural landscape, suggesting the nonhuman world of noise that Eigner is attuned to. These include "The Sky," with its granting of voice to the sea ("the ocean / lifts / what a sound" [*Collected Poems* 3:1079]); "Trees Stand," which observes that "gulls / when they fly they cry" (3:996); and "Birds," which refers with syntactic ambiguity to "powerful breath a ground / target while brooding," the birds perhaps serving as emblems of access to "the world" and "the earth / whole" and "all the dimensions" that the poem keeps referencing (3:945). In fact, this vastness of scope, almost cosmic in scale, is echoed in the tape's poems on outer space and universal scale, like "Common Sense" and "Magnetic Lines," the latter of which refers to the bands of magnetic energy "far out / turning / past the speed of light" (3:992).

There is also in this recording a competing focus on what might be called the obverse of noise and sound. As if to bookend the tape's opening emphasis on "inexpressibles," the final two poems consider the figure of the *listener*. "Contact Communication":

contact communication

explanation

enough and not enough

how far
we keep on (*Collected Poems* 3:1103)

Like "Love Child," this poem opens with what could be an adjectival phrase ("contact communication") but in the reading is decidedly the beginning of a three-word list: Eigner intones these words by leaning heavily on the emphasized syllables (i.e., CON-tact, communi-CA-tion) and leaving comma-pauses between each one. Yet what does this list signify? Coming at the end of a tape concerned with voicing language, the poem interrogates the virtues of "contact" itself, the tautology "enough and not enough" suggesting the indeterminate effects words might have upon listeners. "Everybody Dies," the tape's very last poem, reads in full:

everybody dies
a few listen (*Collected Poems* 3:1010)

Here "listening," an act of aural attentiveness, distinguishes a select few from the mass of equalized humanity—those who die. It's as if Eigner wishes to signal to his tape's listeners that the act of listening—what they've just done, presuming they made it through the tape's 13:05 minutes of sound—is crucial to the poem's "communication" cited above. "There's enough language around (me) so listening gets harder and harder and then impossible," Eigner writes in his short prose piece "Dilemmas by Their Horns" (1980), "quite a barrier to being adequate" (*Areas* 10). For Eigner, the act of listening is a necessary act of attention to achieve "adequacy." By listening to the poems, Eigner's voice is allowed—allowed in its strangeness, allowed flaws and all, allowed goony cadences and rhythms and sounds.

HEARD TOGETHER, Williams and Eigner serve as poets confronting the fact of their disability in a culture of normalcy. For Williams, a heretofore able-bodied modernist, the increasing difficulties in speech led him toward a performance of normalcy abetted by a darting, dynamic graphics of the page and an orientation toward reading that foregrounded his continuing physical ability. For Eigner, born into constrained mobility and range of speech, performing his poems on tape allowed him to wrest his speaking voice free of the many ways in which it was made legible and to sound his incomparably odd voice aloud. Reading aloud let him smudge the line between his many representations in print and his body itself, with its "goon face" and sotto voce. I hope that a cripped version of the late Williams finds its way into future writing on him; and I hope that a voiced Eigner leads toward an acknowledgment of his disability and its role in his life and writing beyond simply questions of syntax and form.

Normalcy and Sixties Poetry Reading

To listen in on Williams and Eigner performing their poems in the dawn of postmodern America is to find ourselves in a world prior to disability consciousness and its location in questions of identity. In fact, for Williams and Eigner, performing poems seemed more about lyric than life. The lyric cripping described above throws the ontology of the poem into question, as both Eigner and Williams work with and against poetic structures and their voicings of them.

Current disability studies, however, is primarily a study of identity. Its main concerns are to unmask an ideology of ableism and to find innovative ways to describe a range of differences that evade the language and consciousness of a negatively constructed subjectivity. Two of the major recent books in the field show this clearly. Tobin Siebers's *Disability Theory* (2008) serves as a defense of identity politics and a call for a "more nuanced" (5) treatment of the ways in which disability is either celebrated or perpetuated in negative terms. Siebers launches two projects in his book: one, to reveal the ideology of ability in its many subtle and all-encompassing maneuverings; and two, to illuminate the many new and productive ways in which disability can be perceived, understood, and valued (9). His argument essentially sets disability studies back on a course of identity investigations that might seem to be in critical eclipse. While Robert McRuer's *Crip Theory* (2006) doesn't make such a frontal claim for its investment in identity, in fact the book serves a similar end. McRuer's aim is not only to expose an able-bodied ideology but also to see how it intersects with heteronormativity. Conflating able-bodiedness and heterosexuality, each of which "still largely masquerades as a nonidentity" (1), leads McRuer to an argument in favor of "flexible subjects" (17) who can more easily accommodate various perspectives and positions. It can be reasonably argued that these two books metonymically stand for the aims of this newly emergent field: to denaturalize ableism by revealing disability's constructivist core and to articulate experiences of disability that have yet to be fully or adequately represented.[11]

And yet for the two poets discussed above, disability consciousness was in its burgeoning stages, and the kinds of questions that drive identity studies in disability—Who am I as a disabled person? What (if anything) do I share with other disabled people? How has the way I've been treated shaped my sense of self? How has disability subjectivity been forged by medical and other social discourses?—were less culturally operative. Certainly it's true that the mid-1950s through the early 1960s, when Williams was reading, saw some early institutionalizing efforts at addressing disability rights. In 1956 the federal government established disability insurance. The year 1961 saw the founding of the American Council of the Blind. Still, the watershed events of the disability rights movement itself were years off. In fact, the pivotal lawsuit by Edward Roberts, a quadriplegic who successfully sued the University of California, Berkeley, for admission occurred in 1962, less than a year before Williams's death. Roberts's activism snowballed from that early victory, and, working alongside other sixties agitations for civil liberties like the civil rights movement, the Free Speech Movement at Berkeley, and the women's movement, Roberts went on to found the Disabled Students Program (DSP) at Berkeley and a disabled gang of sorts, the Rolling Quads, who made their wheelchaired presence known on the college campus (Fleischer and Zames 39). Ultimately, Berkeley became ground zero for the DRM and saw the founding of the Center for Independent Living in 1972 and, as recently as 2011, the founding of disability studies as an undergraduate course of study. Nevertheless, this sweep of history largely missed Williams and even Larry Eigner, who relocated to Berkeley only in 1978, in the movement's full swing. He then took an active part in the DRM, and his tape recording itself was motivated by what might be called a drive toward disability activism after experiences of marginalization by ableist culture. Still, Eigner's real experiences with social movements establishing disability identity occurred years after his recording and schedule of readings began.

For Williams, and to a lesser and progressively diminishing sense Eigner, more dominant and relevant was a postwar culture of normalcy itself, the obverse of the 1960s culture of spontaneity and presence. This was the very thing—in its institutionally bureaucratized incarnation—at which Mario Savio was gnashing his teeth on the steps of Berkeley's Sproul Hall, against which Ginsberg was howling invective. As was described in chapter 1 and as goes the decade's standard narrative, a 1960s culture of authenticity shook its hoary locks in the face of incursions on desire and the ideological construction of American consumption and inauthentic living. This was a state of affairs well described by relatively popular midcentury sociologists and cultural critics, perhaps most notably David Riesman in his book *The Lonely Crowd*. Originally published in 1950, its lasting impact was actually the result of its two reissues in the 1960s, the first in 1961 and the second in 1969. Riesman famously argued that postwar American culture was shifting toward "other-directedness," a social normalizing of behavioral conformity. Whereas in earlier, preindustrial "inner-directed" cultures, individual character worked in concert with external demands, the other-directed individual was attuned to "an exceptional sensitivity to the actions and wishes of others" (21) more than the self. Despite Riesman's assertion that some such orthodoxy was a necessary aspect of *all* cultural development, the very word "conformity" became a shibboleth of 1960s resistance. In his 1969 preface, Riesman himself understood how much contemporary ideals of "moral or intellectual nonconformity" had derived from his work and lamented the fact (xxii). In the popular imagination, *The Lonely Crowd* foretold cultural anomie: a pervading obsession with others was desecrating American individualism. Successfully norming oneself to the standard of others had become, in a nation of individuals, a perverted cultural ideal.

The field of disability studies has turned a critical eye on the very idea of such normalcy and for this reason is in close conversation with early, rather than late, postwar American culture. What is normal? And how does normalcy serve to produce, in an ideological fashion, the limits of disability? A point of agreement is that disability should be viewed in much the same light as the "race, class, and gender mantra," as Lennard Davis phrases it, the long-standing targets of reformist academia's analytical gaze: all are systems of representation that naturalize constructed social categories. Some of the field's canonical texts, including works by Davis and Garland-Thomson, describe disability as a highly constructed, conceptually driven modality similar to race and gender—not an essentialist state of being but a "social process" that produces rather than discovers its subjects (Davis, *Enforcing* 2). This is the "social model" of disability, which has an institutional history dating from the early 1970s, along with the birth of the DRM itself.[12] Yet by the time disability theorists took up the ideology of normalcy, its effects had been lived for decades, centuries. By reading Williams and Eigner against this social and historical backdrop, it's clear that while neither poet conceived of himself in terms of disability identity, both established a lineage of lyric cripping that dates crip consciousness farther back than has previously been imagined and in a different way—more focused on the ways poetry might respond to or accommodate physical difference. (While it may be strange to think of Williams as a precursor figure of disability to later poets like Eigner, it's worth remembering that one of Eigner's early encounters with poetry reading was a Williams poststroke reading in 1954 and that he was generally influential to Eigner.) While none of Eigner's readings mentioned above makes explicit claims to disability activism, their cripping of speech in performance should be heard within this context, in which older standards of conformist normalcy were butting against vital but burgeoning social stances against such standards. Disability, while not a fully conscious identity position, was in fact operative at the lower frequencies in 1960s cultures of reading, which took no deliberate interest in it. To listen to Williams and Eigner is to remember that the 1960s and early 1970s saw lyric cripping without the claims to identity positions; it's this difference that makes them hard to hear now as fully invested in the poetics of disability, even though they were.

If sixties reading is thought of as authentic or saturated with new forms of the poet's presence, if it has been understood as offering poets new ways to connect with audiences and shape their work and reception, listening to Williams and Eigner complicates that picture. Skeptical and wary, cautious and cantankerous, both poets read as disabled poets in an ableist world and found themselves quite far from the sorts of explosive and celebratory humanist reading described elsewhere in this book. They also lead us to ask, Who else was cripping their work against normalcy before such gestures became overt? Josephine Miles was a disabled poet situated right in sixties Berkeley, and Vassar Miller—like Eigner, a poet with *Collected Poems* and nominated for the Pulitzer Prize in 1961—is another. Yet no matter who gets read and reread or is written about or sanctified by the college syllabus, the project of listening in on disabled poets reading in the heyday of reading itself should and can tell us something important about the act of reading itself. It wasn't incidental, it was necessary. It was, truly, putting one's body on the line.

Conclusion | Notes on Gender

On July 17, 1961, Sylvia Plath read a single poem, "Tulips," from the stage of the Mermaid Theatre in London. The occasion was a poetry festival, and Plath was the sole female reader among twelve men, including her husband, Ted Hughes. Plath's introducer, in the surviving recording, notes the distinction this way: "It's a pleasure to present a *woman* poet. We have such a predominantly masculine week here, a fact that didn't really strike me till the programming was complete. What it shows about my taste I don't know, but I'm very glad that we have, at any rate, one very fine woman poet this evening, uh, Miss Sylvia Plath, as I refer to her by her maiden name before she was Mrs. Ted Hughes" (*The Spoken Word*). It was surely no surprise to Plath to hear herself served up, married name and all, as the sole female curio, though hearing this today underscores a set of conditions essential to square with any full assessment of the period's public poetry.

I've spent this book arguing that though poetry readings were articulated as occasions for establishing presence and authenticity, they often deflected and deflated such ambitions; in the antinomies of sixties reading, poets both courted and defied a new public ethos, one that promised liberation and exposure even as it foretold a loss of lyric purity. And yet if we are to take full measure of sixties reading, it's worth turning one eye a bit more definitely toward the effects of gender on performance as well as on composition itself. We've already seen Brooks confront the "shy housewife" persona and negotiate her way through a largely masculine community of writers; and Charles Olson's blusterings in Berkeley reveal his preoccupation with the show of untainted masculinity. Yet there is no better example than Sylvia Plath speaking her poems into those patriarchal English microphones to further highlight the way gender inflected and informed many sixties readers. In the recordings that remain of Plath's voice, the terms of skeptical humanism are replayed, though in a somewhat different key. Where poets like Ginsberg and Frost, Olson and Brooks sought and then ultimately undercut an oral aura in their performances, Plath's voice, which grows in force and control as she nears the end of her life, sets up a somewhat different conflict: between masculine authority, with its repressive effects, on the one hand, and a liberating, fierce feminine agency breaking through, on the other.

Plath was not as frequent a reader as other poets discussed previously, though she did leave behind a batch of significant recordings and a few essential interviews. Plath's recordings reveal that reading was for her a deeply gendered activity. For one thing, when talking on tape she often cast poetry itself in masculine terms. On October 30, 1962—just weeks before her death in February 1963—Plath read fifteen poems from *Ariel* followed by a substantial interview with Peter Orr, a sound archivist who made numerous such recordings of poets.[1] This is Plath's most significant tape, made after her breakup with Ted Hughes and in the midst of the flurry of composition that would become *Ariel* (Moses 105). Discussing the differences between British and American culture, Plath explains that in Britain, writing as a woman is a fraught activity. When she was first at Cambridge, "[y]oung women would come up to me and say, 'How do you dare to write, how do you dare to publish a poem, because of the criticism, the terrible criticism, that falls upon one if one does publish?'" But if poetry was essentially a masculine domain, amply demonstrated by her introduction at the Mermaid Theatre, then publishing was, for Plath, an act of female bravery. Here, pointing up to Orr the difference between poetry and prose, Plath describes poetry as "tyrannical" when opposed to the intimacies and trivialities allowed in the more feminine realm of prose: "Poetry, I feel, is a tyrannical discipline, you've got to go so far, so fast, in such a small space that you've just got to turn away all the peripherals. And I miss them! I'm a woman, I like my little *Lares* and *Penates*, I like trivia, and

I find that in a novel I can get more of life, perhaps not such intense life, but certainly more of life, and so I've become very interested in novel writing as a result" (Plath, *Plath Reads Plath*). Plath associates the domestic "small space" (rather than an expansive masculine field, as someone like Olson would have it) with a kind of male despotism. For Plath, it's not poetry but prose that allows for the cultivation of household gods, freedom from oversight and control, and feminine knickknackery.

This is not simply a matter of Plath noting the ways in which poetry and prose imply gendered forms; in the early sixties, the voice itself—both audible, spoken language and representations of audible, spoken language—became her central mode of counterstatement to such ranged forces. When Orr asks her about reading poetry aloud, Plath notes how essential voice is at this crucial moment in her writing, which coincides, roughly speaking, with the *Ariel* period. Orr asks, "[D]o you consciously design your poems to be both lucid and to be effective when they are read aloud?" Plath answers by framing her recent work as distinctly oral:

> No, I don't. May I say this, that the ones I read are very recent and I have found myself having to read them aloud to myself, saying them to myself. Now this is something I didn't do, for example my first book, *The Colossus*, I can't read any of the poems aloud now. I didn't write them to be read aloud. They, in fact, quite, quite privately, bore me. Now these ones that I have just read, the ones that are very recent, I've got to say them, I speak them to myself, and I think that this in my own writing development is quite a new thing with me, and whatever lucidity they may have comes from the fact that I say them to myself, I say them aloud. (Plath, *Plath Reads Plath*)

Plath's sense of reading here isn't performative, it's compositional: speaking aloud is for her analogous to speaking out *Ariel*'s furious—or in this case "lucid"—contents. Perhaps for this reason, crying, wailing, and particularly shrieking suffuse the *Ariel* poems, which figure sound as an explosive, destructive, aggressive kind of expression that also contains a liberating agency.

Such voices are so contradictory and raw, projecting both the threat of love and the promise of terror, they might actually be seen as the dominant thematic unity in the entire collection.[2] The book's opening poem, "Morning Song," for instance, begins with the baby's "bald cry" and ends with her "handful of notes; / The clear vowels rise like balloons" (*Ariel* 5). Chiming with this opening gesture, cries of children punctuate the volume. In "Ariel," the speaker, hurtling through space, explains how "The child's cry // Melts in the wall" (33–34). "Stopped Dead" opens with a grim nexus of skidding airplane tires and a baby's wail—"A squeal of brakes. / Or is it a birth cry?" (43)—and continues by noting the grating sounds of a child's howling:

> With a goddam baby screaming off somewhere.
> There's always a bloody baby in the air.
> I'd call it a sunset, but
> Whoever heard a sunset yowl like that? (*Ariel* 43)

"A Birthday Present" further captures the strange linkage between violence and purity associated with children's cries in the image of a knife, death itself, which ends the poem: "And the knife not carve, but enter // Pure and clean as the cry of a baby" (*Ariel* 68). In fact, the voice here could be heard as rattling the association of femininity and nurturing, children and innocent benignity. When not associated with babies and children, the voice in *Ariel* is often muffled or bursting violently forth. In "Daddy," "I could never talk to you. / The tongue stuck in my jaw. // It stuck in the barb wire snare. / Ich, ich, ich, ich. / I could hardly speak" (74–75); in "The Rabbit Catcher" (once considered for the title to the volume as a whole), the wind is "gagging my mouth with my own blown hair, / Tearing off my voice" (7). "Medusa" has its "landspit of stony mouth-plugs" (60), "Purdah" its "mouth / veil" (62–63). And then many poems simply shriek aloud, sounding cries against enforced silences. In "Elm," the speaker wonders, "Is it the sea you hear in me, / Its dissatisfactions? / Or the voice of nothing, that was your madness?" before figuring voice as hurricane: "A wind of such violence / Will tolerate no bystanding: I must shriek" (27). "I am inhabited by a cry," the speaker goes on. "Nightly it flaps out / Looking, with its hooks, for something to love" (28). In "The Other," "Navel cords, blue-red and lucent, // Shriek from my belly like arrows" (41). "Purdah" ends:

> I shall unloose—
> From the small jeweled
> Doll he guards like a heart—

The lioness,
The shriek in the bath,
The cloak of holes. (*Ariel* 64)

In the context of Plath's own sense of her voice's importance to writing, it's hard not to hear in these images and situations a link between female speech and liberating, if not also destructive and violent, power. I think that the struggle in these poems is not one between demonstrating or challenging presence and authenticity in the sixties manner but rather devising a way to embody feminine presence in a language that was, to some extent, and surely to Plath, tyrannically male. In figurative and literal terms, voice was the means toward this end.

Of all the poems in *Ariel*, perhaps "The Courage of Shutting-Up" (in early drafts titled "The Courage of Quietness") most neatly aligns the voice to the newly minted forms of reading and recording that Plath was beginning to appreciate. Speaking to Orr, Plath remarks, "I feel that this development of recording poems, of speaking poems at readings, of having records of poets, I think this is a wonderful thing. I'm very excited by it. In a sense, there's a return, isn't there, to the old role of the poet, which was to speak to a group of people, to, to come across" (Plath, *Plath Reads Plath*). "Shutting-Up" imagines a voice of violent protest in the image of black vinyl LPs. If the shut mouth in the poem is described as "The line pink and quiet, a worm, basking," it contrasts the "black discs," "the discs of outrage" that contain the speaker's implicit vocalizing (*Ariel* 45). The LP record here represents some smoldering capacity for long-repressed voice to sound itself. Even the record needle itself is conceived as a mythic "beast" in a forbidding landscape, and the poem as a whole offers an insight into Plath's sense of audiographic possibilities:

The discs revolve, they ask to be heard,

Loaded, as they are, with accounts of bastardies.
Bastardies, usages, desertions and doubleness,
The needle journeying in its groove,
Silver beast between two dark canyons (*Ariel* 45)

Recordings hold the contradictory, illicit, wily, and unruly voice in all its "doubleness"—the poetic voice itself—within its heavily eroticized and feminine "dark canyons." (The poem also pictures the tongue: "It has nine tails, it is dangerous. / And the noise it flays from the air, once it gets going" [*Ariel* 45].) Recording and its physical paraphernalia, as well as the voice out loud, had become crucial means toward illicit, unregulated, and bastard forms of expression.

The Orr recording is Plath's penultimate recorded performance, and it is perhaps the most powerful she gave. It was preceded, however, by numerous other readings, including many for the BBC. At her best, largely in the recordings from 1962, Plath's is the most charged, fascinating, effective reading voice of the 1960s. It's also a force of distinctly feminine power, spoken against a lyric tradition and contemporary culture that was, as she saw it, masculine and repressive. Her actual voice is a study in itself—decidedly mannered, larded with British cadences and a theatrical accent, though Plath also retains American speech sounds and flat Boston vowels. It's a crazy quilt, really, a transatlantic vocal patchwork; Plath herself referred to it as "my odd accent" (*Spoken Word* liner notes). But accent is only a piece of it; there are oddities aplenty. Sometimes she sounds almost elderly, quivering and shaky and slow—pitched a little high in the early BBC recordings but growing lower and more guttural as the months wore on—and yet her poised timbre and modulated balance mark her voice clearly as that of a young mouth speaking out a fiercely intelligent consciousness. Perhaps most fascinating is the way Plath's voice develops over the course of a few years, from something controlled and perhaps even stiff into a scorching, searing lyric unction. On June 5, 1961, Plath read a series of poems on women for a BBC program titled *The Living Poet*, each one preceded by a short introduction: "The Disquieting Muses," "Spinster," "Parliament Hill Fields," and "The Stones," the final section of her sequence "For a Birthday." The format is somewhat jarring due to some basic contrasts: Plath is clearly in a small space (one can "hear the room," the closeness of the walls, due to the recording's marginal quality) and read from prepared remarks in a careful voice. Yet the poems themselves serve as an anthology of feminine identity and grow in force and slow in speed as she moves forward.

Plath prefaces this reading in measured terms that are, in their prosy exactitude and balance, comically at odds with the fierceness that follows: "They are, quite emphatically, about the things of this world. When I say 'this world,' I include of course such feelings as fear and despair and barrenness, as well as domestic love and delight in nature. These darker emotions may well put on the masks of quite unworldly things, such as ghosts and trolls and antique gods" (*Spoken Word*). The reading begins, and Plath moves gingerly through the lines, the first two poems read well though not with great fervor. And then, in "Parliament Hill Fields," some of what would become her later style begins to emerge. She slows, leaving long, surprising pauses between lines and stanzas. The final poem, "The Stones," draws down the pace more, and when Plath gets to the final stanza, her voice falters, especially at the line "My mendings itch," which she reads with an audible sigh and exhalation, as if the speaking poet—Plath herself—dropped the speakerly persona and let it all out. I know: one can't begin parsing what's "real" and what's "performed" in a reading—the very act of reading is predicated on blurring such distinctions—but the recording does presage Plath's later reading with Orr, in which she seethes with an attractive, sexual, and incantatory malice. It's the effect of Plath's voice, rather than any clear intention, that gets captured here, that oozes from the recorded track.

And it's just such a difference that makes the Orr recording special. Plath reads this sequence of poems with a ferocity that is surprising when contrasted to her BBC recordings. In fact, Plath's attitude toward the Orr recording seems to have been different from her attitude toward the recordings for the BBC, which she saw as part of her publication record. The facsimile of *Ariel*'s table of contents, reproduced in the restored edition, includes notes jotted in pen next to each poem that had been previously published, presumably to keep account of a planned acknowledgments page. Alongside names of periodicals like the *Partisan Review*, the *Atlantic Monthly*, *Poetry*, and the *New Yorker* were scribbled the letters "BBC," indicating poems she read in *The Living Poet* broadcast, along with a number of other broadcasts she made there. She also cites her reading at the Mermaid Theatre, mentioned earlier. Yet the Orr reading isn't included in these jottings, suggesting that Plath saw this performance as something other than publication, something less permanent or official. Many of these poems were so new on the day of the recording—above Plath calls them "very recent," somewhat of an understatement—that she may well have not seen them as complete. "Nick and the Candlestick," "Purdah," and "Lady Lazarus," for example, had all been finished on October 29, the day before she sat down with Orr; mere hours, in this case, stood between composition and performance. Perhaps what she saw as a marginal space for her reading—into a tape machine, not knowing where her voice would end up—allowed her a freedom unachieved in reading for the august institution of the BBC.

The Orr reading seethes. Now the pace is quick again, tense and alive, but Plath's voice shivers with emotion. In "Poppies in October," even the title is spat out. The line "Utterly unasked for" sounds as though spoken in an argument; it has the ring of contentious verbal sparring. "Igniting its carbon monoxides" shakes a little, barely stable. Plath's reading of "Purdah," which refers to the Islamic practice of covering the female body, is equally engorged with emotion. In fact, Plath begins to "sigh" words in this poem in the manner of Robert Frost's emotive trills, lengthening some words and raising her voice a notch. The lines "My eye / Veil" is sighed; the phrase "O chatterers" is shot through with an arch, condescending resonance. When Plath reads the poem's final line—"The cloak of holes"—it sounds as though she is about to burst into tears.

Coming at the end of this study, which encourages deep skepticism regarding the performance of authenticity in the reading of the 1960s, I feel I must tread cautiously regarding this point. On the one hand, I don't want to suggest by this analysis that Plath found in speaking her poems aloud something purely liberating and able to communicate freely and presently—"to come across," as she phrases it to Orr, in a full flower of unmediated emotion and presence. Such is the stuff of humanist mythmaking. Yet it's also true that for Plath, reading aloud had become for her a fundamental activity at the very time her poetry leapt into its new register, into "the *Ariel* voice" (*Ariel* xii), as her daughter Frieda Hughes puts it. This may not be a coincidence, and it's worth considering how much reading aloud not only served Plath's performances of the poems but contributed to their very existence. Reading coincides, roughly speaking, with Plath's post-*Colossus* writing: both began around 1961.[3] As Plath says above, "I can't read any of the [*Colossus*] poems aloud now," as something fundamental had changed. Plath's reading onstage syncs up nicely with her growing sense of her voice's power, which grew in force over her final years and suffused, in figurative terms, her last, most important book. And the terms of her concern weren't necessarily poetry and its newly shifting status, its warped and warping life in the public sphere, the conflicts of skeptical humanism; rather, it may more fundamentally concern her role as a woman, living in England, writing in a poetic tradition most wholly sanctified, in her eyes, as male.

Because of this gendered perspective on Plath's reading, it's fascinating to see how different things were, months earlier, when Plath was interviewed on the BBC alongside Ted Hughes in a program titled *Two of a Kind: Poets in Partnership*, recorded for broadcast on January 18, 1961. The interview, conducted by Owen Leeming, focused at times on the couple's domestic arrangements and writing habits. Notable is how fiercely Plath articulates herself in domestic terms. She fields the questions about their household, doing chores, the state of the household finances. "I always can take up a secretarial job or a part-time job if we get close to starving or finding the larder too bare," Plath avers. "Being a very practical and domestic housewife as I am, I think the advantages are too great to want to change," she claims. "I think we're both very much family oriented. I mean, I envision a large house stocked with small children and small animals." Hughes mumbles laconically, saying less, a little diffident in comparison to Plath's vocal adrenaline. At the end of the recording, Plath reads "Mushrooms," a poem that—in this context—sounds like a deferral to meekness. "Perfectly voiceless," the mushrooms speak in unison, "we are meek, / We are edible" (*Collected Poems* 139). One might argue that the mushrooms display a canny rhetorical force, claiming supplication but demonstrating a threat of "Soft fists" and "Our hammers, our rams"—and yet the poem's final lines contain a Christ-like paean to patience and withdrawal: "We shall by morning / Inherit the earth" (140). If Plath grows in power and gendered inclination as she reads poetry aloud, on radio, and into microphones over the coming years, the BBC interview with Hughes shows how much she articulated herself as a woman, and as a married woman in an English recording studio, talking alongside her husband.

Listening in to Plath's voice helps us ask how reading served to address what it was like being a female poet in the early 1960s. Of course, all of these readings took place in England, away from the immediate context of the burgeoning social crises that would end up defining sixties culture more broadly. This is one reason I've not focused on Plath in this book, though another is that her work is more fundamentally associated with so-called confessional poetry, which itself contains a set of controlling ideas about revelation, honesty, presence, and authentic speech, ones that are different—or at least, distinct—from the kinds described in previous chapters.

Yet by putting our ears in this manner to the tweeters and woofers of other sixties readers, a similar emphasis on gendered concern appears, though in ways distinct from Plath's feminist mode. For a gay poet like Frank O'Hara, some readings certainly sounded conventional, as a number of poems accessible on his Random House Voice of the Poet compilation CD attest—poems like "Having a Coke with You," "Ave Maria," and "Blocks." Yet when O'Hara reads "To the Film Industry in Crisis," something interesting happens. The poem itself is a camp ode to Hollywood, its elaborately overblown syntax signifying right off the bat the kind of fey tomfoolery O'Hara's poems are sometimes mistakenly thought to embody as a primary virtue:

> Not you, lean quarterlies and swarthy periodicals
> with your studious incursions toward the pomposity of ants,
> nor you, experimental theatre in which Emotive Fruition
> is wedding Poetic Insight perpetually, nor you,
> promenading Grand Opera, obvious as an ear (though you
> are close to my heart), but you, Motion Picture Industry,
> it's you I love! (*Selected Poems* 92)

The phrases strain credulity, the high-blown constructions tirelessly winking at us, and in the recording—made on May 11, 1959—O'Hara begins loosely, his tone suggesting this is all for fun. It's a *blague*, a jest. In fact, to signal this, prior to the poem actually beginning we hear the famous theme song of Twentieth Century Fox, its blaze of horns, and then O'Hara's voice begins, casually navigating the many overcooked syllables. And then, in the midst of the long second stanza, a piano begins playing a jaunty music hall rag, right at the first mention of a Hollywood personality, the now-forgotten film star Richard Barthelmess. And then Jane Freilicher, O'Hara's close friend and muse and New York School scenester, begins trading lines with him. Her voice, even more than his, suggests a comic lassitude, and in lines like "Ginger Rogers with her pageboy bob like a sausage on her shuffling shoulders," she ekes out a kind of urban, New York–accented, working-girl faux melancholy that jibes against the stuffed-owl diction. It's a hilarious performance, and as O'Hara and Freilicher move through the poem trading fours, as it were—and sometimes reading a line together, as in "The Tarzans"—a listener realizes how far from any other kind of serious poetry in performance this is. It's pure camp, a production more than a reading—the back-and-forth between O'Hara and Freilicher implies a series of practices and a fair amount of prereading preparation, hardly a spontaneous bid at authentic presence, though also an intervention into the high seriousness with which readings were being staged.

Other poems attest to this. O'Hara seems to puncture pretentiousness when, by way of preface to his reading of "Poem (Lana Turner Has Collapsed)," he refers to it as a "sort of walking-around-New-York type" poem—now a common way to describe O'Hara's poems, but then somewhat more fresh. In fact, the story of this poem's composition has become a stock bit of lore about the antipretentiousness and deliberately unserious approach to writing adopted by poets of the New York School. O'Hara claimed he wrote the poem on the ferry coming to a poetry reading on Staten Island.[4] I would add to this common wisdom on O'Hara's compositional looseness and resistance to the high literary mode that he is also performing, in these moments, as a gay man in a deeply masculine scene (the Lana Turner anecdote derives from O'Hara's oddly paired reading on Staten Island with the Brahmin Robert Lowell). Note 51 of Susan Sontag's "Notes on 'Camp,'" the baptismal 1964 source on the subject, suggests an indelible line linking camp and queer: "The peculiar relation between Camp taste and homosexuality has to be explained. While it's not true that Camp taste *is* homosexual taste, there is no doubt a peculiar affinity and overlap" (285). O'Hara's production of the "Film Industry" puff is an effort at gay camp deflation, an intervention into the growing high (masculine?) seriousness of the reading scene.

If we miss the effects of O'Hara's queer productions, and if we don't listen in to Plath's contrapuntal voice, we might imagine the antinomies of sixties reading concerned only with such things as Frost and Olson deconstructing lyric presence in front of grim-spectacled audiences taking careful note. While this was the major strain of reading that characterizes the 1960s staged and recorded performance, Plath and O'Hara embody a different way of showing up, of putting one's body on the line. For O'Hara, reading wasn't a performance of strength or an authentic bid at presence or orality or anything particularly theoretically coherent but rather a courting of evasion and roundabout expression of a new, urban, gay sensibility present in mainstream readings but sub rosa, contained. Like Plath, O'Hara saw possibilities in voice and voicing that allowed him to push back against the idea of a totalized masculine speaker, a monolithic culture of voiced poetry. Plath turned on the patriarchal diocese, O'Hara chuckled blithely in the hetero-utopia of postwar Manhattan, each reading as a woman or a queer and using the reading to do things unavailable in print alone. There are many more examples like these, other antinomies of sixties reading out there, still waiting their turn to be heard.

Appendix | Online Audio Resources

While a number of recordings discussed in this book are available only in archives, many are accessible online, and the bank of publicly available streaming audio grows by the day. Following are some major Websites featuring audio and video files, ranked in descending order of largeness, accessibility, and usefulness.

PennSound

http://writing.upenn.edu/pennsound/

Founded in 2005, PennSound is the most significant Web-based resource for poetry recordings. It features easily accessible MP3 files of hundreds of poets, including major modernist figures, and emphasizes postwar and contemporary poetries.

The Woodberry Poetry Room

http://hcl.harvard.edu/poetryroom/listeningbooth/index.cfm#

The Listening Booth portion of the Woodberry Room's Website features numerous streaming files of readings that took place on Harvard's campus. While the Woodberry's physical holdings are far greater, due to copyright restrictions some of this material is not publicly accessible online (all of it may be accessed on-site by visitors). The Vocarium section of the site includes recordings of discussion panels, group readings, and other nontraditional formats.

UbuWeb

http://www.ubu.com/

UbuWeb is a unique, sprawling site that offers a huge number of sound and video files. It serves as an online archive but also a contemporary publishing hub and is exclusively dedicated to the avant-garde.

Naropa University

http://www.naropa.edu/allen-ginsberg-library/about-the-library/special-collections/#recordings

Like the Woodberry Room, the core of Naropa's collection of sound recordings is drawn from taped events that took place on campus. Founded in 1974, Naropa University is closely associated with the Beat poets and features a strong collection of their readings, though more recently it's become associated with experimental poetries. Many tapes have been digitized and are searchable for streaming.

The Academy of American Poets

http://www.poets.org/page.php/prmID/36

While not as extensive as PennSound or UbuWeb, this site features recordings of some major American poets. The Website includes streaming audio and video files, though some complete recordings must be purchased.

Poets House

http://www.poetshouse.org/watch-listen-and-discuss/listen

Poets House contains a limited number of recordings, audio and visual, all accessible online. Formats include traditional readings by single poets, panel discussions, lectures, and craft talks.

The Poetry Foundation

http://www.poetryfoundation.org/features/audio/all

The Website for the Poetry Foundation, publisher of *Poetry* magazine, includes numerous readings of single poems from their Poem of the Day feature, as well as podcasts and talks.

Notes

Chapter 1

1. Daniel Kane refers to "the sociability of poetry readings" (30) on the Lower East Side during the early 1960s. According to Kane, such readings should be distinguished from the kind of academic stage performance featuring a solitary, intoning poet; instead, they "tended to focus as much on the immediate community at the readings as they did on the poet reading" (31) and featured a "preponderance of extraliterary speech" (31). Rather than serving simply as occasions for individual authors to read, they were "social, aesthetic, and experimental meeting grounds for a community of people whose main organizing principle was poetry" (33). The Ashbery tape conforms to Kane's description of these readings, particularly in terms of its "sociability" and communal aura.

2. Other key full-length studies include (as previously mentioned) Kane; Somers-Willett. See also Perloff and Dworkin, whose anthology addresses questions of performance, the avant-garde, recording technologies, and aural voice as a corrective to the relegation of voice to, as Perloff rightly puts it, "a kind of sideline" (9).

3. See Rubin for a detailed account of this history. Also see Szefel for a different perspective on the role of institutions in shaping reading practices in the early twentieth century.

4. Ed Sanders's mimeographed magazine *Poets at Les Deux Mégots* and Ted Berrigan's *C: A Journal of Poetry*—originally titled *Censored Review* because it was founded after Berrigan's poetry, which included the word "fuck," was rejected on grounds of obscenity by the *Columbia Review*—are two more examples of poets' quick and canny use of cheap modes of publication, many of which served the goal of immediate circulation. Both of these examples are drawn from Kane xv, 100–22. This was not a phenomenon unique to the 1960s. For an excellent history of the material history of earlier political poetry, see Nelson.

5. The field of lyric theory has more recently taken up with vigorous and conflicting debate questions of poetry's ontology. For two recent and conflicting examples, see Blasing; Jackson, *Dickinson's Misery*.

6. Charles Bernstein, along with Al Filreis the cofounder of PennSound, emphasizes the need for preserving disintegrating audio sources in his press release for the Website itself (PennSound). For a thoughtful discussion of pedagogical implications of poetry sound recording, see Furr 151–66.

7. For a full discussion of Antin's method, see Allison. Michael Davidson offers another such example in his description of Paul Blackburn's use of the tape recorder as a "dimension of his material text" (*Ghostlier* 107).

8. Two recent books do begin to address modernist poets more fully: see Wheeler, *Voicing*, which includes chapters on Edna St. Vincent Millay and Langston Hughes; and Furr. Christopher Grobe's recent essay in *PMLA* argues that confessional poets, including Lowell and Plath, were in fact creating a performance genre.

Chapter 2

1. Monteiro cites a *New York Times* review of Frost's 1962 book *In the Clearing* that reveals just how plain this link was to most readers: "Old-stone savage or new-power-hungry savage . . . the good-fences-make-good-neighbors philosophy is riddled again in Berlin" ("Frost's Politics" 236).

2. While there is no major critical literature that theorizes Frost's voice, it is common to make mention of it. Two of Frost's biographers, Lawrance Thompson and Jay Parini, often describe Frost's readings, and Evans and Newdick comment on Frost's reading persona and performance. Numerous monographs mention asides at readings, though none take up the subject of the readings themselves. Beyond the recordings at Harvard and the LOC, many of Frost's readings are preserved today on audiotape. Frost held posts of consultant in poetry and the humanities to the Library of Congress from 1958 to 1963, which means many of his late readings, press conferences, and speeches at festivals and celebratory dinners were recorded and are now housed there. Frost also made three studio recordings for the Archive of Recorded Poetry and Literature at the Library of Congress in 1948, 1953, and 1959. The LOC holds recordings of public readings Frost gave there as well, including speeches at dinners and press conferences held after his trip to the U.S.S.R. Furthermore, Frost's association with a number of educational institutions—including Harvard University, Amherst College, the University of Michigan, Middlebury College (through Bread Loaf), and Dartmouth College—led to his poetry being recorded even more. And not all Frost's recordings are archival: Frost pressed his own Caedmon vinyl, *Robert Frost in Recital*, in 1976, and today his work enjoys representation on CD.

3. While Frost does share a number of elements of platform poet-performers like Lindsay and Riley (he is folksy, entertaining, comfortably bucolic, and anecdotal, and he exploits reading for financial gain), in a caveat that has broad implications for

Frost, the "actual" speaking voices of poets like Lindsay and Riley betray a different set of reading conventions. Lindsay's reading voice is a highly affected, trilling rococo, especially when reading poems like "The Congo," when he actually sings lines like "never again will we hoodoo you" in mock-chant, and throughout his performance he howls, screeches, and ranges between at least two octaves. A rare 1911 recording of Riley reading "Knee-Deep in June" reveals a striking resemblance to Frost's typical reading of "The Witch of Coös," in which Frost impersonates the Mother and Son of that poem by emphasizing their sharp New England accents. The difference is that where Riley seems to take the voice of a country farmer on as his own in a sort of full-character impersonation, Frost maintains his own difference as a speaker, which is clearly distinct from the "characters" he imitates. Whereas platform poets embody their subjects, Frost represents them.

4. Yopie Prins has made a similar argument about Victorian poetry in general, which, as she says, "circulated as 'acoustic devices' for the mediation of voice, preceding and perhaps even predicting the sound reproduction technologies that emerged in the course of the nineteenth century" (44).

5. It should be stressed that "humanism" as I'm using it is distinct from the term's use during Frost's lifetime, especially as popularized by the work of the conservative cultural and literary critic Irving Babbitt. Indeed, Frost was so displeased by his friend Gorham Munson's association of himself with Babbitt's "New Humanism" in his 1927 book *Robert Frost: A Study in Sensibility and Good Sense* (and then again later in his 1930 article "Robert Frost and the Humanist Temper") that it caused a permanent rift in their friendship. Babbitt's humanism was an assault on the legacy of Romanticism, and particularly the work of Rousseau as described in *Rousseau and Romanticism* (1919). Babbitt argued that modern culture post-Rousseau was a "struggle between the general sense and the sense of the individual" and that the weight of the latter was perilously tipping the scales (10). Romanticism, Babbitt argued, had ushered in self-gratifying "imaginative unrestraint" (14), and he called for a return to a "classicism" of "nature, imitation, probability and decorum" (17). In the process of this polemic, Babbitt critiqued the Christian emphasis on heavenly rewards as well as the interior psychology of Frost's erstwhile intellectual mentor, William James. For these reasons alone, Frost had no interest in being part of Babbitt's company. For more on the Babbitt/Munson controversy, see Thompson, *Triumph* 323–27.

6. This is a particularly useful poem to study in this context because its popular reception as earnest advice has been shown to stand at odds with Frost's claim about the poem's true intention—as a "sly jest," as George Monteiro puts it, to his friend Edward Thomas for his often regretful speculations on what might have been (*New England* 47). Thus the poem's reception reveals the poles of sincerity and deflection already at play.

7. There are numerous other poems in which Frost regularly retards his reading pace near the end, including "Two Tramps in Mud Time," "A Soldier," and "A Tuft of Flowers."

8. Referred to in chapter 1, Cameron's reading of the fascicles intervenes into Dickinsonian scholarship by reading poems in textually faithful fascicle versions, which expose the poems as deeply relevant to contexts outside the hermetic lyrics themselves. "I mean to ask how reading the lyric in sequence is different from reading the lyric as independent, for to do the latter is to suppress the context and the relations that govern the lyric in context—a suppression generating that understanding of Dickinson's poems as enigmatic, isolated, culturally incomprehensible phenomena" (19). It's also worth pointing out that Charles Bernstein has made the link between such a textualist claim and readings themselves: "The poem, viewed in terms of its multiple performances, or mutual intertranslatability, has a fundamentally plural existence" (9).

9. Matthew Fike has pointed to the common assumption that Frost wrote the poem as a dedication to his assistant and lover, Kay Morrison, but the reference would hardly be available to nonintimates at the time, turning the nominal poem on sentence-sounds into an oblique and private concern (Fike 109). (For an example of this common assumption, see Thompson, *Triumph* 304.) As Jeffrey Meyers proposes, directly following this poem in *A Witness Tree* Frost placed "The Subverted Flower" to suggest his subsequent conquest of Morrison/Eve (161). When performing in Washington, D.C., around the same time, Frost plunged into biography. After a reading of "A Soldier," Frost introduced his next poem, "Birds' Song," by saying merely, "This is in praise of a lady." Listeners to this reading of "Birds' Song" were directed to regard it as a poem in praise of "a lady," presumably Eve or a code for a private allusion to a lady whose singing is now represented as some beneficent balm ("in praise of") in accord with rather than antagonistic to the birdsong. Whatever the particulars of either reading, Frost's comments organize two exclusive interpretive frames.

Chapter 3

1. This chapter works from three audio recordings, two of which—the Berkeley and Goddard College readings—have been transcribed. *Mutbologos* includes the Berkeley transcript; the Goddard reading has recently been published as a separate, stand-alone volume. I generally refer to these two transcripts when possible, as they are both reliable, and doing so facilitates easy access to these materials.

2. As already mentioned, Libbie Rifkin is an exception to this oversight, as she examines Olson's performances in terms of his avant-garde identity. Olson's biographer

Tom Clark also pays attention to Olson's talks and readings. Because Olson's biography is rife with examples of him teaching (at Black Mountain and at Buffalo), as well as giving readings and talks, critics have indeed drawn upon such evidence on many occasions. However, such events haven't been treated as primary materials as such, and the live events in which Olson actually read are often deemphasized. Davidson, who broadly treats orality in sixties poetry, suggests that literal performance is less important for Olson than the page itself, which remediates it: "Despite the oralist bias of 'Projective Verse,' Olson's primary concern is phenomenological: to create a poetry as close to perception and cognition as possible. The score for such processes was a page that resembled, as closely as possible, physical acts of writing, speaking, and walking" (*Ghostlier* 14).

3. Ralph Maud points out that Olson first reported reading quotations by Malinowski in Carl Jung's *Essays on a Science of Mythology* and that he later assigned Malinowski's *Magic, Science, and Religion, and Other Essays* in his class at Buffalo in 1964–65 (*Reading* 289). Olson also drew upon Malinowski's research in the Trobriand Islands for his lecture "The Special View of History" (1956), given at the end of Olson's tenure at Black Mountain College (Maud, *Reading* 104).

4. In 1955, for example, J. L. Austin gave the William James Lectures at Harvard University; they would eventually be published as *How to Do Things with Words* (1962), which influentially argued against the "'descriptive' fallacy" (3) of purely denotational linguistic functioning, proposing instead language's "performative" capacities (4). Austin's speech act theory analyzes language that is physically productive rather than purely referential, a linguistic functionalism taken up by subsequent major linguistic philosophers like Ludwig Wittgenstein (particularly in the later *Philosophical Investigations*), Jacques Derrida, and John Searle. These debates move far from Olson's concern for a language in which sign and referent are more intimately aligned, though they share the basic concern with reference and embodiment that Olson voices here.

5. Williams discusses his reliance on the typewriter in the foreword to his *Autobiography* (xviii), among other places.

6. Ralph Maud cautions that while "infinitely allusive," most of the references were in fact to people and recent events rather than actual texts, though there are certainly many literary allusions (*Harbor* 171).

7. In a surprising echo, Olson's "Cashes" recalls Wordsworth's positioning of the poet in relationship to the folk voice, what the English poet famously referred to as "the language of men who speak of what they do not understand" (23). Less frequently quoted is Wordsworth's parenthetical aside regarding this language, which he says is "purified indeed from what appear to be its real defects, from all lasting and rational causes of like or disgust" (21).

Chapter 4

1. This episode is frequently mentioned in writing on Brooks's life. For a thorough treatment of the conference itself, see Kent 195–202.

2. See Wheeler's "Heralding the Clear Obscure" and Lindberg for succinct presentations of this critical split. Also see Melhem's references to this "visionary moment" (*Poetry* 12) in Brooks's career. Erkkila frames the split in gendered terms, arguing that "while Brooks's post-1967 transformation led to a new sense of black power and consciousness, her commitment to a strongly male-identified Black Power movement also led to an increased sense of ambivalence about her identity and role as a black woman poet writing in America" (213).

3. From a further vantage, this public/private antinomy is simply a feature of lyric poetry itself, here famously described by Adorno: "For the substance of a poem is not merely an expression of individual impulses and experiences. Those become a matter of art only when they participate in something universal by virtue of the specificity they acquire by being given aesthetic form" (38). For a more recent iteration of this idea, see Blasing, who claims that the lyric "I" isn't an expression of an Enlightenment subjectivity but rather an effect generated by a "microrhetorical" (38) disjunction between sound and sense.

4. Brooks could also be referring to other encounters with the great singer. Robeson appeared in Chicago at least twice. In 1949, when Brooks was thirty-two, he performed at the Tabernacle Baptist Church on the South Side, where Brooks lived (Duberman 375). Then in 1958, Robeson played a concert at the Parkway Ballroom, an event reported in *Jet* magazine (Duberman 457). The Peace Arch concert was taken up by the press and would have been a widely available news item (433). It's also worth mentioning that in 1978, years after this poem was published (in *Family Pictures* in 1970), Brooks was a signatory to a document protesting a Broadway play depicting Robeson and starring James Earl Jones. A folder in Brooks's papers at the Bancroft includes documents showing that the controversy surrounding the play was sparked because Robeson's life had been sanitized and stripped of racial struggle. Among Brooks's papers is a photocopy of a transcription she (or someone else) made of a TV editorial by Pat Collins, a "drama critic" for Channel 2, "as broadcast on Jan. 19, 1978." Collins put it this way: "This play has seemingly been produced with this thought in mind—attract that growing black audience to Broadway but don't alienate the white theatre-goer in the meantime. Frankly, I have no other explanation for a play about Paul Robeson that downplays the topic of home-grown racism. Don't make the audience uncomfortable—give them nostalgia, lots of anecdotes, and keep Robeson's passion for equality to a minimum."

5. Though Brooks disavows "speaking and marching" in the civil rights movement, Brooks's papers include an unpublished poem on the CRM titled "Look at these faces, these scenes," written September 17, 1967—just a few months after the Fisk conference. The poem describes an actual march and ends with an urgent revision to the movement's refrain ending "someday." Here, it's "right now":

Look at these faces, these scenes.
In them: centuries of retch,
roar underbeaten, wound and dismissal,
nervous pianissimo, dangerous crescendo
And the revision of a theme—we shall
overcome, right now.

6. While "De Witt Williams" was banned from the airwaves in 1962, it was read without incident in the 1940s, along with other poems from *A Street in Bronzeville*, on the radio station WNEW in New York City (Melhem, *Poetry* 31).

7. This poem is printed on the Official Inaugural Program for the event. That Brooks wrote such an occasional poem suggests how seriously she took her role as public reader. The poem has not been published before and appears in print here for the first time:

Suddenly

a hand comes.

Help comes.

This Moral Ceiling and Recurrent Giver—

this gymnast of the Fire—

made common sense into a Bread and fed

the people. Said :

Antiquity is not a proof of right.

Said : Right must not be judged by candlelight.

Above old fear, above old height and fibre,

he

is central candor, and a clarity.

8. Programs, pamphlets, and notices for all of these readings are located in Brooks's archive at the Bancroft.

9. While I refer to this reading by its place of occurrence, Asilomar, the recording itself is titled simply "A Poetry Reading."

10. Brooks's appearance at Asilomar was also inflected by gender, something I've not been stressing due to its ample discussion elsewhere (see Erkkila). It's difficult, however, to overlook how Brooks was marginalized by her presence at Asilomar without considering gender. In the reading itself, she performed first, despite the fact of her greater fame and literary success, if measured by prizes, length of career, age, or any other metric. Jones had just two books published by this point, compared to Brooks's three, one of which won the Pulitzer Prize; Brooks had also simply been writing for much longer. Brooks was furthermore not included in *Anger, and Beyond* (1966), the volume of essays compiled after the Asilomar conference by Herbert Hill, the event's organizer. The book includes an essay by Jones titled "Philistinism and the Negro Writer," in which he names only men as important black voices—"W. E. B. Du Bois, Richard Wright, Jean Toomer, Langston Hughes, Ellison, Baldwin, Chester Himes" (58). *Anger* also features "The Afternoon of a Young Poet" by M. Carl Holman, a narrative of poetic coming-of-age by the less-accomplished Holman. It's hard to imagine an explanation for Brooks's exclusion from this volume, and Holman's inclusion, that doesn't ascribe some weight to Brooks's gender.

Chapter 5

1. The word "disabled" is a highly contested one in the field of disability studies, which has been careful to dissociate terms of physical or mental difference and insufficiency. Rather, critics and theorists routinely describe how disability has been fashioned into a defect by assumed standards of able-bodied normalcy. "Disability," writes Rosemarie Garland-Thomson, "is the attribution of corporeal deviance—not so much a property of bodies as a product of cultural rules about what bodies should be or do" (*Extraordinary* 6). In a similar vein, Simi Linton questions the ways in which disability "appears to signify something material and concrete" when it is in fact "an arbitrary designation" (224). Rejected as a marker of essentialized, impaired difference, the word "disability" has been rhetorically transformed by writers such as Thomson and Linton from a natural defect or attribution of physical or cognitive lack to an identity chosen with deliberate intent. As I use them in what follows, the words "disability" and its cognate "disabled" refer not to a secure category of physical difference but more descriptively to each poets' challenges with speech. For a substantive discussion of "disability" and the related term "cripple," see Shapiro 33–34.

2. I had the chance to listen to recordings of Meredith reading at Bread Loaf

during the 1990s from tapes made by Meredith's editor and friend, the poet Michael Collier.

3. McRuer's *Crip Theory*, one of cripping's central theoretical texts (though McRuer calls it "crippin'" [35]), cites the centrality of "transformation" in his term "severe disability." McRuer's central insight is that the heteronormativity and the establishment of heterosexuality as normal and natural, a phenomenon described by queer theorists, is deeply intertwined with what he calls "compulsory able-bodiedness" (2), so much so that "compulsory heterosexuality is contingent on compulsory able-bodiedness, and vice versa" (2).

4. On the performance of disability in everyday life, including references to Belluso's ideas of everyday performance, see Sahndal and Auslander 2; Davidson (*Concerto* 19).

5. While speech itself has been largely overlooked in many cases, it has not in terms of Deaf performance, the subject of widespread critical interest. Beyond Brueggemann, also see Davidson's "Hearing Things: The Scandal of Speech in Deaf Performance," in *Concerto*; and the essays by Rosemarie Garland-Thomson, Jessica Berson, and Jim Ferris collected under the heading "Taxonomies: Disability & Deaf Performances in the Process of Self-Definition," in Sandahl and Auslander.

6. For discussions of the link between Williams's speech problems and formal innovations, see Leibowitz, who refers to tercets as "a kind of speech therapy" (430).

7. Disability studies is rife with counterclaims against the association of disability with negativity, limitation, and lack. One could argue, in fact, that such an uncritical association serves as the root of the critical response to ableist culture that sparked the DRM itself. On this topic, see Garland-Thomson, *Extraordinary* 5–51.

8. "Ableism" refers to the assumption of a nondisabled perspective and the prejudicial and asymmetrical values generated by such a point of view. Linton associates ableism with racism and sexism and adds that "ableism also includes the idea that a person's abilities or characteristics are determined by disability or that people with disabilities as a group are inferior to non-disabled people" (223).

9. Davidson points out that critics have generally not treated, much less mentioned, Eigner's physical status (*Concerto* 121).

10. Copies of this cassette are rare, though the recording itself has been digitized and is available at PennSound. Notes on the physical cassette were taken from the copy in the Thomas J. Dodd Center at the University of Connecticut.

11. Lennard Davis's *Enforcing Normalcy* is an early key text in the field that makes the argument for constructivism. Also see Garland-Thomson, *Extraordinary Bodies*.

12. For more on this, see Shakespeare, "The Social Model of Disability," which outlines the founding of political activity surrounding this deconstructive principle.

Conclusion

1. This recording first appeared on the British Argo label in 1965 and was reissued in the United States as *Plath Reads Plath* (Credo 1975). While there are other hard-copy versions of these audiotexts, numerous online clips make them readily available. For a detailed account of this recording and its context, and other recordings, see Moses.

2. In this discussion I refer to the "restored edition" of *Ariel*, including the facsimile of the book's original manuscript, which contains Plath's arrangement of poems.

3. Plath's first recording for the BBC was made on October 26, 1960. Her final BBC recording was taped on January 10, 1963, just weeks before her death. It's true that Plath did read and get recorded in the late 1950s as well, including a performance at Harvard on June 13, 1958. Yet it's not until midway through Plath's BBC readings that she begins to achieve her true effectiveness as a performer.

4. For the full story, see Lehman 349–50.

Works Cited

Texts

Adorno, Theodor. "On Lyric Poetry and Society." *Notes on Literature*. Vol. 1. New York: Columbia UP, 1991. 37–54. Print.

Allen, Donald, ed. *The New American Poetry: 1945–1960*. Berkeley: U of California P, 1960. Print.

Allison, Raphael. "David Antin's Pragmatist Technophobia." *Journal of Modern Literature* 28.4 (2005): 110–34. Print.

Altieri, Charles. *Enlarging the Temple: New Directions in American Poetry in the 1960s*. Lewisburg: Bucknell UP, 1979. Print.

"Apostrophe." *The New Princeton Encyclopedia of Poetry and Poetics*. Ed. Alex Preminger and T. V. F. Brogan. Princeton: Princeton UP, 1993. Print.

Article (untitled) from the *Chicago Daily News*, May 10, 1965. Gwendolyn Brooks Papers, BANC MSS 2001/83 z. Bancroft Library, University of California, Berkeley.

Article (untitled) from the *Daily Illini*, May 19, 1972. Gwendolyn Brooks Papers, BANC MSS 2001/83 z. Bancroft Library, University of California, Berkeley.

Article (untitled) from the *Kansas City Star*, Apr. 14, 1964. Gwendolyn Brooks Papers, BANC MSS 2001/83 z. Bancroft Library, University of California, Berkeley.

Ashbery, John. *Rivers and Mountains*. New York: Holt, Rinehart and Winston, 1966. Print.

———. *The Tennis Court Oath*. Middletown, CT: Wesleyan UP, 1962. Print.

Auslander, Philip. "Liveness: Performance and the Anxiety of Simulation." *Performance and Cultural Politics*. Ed. Elin Diamond. New York: Routledge, 1996. 198–218. Print.

Austin, J. L. *How to Do Things with Words*. Ed. J. O. Urmson and Marina Sbisá. 1962. Cambridge: Harvard UP, 1975. Print.

Babbitt, Irving. *Rousseau and Romanticism*. 1919. Introduction by Claes G. Ryn. New Brunswick, NJ: Transaction Publishers, 1991. Print.

Baker, Houston. "From 'The Florescence of Nationalism in the 1960s and 1970s.'" *On Gwendolyn Brooks: Reliant Contemplation.* Ed. Stephen Caldwell Wright. Ann Arbor: U of Michigan P, 2001. 116–23. Print.

Bakhtin, M. M. *The Dialogic Imagination: Four Essays.* Austin: U of Texas P, 1982. Print.

Barthes, Roland. "From Work to Text." *Image, Music, Text.* Trans. Stephen Heath. New York: Hill and Wang, 1977. 155–64. Print.

Belgrad, Daniel. *The Culture of Improvisation: Improvisation and the Arts in Post-war America.* Chicago: U of Chicago P, 1998. Print.

Berg, Peter. "The Digger." *Generation on Fire: Voices of Protest from the 1960s, an Oral History.* Ed. Jeff Kisseloff. Lexington: U of Kentucky P, 2007. 137–51. Print.

Bernstein, Charles. Introduction. *Close Listening: Poetry and the Performed Word.* Ed. Charles Bernstein. New York: Oxford UP, 1998. 3–26. Print.

Berry, Eleanor. "The Emergence of Charles Olson's Prosody of the Page Space." *Journal of English Linguistics* 30.1 (2002): 51–72. Print.

———. "William Carlos Williams' Triadic-Line Verse: An Analysis of Its Prosody." *Twentieth-Century Literature* 35.3 (1989): 354–70. Print.

Bibby, Michael. *Hearts and Minds: Bodies, Poetry, and Resistance in the Vietnam Era.* New Brunswick, NJ: Rutgers UP, 1996. Print.

Blasing, Mutlu Konuk. *Lyric Poetry: The Pain and Pleasure of Words.* Princeton: Princeton UP, 2007. Print.

Book Bulletin (Chicago Public Library) 33.1 (1951). Gwendolyn Brooks Papers, BANC MSS 2001/83 z. Bancroft Library, University of California, Berkeley.

Brooks, Gwendolyn. *Blacks.* Chicago: Third World, 1991. Print.

———. *Conversations with Gwendolyn Brooks.* Ed. Gloria Wade Gayles. Jackson: U of Mississippi P, 2003. Print.

———. "Dear Mrs. Bitterman." Letter, undated. Gwendolyn Brooks Papers, BANC MSS 2001/83 z. Bancroft Library, University of California, Berkeley.

———. Foreword. *New Negro Poets U.S.A.* Ed. Langston Hughes. Bloomington: Indiana UP, 1964. 13–15. Print.

———. "How I Think Poetry Should Be Written." Sept. 11, 1938. Gwendolyn Brooks Papers, BANC MSS 2001/83 z. Bancroft Library, University of California, Berkeley.

———. Introduction. *Jump Bad: A New Chicago Anthology.* Ed. Gwendolyn Brooks. Detroit: Broadside, 1971. 3–10. Print.

———, ed. *Jump Bad: A New Chicago Anthology.* Detroit: Broadside, 1971. Print.

———. "Look at these faces, these scenes." Gwendolyn Brooks Papers, BANC MSS 2001/83 z. Bancroft Library, University of California, Berkeley.

———. "Poets Who Are Negroes." *The Negro in Literature*. Spec. issue of *Phylon* 11.4 (1950): 296. Print.

———. *Report from Part One*. Detroit: Broadside, 1972. Print.

———. *Report from Part Two*. Chicago: Third World, 1996. Print.

———. "Richard Gordon Hatcher." Pamphlet for the City of Gary Official Inaugural Program. Gwendolyn Brooks Papers, BANC MSS 2001/83 z. Bancroft Library, University of California, Berkeley.

———. *Selected Poems*. New York: Harper Perennial, 1963. Print.

Brooks, Gwendolyn, Keorapetse Kgositsile, Haki R. Madhubuti, and Dudley Randall, eds. *A Capsule Course in Black Poetry Writing*. Detroit: Broadside, 1975. Print.

Brueggemann, Brenda Jo. "Delivering Disability, Willing Speech." *Bodies in Commotion: Disability and Performance*. Ed. Carrie Sandahl and Philip Auslander. Ann Arbor: U of Michigan P, 2005. 17–29. Print.

Butterick, George F. *A Guide to "The Maximus Poems" of Charles Olson*. Berkeley: U of California P, 1981. Print.

———. Introduction. *Muthologos: The Collected Lectures and Interviews*. Ed. George F. Butterick. Vol. 1. Bolinas: Four Seasons Foundation, 1979. ix–x. Print.

Caleb, John Rufus. "Voices of Things Black." *Dickinsonian*, Apr. 19, 1974. Gwendolyn Brooks Papers, BANC MSS 2001/83 z. Bancroft Library, University of California, Berkeley.

Cameron, Sharon. *Choosing Not Choosing: Dickinson's Fascicles*. Chicago: U of Chicago P, 1992. Print.

Carina, Sister M. Letter, dated Oct. 22, 1968. Gwendolyn Brooks Papers, BANC MSS 2001/83 z. Bancroft Library, University of California, Berkeley.

Chafe, William H. *Civilities and Civil Rights: Greensboro, North Carolina, and the Black Struggle for Freedom*. New York: Oxford UP, 1980. Print.

Clark, Tom. *Charles Olson: The Allegory of a Poet's Life*. New York: Norton, 1991. Print.

Conte, Joseph M. *Unending Design: The Forms of Postmodern Poetry*. Ithaca, NY: Cornell UP, 1991. Print.

Cruse, Harold. *The Crisis of the Negro Intellectual*. New York: Morrow, 1967. Print.

Culler, Jonathan. *The Pursuit of Signs: Semiotics, Literature, Deconstruction*. 1981. Ithaca, NY: Cornell UP, 2002. Print.

Damon, Maria. "Was That 'Different,' 'Dissident' or 'Dissonant'? Poetry (n) the Public Spear: Slams, Open Readings, and Dissident Traditions." *Close Listening: Poetry and the Performed Word*. Ed. Charles Bernstein. New York: Oxford UP, 1998. 324–42. Print.

Davidson, Michael. *Concerto for the Left Hand: Disability and the Defamiliar Body.* Ann Arbor: U of Michigan P, 2008. Print.

———. *Ghostlier Demarcations: Modern Poetry and the Material World.* Berkeley: U of California P, 1997. Print.

———. "Missing Larry: The Poetics of Disability in Larry Eigner." *Concerto for the Left Hand* 116–41. Print.

———. "Technologies of Presence: Orality and the Tapevoice of Contemporary Poetics." *Sound States: Innovative Poetics and Acoustical Technologies.* Ed. Adalaide Morris. Chapel Hill: U of North Carolina P, 1997. 97–126. Print.

Davis, Garick, ed. *Praising It New: The Best of the New Criticism.* Foreword by William Logan. Athens: Ohio UP, 2008. Print.

Davis, Lennard J. *Enforcing Normalcy: Disability, Deafness, and the Body.* New York: Verso, 1995. Print.

Davis, Ruby Dee. Letter, dated Sept. 15, 1964. Gwendolyn Brooks Papers, BANC MSS 2001/83 z. Bancroft Library, University of California, Berkeley.

Derrida, Jacques. "Ellipsis." *Writing and Difference.* Trans. Alan Bass. Chicago: U of Chicago P, 1978. Print.

Dotson, John. Letter, dated Aug. 6, 1972. Gwendolyn Brooks Papers, BANC MSS 2001/83 z. Bancroft Library, University of California, Berkeley.

Duberman, Martin Bauml. *Paul Robeson.* New York: Knopf, 1988. Print.

Duffy, Bernard. *A Poetry of Presence: The Writing of William Carlos Williams.* Madison: U of Wisconsin P, 1986. Print.

Dunning, John. *On the Air: The Encyclopedia of Old-Time Radio.* New York: Oxford UP, 1998. Print.

Eigner, Larry. *Areas/Lights/Heights: Writings 1954–1989.* Ed. Benjamin Friedlander. New York: Roof Books, 1989. Print.

———. *The Collected Poems of Larry Eigner.* Ed. Curtis Faville and Robert Grenier. 4 vols. Stanford, CA: Stanford UP, 2010. Print.

———. Letter to David and Maria Gitin, dated May 9, 1973. Larry Eigner Papers. Archives & Special Collections at the Thomas J. Dodd Research Center, University of Connecticut Libraries.

———. Letter to David and Maria Gitin, dated Jan. 23, 1975. Larry Eigner Papers. Archives & Special Collections at the Thomas J. Dodd Research Center, University of Connecticut Libraries.

———. *The World and Its Streets, Places.* Santa Barbara, CA: Black Sparrow, 1977. Print.

Emerson, Ralph Waldo. "The Poet." *Ralph Waldo Emerson: Essays & Poems.* New York: Library of America, 1996. 447–468. Print.

Erkkila, Betsy. *The Wicked Sisters: Women Poets, Literary History, and Discord.* New York: Oxford UP, 1992. Print.

Evans, William R. "Frost's 'Sound of Sense' and a Popular Audience." *American Literature* 53.1 (1981): 116–23. Print.

Ferris, Jim. "Crip Poetry, or How I Learned to Love the Limp." *Wordgathering: A Journal of Disability Poetry* 2.1 (2007). Web.

Fike, Matthew A. "Never Again Would Birds' Song Be the Same." *Explicator* 49.2 (1991): 108–12. Web.

Finkelstein, Norman. "The Crisis of Language and Poetic Identity in Williams's 'The Desert Music.'" *William Carlos Williams and the Language of Poetry.* Ed. Burton Hatlen and Demetres Tryphonopoulos. Orono, ME: National Poetry Foundation, 2002. 273–82. Print.

Fleischer, Doris Zames, and Frieda Zames. *The Disability Rights Movement: From Charity to Confrontation.* Philadelphia: Temple UP, 2001. Print.

Ford, Nick Aaron. "From 'Battle of the Books': A Critical Survey of Significant Books by and about Negroes Published in 1960." *On Gwendolyn Brooks: Reliant Contemplation.* Ed. Stephen Caldwell Wright. Ann Arbor: U of Michigan P, 2001. 17–18. Print.

Fredman, Stephen. *The Grounding of American Poetry: Charles Olson and the Emersonian Tradition.* New York: Cambridge UP, 1993. Print.

Friedlander, Benjamin. "Larry Eigner (1926–1996)." *American Poets since World War II, 6th series.* Ed. Joseph Conte. Detroit: Gale Research, 1998. 114–26. Print.

Fries, Kenny, ed. *Staring Back: The Disability Experience from the Inside Out.* New York: Penguin, 1997. Print.

Frobenius, Leo. "The Story of Rock Picture Research." *Prehistoric Rock Pictures in Europe and Africa: From Materials in the Archives of the Research Institute for the Morphology of Civilization.* Ed. Leo Frobenius and Douglas C. Fox. 1937. New York: Museum of Modern Art/Arno, 1972. 13–28. Print.

Frost, Robert. *The Collected Prose of Robert Frost.* Ed. Mark Richardson. Cambridge, MA: Belknap, 2007. Print.

———. *The Poetry of Robert Frost.* Ed. Edward Connery Lathem. New York: Holt, Rinehart and Winston, 1969. Print.

———. *Robert Frost: Speaking on Campus: Excerpts from His Talks, 1949–1962.* Ed. Edward Connery Lathem. New York: W. W. Norton, 2009. Print.

———. *Selected Letters of Robert Frost.* Ed. Lawrance Thompson. New York: Holt, Rinehart and Winston, 1964. Print.

Fuller, Hoyt W. Letter, dated Jan. 26, 1971. Gwendolyn Brooks Papers, BANC MSS 2001/83 z. Bancroft Library, University of California, Berkeley.

Furr, Derek. *Recorded Poetry and Poetic Reception from Edna Millay to the Circle of Robert Lowell.* New York: Palgrave Macmillan, 2010. Print.

Garland-Thomson, Rosemarie. "Beholding." *The Disability Studies Reader.* 3rd ed. Ed. Lennard J. Davis. New York: Routledge, 2010. Print.

———. *Extraordinary Bodies: Figuring Physical Disability in American Culture and Literature.* New York: Columbia UP, 1997. 199–208. Print.

Gates, Henry Louis, Jr. "Phillis Wheatley on Trial: In 1772, a Slave Girl Had to Prove She Was a Poet. She's Had to Do So Ever Since." *New Yorker* Jan. 20, 2003: 82–87. Print.

Ginsberg, Allen. *Collected Poems: 1947–1980.* New York: Harper & Row, 1984. Print.

———. *Deliberate Prose: Selected Essays 1952–1995.* Ed. Bill Morgan. New York: HarperCollins, 2000. Print.

———. *Howl: Original Draft Facsimile, Transcript & Variant Versions, Fully Annotated by the Author, with Contemporaneous Correspondence, Account of First Public Reading, Legal Skirmishes, Precursor Texts & Bibliography.* Ed. Barry Miles. 1956. New York: Harper & Row, 1986. Print.

———. "Notes on Finally Recording 'Howl.'" *On the Poetry of Allen Ginsberg.* Ed. Lewis Hyde. Ann Arbor: U of Michigan P, 1985. 80–84. Print.

Gitlin, Todd. *The Sixties: Years of Hope, Days of Rage.* New York: Bantam Books, 1987. Print.

Goffman, Erving. *The Presentation of Self in Everyday Life.* 1959. Woodstock, NY: Overlook, 1973. Print.

Gray, Francine du Plessix. "Black Mountain: The Breaking (Making) of a Writer." *Black Mountain College: Sprouted Seeds. An Anthology of Personal Accounts.* Ed. Mervin Lane. Knoxville: U of Tennessee P, 1990. Print.

Grobe, Christopher. "The Breath of the Poem: Confessional Print/Performance circa 1959." *PMLA* 127.2 (2012): 215–30. Print.

Hall, Donald. Column in *American Poetry Review* 34.2 (2005): 11–12. Print.

Hall, James C. *Mercy, Mercy Me: African-American Culture and the American Sixties.* New York: Oxford UP, 2001. Print.

Hart, George. "'Enough Defined': Disability, Ecopoetics, and Larry Eigner." *Contemporary Literature* 51.1 (2010): 152–79. Web.

Henderson, Winston T. "The Sundays of Satin Legs Smith." Gwendolyn Brooks Papers, BANC MSS 2001/83 z. Bancroft Library, University of California, Berkeley. Screenplay.

Hill, Herbert, ed. *Anger, and Beyond: The Negro Writer in the United States.* New York: Harper & Row, 1966. Print.

Hill-Lubin, Mildred A. Letter, dated Feb. 18, 1980. Gwendolyn Brooks Papers, BANC MSS 2001/83 z. Bancroft Library, University of California, Berkeley.

Hoffman, Tyler. *American Poetry in Performance: From Walt Whitman to Hip Hop*. Ann Arbor: U of Michigan P, 2011. Print.

———. *Robert Frost and the Politics of Poetry*. Middlebury, VT: Middlebury College P, 2001. Print.

Hoover, Paul. *Postmodern American Poetry: A Norton Anthology*. New York: Norton, 1994. Print.

Jackson, Virginia. *Dickinson's Misery: A Theory of Lyric Reading*. Princeton, NJ: Princeton UP, 2005. Print.

———. "Who Reads Poetry?" *PMLA* 123.1 (2008): 181–87. Print.

Johnson, Harriet McBryde. "Unspeakable Conversations." *The Disability Studies Reader*. 3rd ed. Ed. Lennard J. Davis. New York: Routledge, 2010. 573–85. Print.

Kane, Daniel. *All Poets Welcome: The Lower East Side Poetry Scene in the 1960s*. Berkeley: U of California P, 2003. Print.

Kearns, Katherine. "The Serpent's Tail: Robert Frost and a Poetics of Appetite." *Western Humanities Review* 47.2 (1993): 110–31. Print.

Kent, George E. *A Life of Gwendolyn Brooks*. Lexington: UP of Kentucky, 1990. Print.

Kerr, Clark. *The Uses of the University*. 1963. Cambridge, MA: Harvard UP, 2003. Print.

King, Willie Marvel. Letter, undated. Gwendolyn Brooks Papers, BANC MSS 2001/83 z. Bancroft Library, University of California, Berkeley.

Koehler, Stanley. "William Carlos Williams, the Art of Poetry No. 6." Interview. *Paris Review* 32 (Summer–Fall 1962). Web.

Kuppers, Petra. *Disability and Contemporary Performance: Bodies on Edge*. New York: Routledge, 2003. Print.

Laing, R. D. *The Politics of Experience*. New York: Pantheon, 1967. Print.

Lake, Paul. "Verse That Print Bred." *After New Formalism: Poets on Form, Narrative, and Tradition*. Ed. Annie Finch. Ashland, OR: Story Line, 1999. 25–30. Print.

Laws, Pamela Combs. Letter, dated Apr. 30, 1979. Gwendolyn Brooks Papers, BANC MSS 2001/83 z. Bancroft Library, University of California, Berkeley.

Lehman, David. *The Last Avant-Garde: The Making of the New York School*. New York: Anchor Books, 1999. Print.

Leibowitz, Herbert. *"Something Urgent I Have to Say to You": The Life and Works of William Carlos Williams*. New York: Farrar, Straus and Giroux, 2011. Print.

Lerner, Ben. *Leaving the Atocha Station*. New York: Coffee House, 2011. Print.

Lesser, Wendy. "Elegy for Mario Savio." *The Free Speech Movement: Reflections on Berkeley in the 1960s*. Ed. Robert Cohen and Reginald E. Zelnik. Berkeley: U of California P, 2002. 563–65. Print.

Levine, Lawrence W. "From the Big Apple to Berkeley: Perspectives of a Junior Faculty Member." *The Free Speech Movement: Reflections on Berkeley in the 1960s*. Ed. Robert Cohen and Reginald E. Zelnik. Berkeley: U of California P, 2002. 339–44. Print.

Lindberg, Kathryne V. "Whose Canon? Gwendolyn Brooks: Founder at the Center of the 'Margins.'" *Gendered Modernisms: American Women Poets and Their Readers*. Ed. Margaret Dickle and Thomas Travisano. Philadelphia: U of Pennsylvania P, 1996. 283–311. Print.

Linton, Simi. "Reassigning Meaning." *The Disability Studies Reader*. 3rd ed. Ed. Lennard J. Davis. New York: Routledge, 2010. 223–36. Print.

Lustig, Jeff. "The FSM and the Vision of a New Left." *The Free Speech Movement: Reflections on Berkeley in the 1960s*. Ed. Robert Cohen and Reginald E. Zelnik. Berkeley: U of California P, 2002. 215–26. Print.

MacArthur, Marit J. *The American Landscape in the Poetry of Frost, Bishop, and Ashbery: The House Abandoned*. New York: Palgrave Macmillan, 2008. Print.

Mackey, Nathaniel. *Discrepant Engagement*. Cambridge: Cambridge UP, 1993. Print.

Madhubuti, Haki R. "Gwendolyn Brooks: Beyond the Wordmaker—the Making of an African Poet." *On Gwendolyn Brooks: Reliant Contemplation*. Ed. Stephen Caldwell Wright. Ann Arbor: U of Michigan P, 1996. 81–96. Print.

Malinowski, Bronisław. "The Problem of Meaning in Primitive Languages." *The Meaning of Meaning: A Study of the Influence of Language upon Thought and of the Science of Symbolism*. Ed. C. K. Ogden and I. A. Richards. New York: Harcourt, Brace, 1938. 296–336. Print.

Marcuse, Herbert. *One-Dimensional Man: Studies in the Ideology of Advanced Industrial Society*. Boston: Beacon, 1964. Print.

Mariani, Paul. *William Carlos Williams: A New World Naked*. New York: McGraw-Hill, 1981. Print.

Martin, Waldo. "Holding One Another: Mario Savio and the Freedom Struggle in Mississippi and Berkeley." *The Free Speech Movement: Reflections on Berkeley in the 1960s*. Ed. Robert Cohen and Reginald E. Zelnik. Berkeley: U of California P, 2002. 83–102. Print.

Maud, Ralph. *Charles Olson at the Harbor*. Vancouver, BC: Talonbooks, 2008. Print.

———. *Charles Olson's Reading: A Biography*. Carbondale: Southern Illinois UP, 1996. Print.

McClure, Michael. *Scratching the Beat Surface: Essays on New Vision from Blake to Kerouac*. New York: Penguin, 1994. Print.

McGann, Jerome. *The Textual Condition*. Princeton, NJ: Princeton UP, 1991. Print.

McLuhan, Marshall. *The Gutenberg Galaxy: The Making of Typographic Man*. Toronto: U of Toronto P, 1962. Print.

McRuer, Robert. *Crip Theory: Cultural Signs of Queerness and Disability*. New York: New York UP, 2006. Print.

Melhem, D. H. Afterword. *Report from Part Two*. Chicago: Third World, 1996. 146–60. Print.

———. *Gwendolyn Brooks: Poetry and the Heroic Voice*. Lexington: UP of Kentucky, 1987. Print.

Meyers, Jeffrey. *Robert Frost: A Biography*. New York: Houghton Mifflin, 1996. Print.

Middleton, Peter. "The Contemporary Poetry Reading." *Close Listening: Poetry and the Performed Word*. Ed. Charles Bernstein. New York: Oxford UP, 1998. 262–99. Print.

———. *Distant Reading: Performance, Readership, and Consumption in Contemporary Poetry*. Tuscaloosa: U of Alabama P, 2005. Print.

Millard, Andre. *America on Record: A History of Recorded Sound*. New York: Cambridge UP, 1995. Print.

Moffet, Penelope. "A Poet's Slant on South Africa: Gwendolyn Brooks Captures the Agony of Apartheid." *Los Angeles Times*, Nov. 6, 1987. Web.

Monteiro, George. "Frost's Politics and the Cold War." *The Cambridge Companion to Robert Frost*. New York: Cambridge UP, 2001. 221–40. Print.

———. *Robert Frost and the New England Renaissance*. Lexington: UP of Kentucky, 1988. Print.

Morris, Adalaide, ed. *Sound States: Innovative Poetics and Acoustical Technologies*. Chapel Hill: U of North Carolina P, 1997. Print.

Morton, David. *Off the Record: The Technology and Culture of Sound Recording in America*. New Brunswick, NJ: Rutgers UP, 2000. Print.

Moses, Kate. "Sylvia Plath's Voice, Annotated." *The Unraveling Archive: Essays on Sylvia Plath*. Ed. Anita Helle. Ann Arbor: U of Michigan P, 2007. 89–117. Print.

Munson, Gorham. *Robert Frost: A Study in Sensibility and Good Sense*. 1927. New York: Haskell House, 1973. Print.

Nelson, Cary. *Repression and Recovery: Modern American Poetry and the Politics of Cultural Memory, 1910–1945*. Madison: U of Wisconsin P, 1989. Print.

Newdick, Robert S. "Robert Frost and the Sound of Sense." *American Literature* 9.3 (1937): 289–300. Print.

O'Hara, Frank. *Selected Poems*. New York: Knopf, 2009. Print.

Olson, Charles. *Charles Olson at Goddard College: April 12–14, Plainfield, Vermont.* Foreword by Basil King. Ed. Kyle Schlesinger. Victoria, TX: Cuneiform, 2011. Print.

———. *The Complete Poems of Charles Olson.* Ed. George F. Butterick. Berkeley: U of California P, 1997. Print.

———. "Human Universe." *Human Universe and Other Essays.* New York: Grove, 1967. 3–15. Print.

———. *The Maximus Poems.* Ed. George F. Butterick. Berkeley: U of California P, 1985. Print.

———. *Mayan Letters.* Ed. Robert Creeley. London: Jonathan Cape, 1968. Print.

———. *Muthologos: The Collected Lectures and Interviews.* Ed. George F. Butterick. Vol. 1. Bolinas: Four Seasons Foundation, 1979. Print.

———. "Projective Verse." *Human Universe and Other Essays.* New York: Grove, 1967. 51–61. Print.

Ong, Walter J. *Orality and Literacy: The Technologizing of the Word.* New York: Routledge, 1982. Print.

———. *The Presence of the Word: Some Prolegomena for Cultural and Religious History.* New Haven, CT: Yale UP, 1967. Print.

Oster, Judith. *Toward Robert Frost: The Reader and the Poet.* Athens: U of Georgia P, 1991. Print.

Parini, Jay. *Robert Frost: A Life.* New York: Henry Holt, 1999. Print.

Pearlman, Ellen. "Anne Waldman, as Told to Ellen Pearlman." *Brooklyn Rail* 1 Feb. 2004. Web.

"PennSound: All the Free Poetry You Care to Download." Press release. Jan. 5, 2005. PennSound. Web.

Perelman, Bob. "Speech Effects: The Talk as a Genre." *Close Listening: Poetry and the Performed Word.* Ed. Charles Bernstein. New York: Oxford UP, 1998. 200–16. Print.

Perloff, Marjorie. "Language Poetry and the Lyric Subject: Ron Silliman's Albany, Susan Howe's Buffalo." *Critical Inquiry* 25.3 (1999): 405–34. Web.

———. *The Poetics of Indeterminacy: Rimbaud to Cage.* Princeton, NJ: Princeton UP, 1981. Print.

Perloff, Marjorie, and Craig Dworkin, eds. *The Sound of Poetry/The Poetry of Sound.* Chicago: U of Chicago P, 2009. Print.

Phelan, Peggy. *Unmarked: The Politics of Performance.* New York: Routledge, 1993. Print.

Picker, John. "The Two Voices." *Victorian Poetry* 41.4 (2003): 642–45. Print.

Piombino, Nick. "The Aural Ellipsis and the Nature of Listening in Contemporary

Poetry." *Close Listening: Poetry and the Performed Word*. Ed. Charles Bernstein. New York: Oxford UP, 1998. 53–72. Print.

Plath, Sylvia. *Ariel: The Restored Edition*. Foreword by Frieda Hughes. New York: Harper Collins, 2004. Print.

———. *The Collected Poems*. Ed. Ted Hughes. New York: Harper & Row, 1981. Print.

Poirier, Richard. *Poetry and Pragmatism: Inventories of the Present*. Cambridge, MA: Harvard UP, 1992. Print.

———. *Robert Frost: The Work of Knowing*. Stanford, CA: Stanford UP, 1990. Print.

Prettow, Rhonda A. Letter, dated Apr. 10, 1979. Gwendolyn Brooks Papers, BANC MSS 2001/83 z. Bancroft Library, University of California, Berkeley.

Prins, Yopie. "Voice Inverse." *Victorian Poetry* 42.1 (2000): 42–59. Print.

Queen, Laurence. Letter, dated Apr. 25, 1979. Gwendolyn Brooks Papers, BANC MSS 2001/83 z. Bancroft Library, University of California, Berkeley.

Radner, Joan Newlon. "'The Speaking Eye and the Listening Ear': Orality, Literacy, and Manuscript Traditions in Northern New England Villages." *Cultural Narratives: Textuality and Performance in American Culture before 1900*. Ed. Sandra M. Gustafson and Caroline F. Sloat. Notre Dame, IN: U of Notre Dame P, 2010. 175–99. Print.

Ransom, John Crowe. "Poetry: A Note on Ontology." *The World's Body*. New York: Charles Scribner's Sons, 1938. 112–39. Print.

Rasula, Jed. "Understanding the Sound of Not Understanding." *Close Listening: Poetry and the Performed Word*. Ed. Charles Bernstein. New York: Oxford UP, 1998. 233–61. Print.

Richardson, Mark. *The Ordeal of Robert Frost: The Poet and His Poetics*. Chicago: U of Illinois P, 1997. Print.

Riesman, David, Nathan Glazer, and Reuel Denney. *The Lonely Crowd: A Study of the Changing American Character*. 1969. New Haven, CT: Yale UP, 2001. Print.

Rifkin, Libbie. *Career Moves: Olson, Creeley, Zukofsky, Berrigan, and the American Avant-Garde*. Madison: U of Wisconsin P, 2000. Print.

Roach, Joseph. "Performance: The Blunders of Orpheus." *PMLA* 125.4 (2010): 1078–86. Print.

Robinson, Scott. Article clipping, unidentified publication, Mar. 4, 1981. Gwendolyn Brooks Papers, BANC MSS 2001/83 z. Bancroft Library, U of California, Berkeley.

Rossinow, Doug. *The Politics of Authenticity: Liberalism, Christianity, and the New Left in America*. New York: Columbia UP, 1998. Print.

Roubaud, Jacques. "Prelude: Poetry and Orality." Trans. Jean-Jacques Poucel. *The*

Sound of Poetry/The Poetry of Sound. Ed. Marjorie Perloff and Craig Dworkin. Chicago: U of Chicago P, 2009. 18–28. Print.

Rubin, Joan Shelley. *Songs of Ourselves: The Uses of Poetry in America*. Cambridge, MA: Belknap, 2007. Print.

Sandahl, Carrie, and Philip Auslander. *Bodies in Commotion: Disability and Performance*. Ann Arbor: U of Michigan P, 2005. Print.

Satelmajer, Ingrid. "Print Poetry as Oral 'Event' in Nineteenth-Century American Periodicals." *Cultural Narratives: Textuality and Performance in American Culture before 1900*. Ed. Sandra M. Gustafson and Caroline F. Sloat. Notre Dame, IN: U of Notre Dame P, 2010. 200–19. Print.

Sayres, Sohnya, Anders Stephanson, Stanley Aronowitz, and Fredric Jameson, eds. *The 60s without Apology*. Minneapolis: U of Minnesota P, in cooperation with Social Text, 1984. Print.

Schlesinger, Kyle. Introduction. *Charles Olson at Goddard College: April 12–14, Plainfield, Vermont*. Foreword by Basil King. Ed. Kyle Schlesinger. Victoria, TX: Cuneiform, 2011. Print.

Schumacher, Michael. *Dharma Lion: A Critical Biography of Allen Ginsberg*. New York: St. Martin's, 1992. Print.

Scroggins, Mark. "US Modernism II: The Other Tradition—Williams, Zukofsky, and Olson." *The Cambridge Companion to Modernist Poetry*. Ed. Alex Davis and Lee M. Jenkins. Cambridge: Cambridge UP, 2007. 181–94. Print.

"SDS Calls for a March on Washington." *"Takin' It to the Streets": A Sixties Reader*. Ed. Alexander Bloom and Wini Breines. New York: Oxford UP, 2011. 191–92. Print.

Shakespeare, Tom. "The Social Model of Disability." *The Disability Studies Reader*. 3rd ed. Ed. Lennard J. Davis. New York: Routledge, 1997. 266–73. Print.

Shapiro, Joseph P. *No Pity: People with Disabilities Forging a New Civil Rights Movement*. New York: Times Books/Random House, 1993. Print.

Shribman, David M. Introduction. *Robert Frost: Speaking on Campus: Excerpts from His Talks, 1949–1962*. Ed. Edward Connery Lathem. New York: W. W. Norton, 2009. v–xxv. Print.

Shulman, Grace. Liner notes. *Robert Frost in Recital: As Originally Recorded at the Poetry Center of the 92nd Street Y*. New York: Caedmon, 1976. Audio recording.

Siebers, Tobin. *Disability Theory*. Ann Arbor: U of Michigan P, 2008. Print.

Silliman, Ron. "Afterword: Who Speaks: Ventriloquism and the Self in the Poetry Reading." *Close Listening: Poetry and the Performed Word*. Ed. Charles Bernstein. New York: Oxford UP, 1998. 360–78. Print.

———. Introduction. *In the American Tree*. Orono, ME: National Poetry Foundation, 1986. v–xxii. Print.

Sokol, B. J. "Poet in the Atomic Age: Robert Frost's 'That Millikan Mote' Expanded." *Annals of Science* 53 (1996): 399–411. Print.

Somers-Willett, Susan B. A. *The Cultural Politics of Slam Poetry: Race, Identity, and the Performance of Popular Verse in America.* Ann Arbor: U of Michigan P, 2009. Print.

Sontag, Susan. "Notes on 'Camp.'" *Against Interpretation and Other Essays.* New York: Picador, 1966. 275–92. Print.

Spelius, Carol. Letter, dated May 23, 1964. Gwendolyn Brooks Papers, BANC MSS 2001/83 z. Bancroft Library, University of California, Berkeley.

Stern, Frederick C. "The Formal Poetry Reading." *Drama Review: A Journal of Performance Studies* 35.3 (1991): 67–84. Print.

Sterne, Jonathan. *The Audible Past: Cultural Origins of Sound Reproduction.* Durham, NC: Duke UP, 2003. Print.

Stewart, Garrett. *Reading Voices: Literature and the Phonotext.* Berkeley: U of California P, 1990. Print.

Stewart, Susan. *Poetry and the Fate of the Senses.* Chicago: U of Chicago P, 2002. Print.

Swigg, Richard. "Sounding The Waste Land: T. S. Eliot's 1935 Recording." *PN Review* 28.1 (2001): 54–61. Print.

Szalay, Michael. *New Deal Modernism: American Literature and the Invention of the Welfare State.* Durham, NC: Duke UP, 2000. Print.

Szefel, Lisa. *The Gospel of Beauty in the Progressive Era: Reforming American Verse and Values.* New York: Palgrave Macmillan, 2005. Print.

Taylor, Eleanor Ross. "Sylvia Plath's Last Poems." *Poetry* 109.4 (1967): 260–62. Print.

Taylor, Henry. "Gwendolyn Brooks: An Essential Sanity." *On Gwendolyn Brooks: Reliant Contemplation.* Ed. Stephen Caldwell Wright. Ann Arbor: U of Michigan P, 2001. 254–76. Print.

Thomas, Lorenzo. "Neon Griot: The Functional Role of Poetry Readings in the Black Arts Movement." *Close Listening: Poetry and the Performed Word.* Ed. Charles Bernstein. New York: Oxford UP, 1998. 300–23. Print.

Thompson, Lawrance. *Robert Frost: The Early Years 1874–1915.* New York: Holt, Rinehart and Winston, 1966. Print.

———. *Robert Frost: The Years of Triumph 1915–1938.* New York: Holt, Rinehart and Winston, 1970. Print.

Thompson, Lawrance, and R. H. Winnick. *Robert Frost: The Later Years 1938–1963.* New York: Holt, Rinehart and Winston, 1976. Print.

Trilling, Diana. *Claremont Essays.* New York: Harcourt, Brace & World, 1964. Print.

Trilling, Lionel. *Sincerity and Authenticity.* Cambridge, MA: Harvard UP, 1971. Print.

Von Hallberg, Robert. *Charles Olson: The Scholar's Art.* Cambridge, MA: Harvard UP, 1978. Print.

Watten, Barrett. "Missing 'X': Formal Meaning in Crane and Eigner." *Total Syntax.* Carbondale: Southern Illinois UP, 1985. 170–92. Print.

Wheeler, Lesley. "Heralding the Clear Obscure: Gwendolyn Brooks and Apostrophe." *Callaloo* 24.1 (2001): 227–35. Print.

———. *Voicing American Poetry: Sound and Performance from the 1920s to the Present.* Ithaca, NY: Cornell UP, 2008. Print.

Williams, William Carlos. *The Autobiography of William Carlos Williams.* New York: New Directions, 1951. Print.

———. *The Collected Poems of William Carlos Williams.* Ed. Christopher MacGowan. 2 vols. New York: New Directions, 1988. Print.

———. *The Selected Essays of William Carlos Williams.* New York: Random House, 1954. Print.

———. *The Selected Letters of William Carlos Williams.* New York: McDowell, Obolensky, 1957. Print.

Wordsworth, William. "Preface to 'Lyrical Ballads.'" *Poetry and Cultural Studies: A Reader.* Ed. Maria Damon and Ira Livingston. 1802. Urbana: U of Illinois P, 2009. Print.

Ziegler, James. "Charles Olson's American Studies: Call Me Ishmael and the Cold War." *Arizona Quarterly: A Journal of American Literature, Culture, and Theory* 63.2 (2007): 51–80. Print.

Recordings, Films, and Radio Programs

Ashbery, John. "Reading at the Living Theatre." New York, NY. Sept. 16, 1963. PennSound. Poetry reading. Web.

———. "Reading at the Washington Square Art Gallery." New York, NY. Aug. 23, 1964. PennSound. Poetry reading. Web.

———. "Reading at YM-YWHA." Introduced by Richard Howard. New York, NY. Mar. 27, 1967. PennSound. Poetry reading. Web.

Brooks, Gwendolyn. *Gwendolyn Brooks Reading Her Poetry, with an Introductory Poem by Don L. Lee.* New York: Caedmon, 1969. LP record.

Brooks, Gwendolyn, and Amiri Baraka. "A Poetry Reading." *From the Vault.* Pacifica Radio Archives, 1964. Web.

Clifton, Lucille, and Gwendolyn Brooks. "Lucille Clifton and Gwendolyn Brooks." Solomon R. Guggenheim Museum, May 3, 1983. CD.

Eigner, Larry. *around new/sound daily/means: a selection of poems.* S Press Tape no. 37, 1974. Audio tape.
———. *around new/sound daily/means: a selection of poems.* July 1 and 11, 1974, Swampscott, MA, by Michael Köhler. PennSound. Web.
———. "Eigner Reading on November 28, 1978." PennSound. Web.
Frost, Robert. "10/24/55." Sound Reference Center, Library of Congress. Cassette tape.
———. "Columbia University Disc from the Brander Matthews Dramatic Museum. April 5, 1933." Sound Reference Center. LP record.
———. *Robert Frost.* Voice of the Poet series. New York: Random House, 2003. CD.
———. "Robert Frost 1955." Woodberry Poetry Room, Lamont Library, Harvard University. Cassette tape.
———. *Robert Frost in Recital: As Originally Recorded at the Poetry Center of the 92nd Street Y.* New York: Caedmon, 1976. LP record.
———. "Robert Frost: Morris Gray Lecture 12/7/60." Woodberry Poetry Room. Cassette tape.
———. "Robert Frost Poetry Reading 3/13/62." Woodberry Poetry Room. Cassette tape.
———. "Robert Frost Reading 12/2/62." Woodberry Poetry Room. Cassette tape.
———. "Robert Frost Reading His Poems for a Joint Meeting of the Chesapeake Chapter of the American Studies Association, March 31 1959." Sound Reference Center. Cassette tape.
———. "Robert Frost Reads for NBC 3/28/54." Woodberry Poetry Room. Cassette tape.
———. "Robert Frost Speaking in Coolidge Auditorium to High School Honor Students." Sound Reference Center. n.d. Cassette tape.
Ginsberg, Allen. "Big Table Chicago Reading." Chicago, IL. No date given. PennSound. Poetry reading. Web.
———. "Reading at the Intersection for the Arts." San Francisco. Aug. 1971. PennSound. Poetry reading. Web.
———. "Reading at the Poetry Center." San Francisco State University. Oct. 25, 1956. PennSound. Studio recording. Web.
———. "Reading at the Vancouver Poetry Conference." July 31, 1963. PennSound. Poetry reading. Web.
A Hand Is on the Gate. Verve Folkways, 1966. LP record.
"In Celebration of Black Poetry." *Voices of Our People.* KCET, Hollywood, and the Media Forum. Produced and directed by Jim Washburn. 1966. Television.

Lindsay, Vachel. *Vachel Lindsay Reading "The Congo," "Chinese Nightingale," and Other Poems.* New York: Caedmon, n.d. LP record.

O'Hara, Frank. "Poem (Lana Turner Has Collapsed)" and "To the Film Industry in Crisis." No date given. UbuWeb. Poetry reading. Web.

Olson, Charles. "At Goddard College, April 12–14 1962." PennSound. Web.

———. "Reading at the Berkeley Poetry Conference, July 23 1965." PennSound. Web.

———. "Studio Recording at Black Mountain College c. 1954." PennSound. Web.

Plath, Sylvia. *Plath Reads Plath.* Cambridge, MA: Credo Records, 1975. LP record.

———. *The Spoken Word: Sylvia Plath. The Surviving BBC Recordings.* British Library Board, 2010. CD.

"The Poet in Bronzeville." *Destination Freedom.* WMAQ, Chicago, 28 Aug. 1949. Radio.

Riley, James Whitcomb. "Knee Deep in June." Sound Reference Center, 1911. Cassette tape.

Stevens, Wallace. "Wallace Stevens Morris Gray Poetry Reading 5/1/52." Woodberry Poetry Room. Cassette tape.

———. "Wallace Stevens Reading His Poems. Trans-Radio Studio Recording 10/8/54." Woodberry Poetry Room. Cassette tape.

Williams, William Carlos. *Pleasure Dome: An Audible Anthology of Modern Poetry Read by Its Creators.* Columbia Records, 1949. PennSound. LP record. Web.

———. "Poetry Readings (1951)." Listening Booth, Woodberry Poetry Room. Web.

———. "Reading and Commentary at Harvard University." Dec. 4, 1951. PennSound. Web.

———. "Reading and Commentary at UCLA." Nov. 15, 1950. PennSound. Web.

———. "Reading and Commentary at the U of California, Berkeley." May 19, 1955. PennSound. Web.

Index

Contemporary North American Poetry Series

Bodies on the Line: Performance and the Sixties Poetry Reading
By Raphael Allison

Industrial Poetics: Demo Tracks for a Mobile Culture
By Joe Amato

What Are Poets For? An Anthropology of Contemporary Poetry and Poetics
By Gerald L. Bruns

Reading Duncan Reading: Robert Duncan and the Poetics of Derivation
Edited by Stephen Collis and Graham Lyons

Postliterary America: From Bagel Shop Jazz to Micropoetries
By Maria Damon

Among Friends: Engendering the Social Site of Poetry
Edited by Anne Dewey and Libbie Rifkin

Purple Passages: Pound, Eliot, Zukofsky, Olson, Creeley, and the Ends of Patriarchal Poetry
By Rachel Blau DuPlessis

On Mount Vision: Forms of the Sacred in Contemporary American Poetry
By Norman Finkelstein

Form, Power, and Person in Robert Creeley's Life and Work
Edited by Stephen Fredman and Steven McCaffery

Redstart: An Ecological Poetics
By Forrest Gander and John Kinsella

Jorie Graham: Essays on the Poetry
Edited by Thomas Gardner
University of Wisconsin Press, 2005

Gary Snyder and the Pacific Rim: Creating Countercultural Community
By Timothy Gray

Urban Pastoral:
Natural Currents in the
New York School
By Timothy Gray

Racial Things, Racial Forms:
Objecthood in Avant-Garde
Asian American Poetry
By Joseph Jonghyun Jeon

We Saw the Light:
Conversations between the
New American Cinema
and Poetry
By Daniel Kane

History, Memory, and
the Literary Left:
Modern American Poetry,
1935–1968
By John Lowney

Paracritical Hinge:
Essays, Talks, Notes, Interviews
By Nathaniel Mackey
University of Wisconsin Press

Behind the Lines:
War Resistance Poetry on
the American Homefront
By Philip Metres

Hold-Outs:
The Los Angeles Poetry
Renaissance, 1948–1992
By Bill Mohr

In Visible Movement:
Nuyorican Poetry from
the Sixties to Slam
By Urayoán Noel

Frank O'Hara:
The Poetics of Coterie
By Lytle Shaw

Renegade Poetics:
Black Aesthetics and
Formal Innovation in
African American Poetry
By Evie Shockley

Radical Vernacular:
Lorine Niedecker and the
Poetics of Place
Edited by Elizabeth Willis